Theory of Addiction

Addiction Press aims to communicate current ideas and evidence in this expanding field, not only to researchers and practising health professionals, but also to policy makers, students and interested non-specialists. These publications are designed to address the significant challenges that addiction presents to modern society.

Other books in the Addiction Press series

Clinical Handbook of Adolescent Addiction
Edited by R. Rosner
978 0 4709 7234 2

Harm Reduction in Substance Use and High-Risk Behaviour
Edited by R. Pates & D. Riley
978 1 4051 8297 3

Injecting Illicit Drugs
Edited by R. Pates, A. McBride & K. Arnold
978 1 4051 1360 1

Neuroimaging in Addiction
Edited by B. Adinoff & E. Stein
978 0 4706 6014 0

Treating Drinkers and Drug Users in the Community
T. Waller & D. Rumball
978 0 6320 3575 5

Understanding and Treating Addictions: Psychological Assessment and Intervention
Edited by A. Copello
978 1 4051 2417 1

Addiction: Evolution of a Specialist Field
Edited by G. Edwards
978 0 6320 5976 8

Theory of Addiction

Second Edition

Robert West and Jamie Brown

University College London

WILEY Blackwell

Addiction
Press

Registered office: John Wiley & Sons, Ltd, The Atrium, Southern Gate, Chichester, West Sussex,
PO19 8SQ, UK

Editorial offices: 9600 Garsington Road, Oxford, OX4 2DQ, UK
The Atrium, Southern Gate, Chichester, West Sussex, PO19 8SQ, UK
111 River Street, Hoboken, NJ 07030-5774, USA

For details of our global editorial offices, for customer services and for information about how to apply for
permission to reuse the copyright material in this book please see our website at
www.wiley.com/wiley-blackwell

Library of Congress Cataloging-in-Publication Data

West, Robert, 1955–
   Theory of addiction / Robert West and Jamie Brown. – Second edition.
      pages cm
   Includes bibliographical references and index.
   ISBN 978-0-470-67421-5 (pbk. : alk. paper)   1. Substance abuse.   2. Compulsive behavior.
I. Brown, Jamie, 1984–   II. Title.
   RC564.W47 2014
   616.86–dc23

                                                        2013013746

A catalogue record for this book is available from the British Library.

Cover image: www.istockphoto.com/stock_shoppe
Cover design by www.hisandhersdesign.co.uk

Set in 10/12.5pt Sabon by Aptara® Inc., New Delhi, India
Printed and bound in Malaysia by Vivar Printing Sdn Bhd

1   2013

CONTENTS

PREFACE

The first edition of Theory of Addiction summarised the major theoretical approaches that attempt to explain the range of phenomena that we call 'addiction' and synthesise these into an overarching theory that captured their main core features. It was borne out of a need for a single model that could account for features of addiction that involve conscious choice, powerful desires and impulses, and attempts at, and failure of, self-control. It needed to bring in ideas of pleasure-seeking as well as relief from mental and physical discomfort. It needed to account for individual differences in susceptibility to addiction and explain when and why many addicts 'recover' without help but also why some interventions help some addicts. It needed to explain why population-level interventions such as price increases and reductions in availability can influence the prevalence of addiction and why some medicines can help addicts recover without appearing to provide any of the functions provided by the addictive behaviour.

Given that motivation lay at the heart of addiction it became apparent that a theory of addiction needed to be built on a theory of motivation, and that involved creating a synthetic model of motivation. A first draft of a theory was constructed, aiming to be as parsimonious as possible, while still accounting for the full range of 'big observations'. The goal was not only to explain, but also to generate hypotheses about how one might intervene more effectively to combat addiction. It was always intended that the theory would continue to develop, both in order to account for more observations and to make it more useful when it comes to designing interventions.

Since the first edition was published, new findings have accumulated and experience has been gathered in communicating the theory. After 6 years, it seemed appropriate to update the book to take account of this. Important revisions include the following:

1. Updating the definition and conceptualisation of addiction.
2. Updating descriptions of theories in the literature.
3. Providing a functional classification of theories and models of addiction.
4. Providing a description of core concepts involved in these theories.
5. Updating the description of the synthetic theory of addiction (PRIME Theory) to improve clarity and take account of new observations.

6. Assessing PRIME Theory in the light of new evidence.
7. Setting the PRIME Theory motivation in the context of a more general theory of behaviour that also incorporates capability and opportunity.

The theory is still very much 'work in progress'. There is much to be done to fill in gaps, test assumptions and examine how far the theory adds value when designing interventions.

Chapter 1

INTRODUCTION: JOURNEY TO THE CENTRE OF ADDICTION

This book aims to take you on a journey. The starting point is the simplest possible common-sense theory of addiction and the destination will be a theory that accounts for the available evidence on how addiction develops, who becomes addicted, what they become addicted to and how some of them recover. The path is traced by exploring with successive versions of the theory how it needs to be extended or changed to take account of the available evidence. The goal is to arrive at a theory that is comprehensive yet parsimonious, coherent, and above all useful. It aims to stimulate research and to guide clinicians and policy makers in coming up with better ways of tackling this global scourge. This is a continuing journey. As new evidence emerges and better ways of explaining the evidence are brought to light, the theory will need updating.

Preparing for the journey

Many theories but not much progress

The field of addiction is not short on theories. There are psychological theories, biological theories, sociological theories, economic theories, biopsychosocial theories and more. Almost all of the theories in the field of addiction capture important elements of the phenomenon. The problem is that each theory seems to stem from an idea or set of ideas that accounts for a part of the problem but does not account for other features that were previously addressed by other theories. They view addiction from a particular perspective and focus on what is immediately visible from that point of view. They neglect key features that are visible from other points of view. This militates against developing an 'incremental science' of addiction in which new theoretical principles build on what has gone before, correcting areas where they fail to account for data and creating new avenues for exploration.

Theory and observation

Part of the problem appears to be that we have adopted a model of science that does not quite fit the area of study. In behavioural science, we have developed our

Theory of Addiction, Second Edition. Robert West and Jamie Brown.
© 2013 John Wiley & Sons, Ltd. Published 2013 by John Wiley & Sons, Ltd.

methods from the paradigm of the natural sciences; but unfortunately, they have not always served us well. In the prevailing paradigm, the primary source of evidence is the formal study: the survey, the experiment, the semi-structured interview and so forth. Observation of behaviour in the natural habitat is considered 'anecdotal'. The problem with this is that what one might call the 'big' observations about what people do a lot or never do become less important than percentages in surveys, 'significant differences' between groups and 'correlations' between variables. In many cases, these involve rather trivial behaviours in unrealistic laboratory situations or taking at face value people's reports of their attitudes, beliefs and behaviours on questionnaires or in interviews. Very often this gives us an inaccurate portrayal of real behaviour, thoughts and feelings about things that really matter. The responses are too often a pale shadow of, and bear little relationship to, what happens in the world at large.

That is not to say that formal studies are not vital to description, and hypothesis generation and testing. Only that it is important not to lose sight of the value of careful naturalistic observation and detective work when trying to find explanations for behaviour. A simple example can illustrate this. People do not get addicted to listening to music, making the bed or taking aspirin. Listening to music can be very pleasurable; making the bed is functional; and taking aspirin provides relief from pain. A theory of addiction has to be able to explain why these pleasurable, functional and self-medicating behaviours are not addictive while gambling, smoking and drinking alcohol are. As we are aware, no formal study has been done on the addictive qualities of the former but the simple observation is potentially illuminating.

Need for a synthetic theory

The theory developed in this book aims to provide a conceptual framework within which the major insights provided by the existing theories can be placed. It is a synthetic theory in the sense that it attempts to pull together the accumulated wisdom. It does not attempt to explain *everything* there is to explain, but it does seek to explain the 'big observations' and provide a conceptual system in which the existing theories can be located. It aims to be as parsimonious as possible: that is to say, it only brings in additional elements if they are needed. It strives for coherence: the ideas should relate naturally to each other and not be just a list of unconnected assertions.

A guiding principle

In attempting this task, we are mindful of the words of Nick Heather (Heather 1998), which we can do no better than to quote verbatim:

> 'addiction ... is best defined by repeated failures to refrain from drug use despite prior resolutions to do so. This definition is consistent with views of addiction that see decision-making, ambivalence and conflict as central features of the addict's

behaviour and experience. On this basis, a three-level framework of required explanation is (needed) consisting of (1) the level of neuroadaptation, (2) the level of desire for drugs and (3) the level of "akrasia" or failures of resolve … explanatory concepts used at the "lower" levels in this framework can never be held to be sufficient as explanations at higher levels, i.e. the postulation of additional determinants is always required at Levels 2 and 3. In particular, it is a failure to address problems at the highest level in the framework that marks the inadequacy of most existing theories of addiction.' (p. 3)

While addiction as conceived in this book has to be broader than just drug use, Professor Heather's point about the inadequacy of explanations at higher levels seems to us to be well made. Thus, neurophysiological models of the actions of particular addictive drugs on specific brain pathways are important and can help us design medicines to help treat the problem. But it is foolish to imagine that they are theories of addiction given their patent failure to address important observations about social and psychological determinants or indeed other brain mechanisms.

We are also aware of the fact that there already exists in the literature a scholarly and eclectic account in the form of Jim Orford's model 'Excessive Appetites' (Orford 2001). The new theory seeks to build on the work of Professor Orford while paying close attention to the admonitions of Professor Heather.

A psychological orientation

We are psychologists by training and our main field of research is tobacco. Both of these things will inevitably affect our approach and the examples we use. It is difficult for theorists to write convincingly in areas that are not their discipline (e.g. neuropharmacologists or economists writing about psychology), and equally difficult for researchers to demonstrate proficiency in areas of addiction that are not their specialty (the alcohol researcher writing about tobacco or the tobacco researcher writing about cocaine) and many do not even try. But we must try because if we do not, we will fail to grasp what addiction is all about. Since the first edition of this book, we have had the opportunity to discuss the ideas with many colleagues studying different forms of addiction and have been heartened by the extent to which those colleagues have considered that the ideas translate well to their areas of study.

In the end

So the book is a journey from the most common sense and simple explanation of addiction to one that is only as complicated as it needs to be. The narrative is punctuated with references to many of the theories that have been proposed, together with comments on these.

These are not just summaries. In any event, it is not possible to do justice to the theories in the space available; some of them take up whole volumes. We attempt to draw out the theories' unique insights or important lessons that may be drawn from them. Where possible, the developing theory uses concepts that already exist in the minds of well-informed non-specialists and use words that serve non-psychologists well in explaining and predicting each other's behaviour. We try to avoid the pitfall of needlessly constructing new terms or making up new meanings for existing ones.

This book uses the device of putting existing theories that it discusses in boxes. In some cases, the theories are described very briefly and in others, they are considered in much more detail. The level of detail is not related to the complexity or importance of the theory but only to what is required to draw out the lessons for the purposes of taking forward the journey to a comprehensive theory of addiction.

The starting definition of addiction

There are many different ways of defining addiction, by which we mean that there are many different things to which the label addiction can be applied. The next chapter will address this issue in more detail but we need to get started on the right foot, so it should be stated here that we will use the term to refer to a chronic condition in which there is a repeated powerful motivation to engage in a rewarding behaviour, acquired as a result of engaging in that behaviour, that has significant potential for unintended harm. It is not all-or-none, but a matter of degree. Its severity can be assessed, amongst other things, by the severity of subjective urges or cravings, a frequency or intensity of behaviour that is causing harm and failure of serious attempts to limit or cease the activity. This definition differs in some respects from others that are widely used. The reason is that we believe that it captures more precisely the phenomena that most of us working in the field need to be captured and excludes broadly similar phenomena that we would want excluded.

Addiction and motivation

Putting motivation at the heart of addiction means that any theory of addiction needs to be based on a theory of motivation. It makes sense to think of addiction as a disorder of motivation. Although many aspects of motivation are well understood, surprisingly there appears to be no truly synthetic theory that brings them all together. Therefore, this book attempts to provide one. Hopefully, the theory will have value outside the study of addiction.

Establishing base camp

To achieve the goals set out above is no small matter. To bring on board an expert readership made up of researchers who have their own ideas about how addiction should be construed is even more challenging. Nevertheless, the goal seems worthwhile and if the ideas presented are logical and contain enough new insights, perhaps this theory will provide a basis from which we can start an incremental science of addiction research. We can start replacing the parts that are contradicted by evidence with new, better parts, finding more coherent or simpler accounts that explain all the things that this theory explains, or adding new theories within the structure of this one. That is what we sought to do with the draft of the theory set out in the first edition of Theory of Addiction. This edition continues the process of development.

What this book does

Many of the ideas in this book are quite novel and may take some getting used to. To try to help with the process of understanding it, what follows provides some pointers:

- This book develops a draft of a *synthetic theory of addiction* that draws into a single system the mechanisms underlying it: learning through reward and punishment and by associations; feelings of compulsion and desire; the exercise of self-control, beliefs, decisions and plans.

   The theory is based on a *synthetic theory of motivation* that focuses on the *moment-to-moment* control of actions through causal pathways of varying lengths and levels of complexity from simple reflexes, through impulses and inhibitory forces, then desires, drives, and emotional states, to evaluations and plans. It emphasises the fact that for any element to influence behaviour, *it must do so through impulses and inhibitory forces operating at the time*.
- The book argues that the functioning of the brain has evolved to be *inherently unstable*; the motivational system is built like a 'fly-by-wire' aircraft with built-in instability that requires constant balancing input to keep it 'on the straight and narrow'. This has the advantage of making us highly adaptive and cre-ative but the disadvantage that, without balancing inputs, including devices and techniques to stabilise our mental processes, we readily develop maladaptive thought processes and behaviour patterns.
- The book argues that this pattern of activity can be understood in terms of the concepts of the *'epigenetic landscape'* proposed by Waddington (1977) to explain embryological developments, and *chaos theory*, a mathematical approach to modelling systems such as weather patterns. In chaos theory, sys-tems can descend into particular states ('Lorenz attractors' are examples of these) but still switch apparently unpredictably to other states or even move in a *pseudo-random* fashion between them.
- The book argues that addiction develops in susceptible individuals from a failure of balancing inputs leading the *motivational system* concerned into a condition such that particular forces have an unhealthy dominance.
- The book recognises that the disorder of motivation that we call 'addiction' can arise from many different causes. The idea is that addiction is associated with widely varying underlying pathologies and a number of *different syndromes*

(such as the alcohol dependence syndrome). These pathologies involve disorders with varying combinations of abnormally strong impulses, abnormal drives, abnormal emotional states or abnormal mechanisms for restraint.

Sometimes the pathology is present in the individual quite independently of the addictive behaviour. Sometimes the pathology arises from a susceptibility of the individual to the effects of the addictive behaviour or drug. And sometimes it is the individual's environment that is pathological and most 'normal' individuals would succumb in such situations.

Often the pathology shows itself as a syndrome that goes beyond addiction *per se* but involves other classic symptoms (as in the alcohol dependence syndrome already mentioned). But across the different types of addictive behaviour, the pathologies often interact with environmental conditions to result in widely varying manifestations of the symptoms from frequent, low-intensity adoption of the addictive behaviour through to relatively infrequent bingeing. The same drug can lead to different patterns of addictive behaviour in different social and environmental conditions.

- The book proposes a change to the *diagnosis of addiction*. It argues that the assessment should focus on gathering evidence for the degree of dominance of the motivational forces underpinning a behaviour. This is the 'strength' of addiction. It is conceptually necessary to distinguish this from 'severity' which concerns the degree of harm caused by the addiction. There is a move in the American Psychiatric Association's Diagnostic and Statistical Manual V (DSM-V) to combine the two because they are so highly correlated in a given culture. But that leads us to ignore the cultural factors that generate harm from an addictive disorder. For example, if a society chooses to impose draconian punishments on behaviours such as ecstasy use, it can raise the severity without affecting the strength. For clinicians, the next step after diagnosis of addiction would be to try to determine where the pathology or pathologies lie and what are the prospects in the short and medium term for treating these. This would inform the decision about how much emphasis to place on treating the underlying pathology or simply suppressing the symptom (the addictive behaviour).

  Further, if one is to treat the underlying pathology, what are the prospects for an acute treatment episode that will result in a lasting effect, will chronic treatment be required, or is the best model one where treatment episodes are repeated as required? *Symptomatic treatment* involves harnessing additional motives to bolster restraint and minimise the manifestation of the impulses to engage in the behaviour. *Treatment of the underlying pathologies* involves pharmacological and psychological interventions to treat, or permanently normalise, the disorders of the motivational system.

- The book proposes an approach to the development of *population-level interventions* to prevent or control addictive behaviour that takes account of the whole of the motivational system (impulses, desires, evaluations and plans). It states that, equally importantly, interventions should be based on a calculus of the forces operating on individuals *at times when the activity is currently occurring or being planned.*

- This book argues that our existing approach to theory development and testing is not conducive to 'incremental science' but rather a plethora of theories that have much in common but use different formulations or that focus on just one aspect of the matter in hand and fail to address other important aspects. Moreover, the methods we use to test theories, such as correlation coefficients and regression, are often not up to the job. We should also be looking for counter-examples: a single genuine counter-example means that the theory must be wrong and prompts the search for improvements.
- This second edition continues the processes started with the first in 2006 of building an incremental science of addiction, with new theoretical ideas being proposed that do a better job at explaining and predicting behaviour within a common integrative framework, rather than just drawing attention to new insights that explain some things better but fail to address other observations that were adequately explained by previous theories. It also seeks to find better ways of explaining and describing the theory and its application.

The synthetic theory of addiction in brief

To start the ball rolling the following paragraphs will outline some of the statements made by the theory. This will involve some repetition. This is deliberate: ideas often take several exposures in different contexts to be understood—this is just the beginning.

Addiction is

Addiction can arise from many different pathologies, and varies in its strength, severity and manifestations. Addiction involves a chronic condition of the *motivational system* (see next section) in which there is an abnormally and damagingly high priority given to a particular activity.

The pathologies underlying addiction come in *three basic types*:

- Abnormalities in the motivational system that were not directly caused by the addictive activity (e.g. related to chronic anxiety, depression, low self-esteem, poor impulse control, etc.).
- Abnormalities in the motivational system caused by the addictive activity acting on susceptibilities in that system (e.g. sensitisation to the effects of stimulant drugs, tolerance and withdrawal symptoms, and mood disturbance arising from social effects of the behaviour).
- Pathological environments acting on essentially normal motivational systems that are not equipped to cope with them (e.g. sometimes the lifestyle of public icons, particular social relationships and people in chronically distressing circumstances).

In many cases, the underlying pathology involves more than one of these interacting with each other.

The 'motivational system'

The motivational system is the set of brain processes that energise and direct our actions. It consists of five interacting subsystems: (1) the response subsystem generates responses, (2) the impulse–inhibition subsystem generates impulses and inhibitions that feed into this, (3) the motive subsystem generates wants and needs that feed into this, (4) the evaluation subsystem generates beliefs about what is good and bad that feed into this and (5) the planning subsystem generates self-conscious intentions that feed into this.

Motives can influence behaviour only through impulses and inhibitions, evaluations can do so only through motives, and plans operate on motives and evaluations.

Impulses, motives and plans

Leaving aside simple reflex responses, actions result only from *impulses* and *inhibitory forces* operating at that moment in time, and these result from stimuli/ information and from motives operating at that time. Thus, motives operate through impulses and inhibitions, and evaluations operate through motives. We think that plans influence actions primarily through evaluations but it is possible that they may act directly on desires.

The way that the motivational system is structured imparts an inherent (though not paramount) primacy to the immediate environment in terms of influences on our actions and a primacy of desires and urges over evaluations and plans.

Motives and impulses derive from interactions between *external stimuli* and *drives* (e.g. hunger), *generalised emotional states* (e.g. happiness, sadness, excitement) and *targeted emotional states* (e.g. liking, disliking). The strength of a given motive derives from the strength of associated emotions and drives. The direction of the motive derives from the nature of the drives and whether the emotions are positive or negative.

Learning by association

Occurrence and *repetition* of particular associations within the motivational system lead to facilitative links being formed so that when one element occurs the other elements are triggered more readily. This is *associative learning*.

Stimulus–stimulus associations underlie 'Pavlovian (classical) conditioning' while *stimulus–response–outcome* (reward or punishment) associations underpin what is called 'instrumental (operant) learning'. Associative learning is a general property of the brain, which underpins creative thoughts and propositional learning and habits and skills. Thus, what we have come to think of as classical and operant learning are two examples of a wide range of possible types of association between mental activities.

The term *habit* in this view refers to any activity that involves a significant element of automaticity through stimulus–impulse or stimulus–inhibition learning.

The unstable mind

The pathologies underlying addiction develop because the human mind and the physiological systems that give rise to it have evolved to be *inherently unstable* and require constant balancing input to prevent them heading off in unwanted directions. This instability is what makes humans highly responsive to environmental events, creative and adaptable but at the cost of a tendency to descend into maladaptive patterns of thought and behaviour in the absence of balancing input.

A useful way of visualising this is *Waddington's 'epigenetic landscape'*. This characterises the state of an organism as a ball rolling down a contoured landscape with valleys and plains. At bifurcations in the valleys, small environmental forces can lead the ball down one path or another. Addiction represents a particularly deep valley, which would require very powerful sustained input to escape from.

In principle, this approach can be modelled using mathematical concepts of *'chaos theory'*. 'Chaotic systems' (such as weather) exhibit characteristic patterns: they involve periods of short- to medium-term stability punctuated by apparently unpredictable switches in state or periods of violent instability resulting from apparently small events; the paths that two systems follow can diverge markedly as a result of very small differences in their starting points; on occasions, the system can become fixed in a particular state without the possibility of escape under any realistic conditions, while on other occasions, it can apparently show this pattern only to suddenly switch states.

The *motivational system* seems to fit this chaotic adaptive model, and addiction represents a particular kind of activity of the system. For most people under most conditions, the motivational system has checks and balances that prevent any one set of motivational forces dominating for a protracted period. However, some circumstances (a pre-existing pathology in the system, changes to a susceptible system stemming from a given set of actions or a particular set of environmental inputs to the system) lead it to enter a state in which the inputs are not sufficiently balanced for that particular system and it is 'attracted' to an addicted state where a given set of motivational forces are inadequately balanced by competing influences.

This book is an essay. We have tried to communicate the ideas as best as we can, but each chapter could be a book in itself and this text is not attempting to include that level of detail. Instead, we aim to present a wider view of addiction theory. We hope we have done justice to the subject and, even if you do not agree with everything in the book, we still hope you find it stimulating.

References

Heather, N. (1998) A conceptual framework for explaining drug addiction. *J Psychopharmacol* **12**(1): 3–7.

Orford, J. (2001) Addiction as excessive appetite. *Addiction* **96**(1): 15–31.

Waddington, C. (1977) *Tools for Thought: How to Understand and Apply the Latest Scientific Techniques of Problem Solving*, Basic Books, New York.

Chapter 2
DEFINITION, THEORY AND OBSERVATION

This chapter discusses the issue of definitions in the social and behavioural sciences. It develops a definition of addiction based on what appears to be current usage. It then examines what makes a good theory and finishes with a summary of some of the 'big observations' that a theory of addiction needs to accommodate.

Defining addiction (addiction is not an elephant)

This section explores the issue of definition of addiction and related concepts. It accepts the intention behind most major definitions of addiction but suggests a particular wording to achieve this intention.

What are definitions?

When we notice similarities between different 'entities' (things, substances, situations, events or attributes), we give them labels so that they can be thought of as categories and treated similarly. We then describe the features of the category of entity to which the label applies so that we know when to apply the label. Those descriptions are definitions.

Definitions are surprisingly difficult to formulate precisely in a way that covers all eventualities even for concrete objects such as furniture or large mammals such as elephants. For example, we all know what an elephant is. It is a large quadruped with a thick skin, big ears and a long proboscis. But are these absolute defining features? They cannot be. For example, what about an elephant that was born with three legs or that had had its trunk amputated in a freak logging accident? With modern science at our disposal, we could define elephants in terms of their DNA, but for most purposes that would be impracticable and unnecessary. Thus, in practice, we go by what elephants look like and make allowances for the exceptions and we generally know an elephant when we see it – even if it only has three legs.

So what about addiction? Addiction is an abstract concept, like love and fairness. It has no objective existence and boundaries as would, for example, a chair or an elephant. Furthermore, it is socially defined which means that opinions can

Theory of Addiction, Second Edition. Robert West and Jamie Brown.
© 2013 John Wiley & Sons, Ltd. Published 2013 by John Wiley & Sons, Ltd.

legitimately differ about what it is that we want the label to be associated with; it cannot be said that one definition is unequivocally correct and another incorrect, only that one is more useful or is generally agreed upon by 'experts'. Despite this, 'addiction' is an important concept in behavioural and clinical science. According to the US National Library of Medicine database, the word is found in the title or abstract of some 40 000 scholarly articles dating back to 1914.

The changing definitions of addiction

The Oxford English Dictionary traces the term 'addiction' back to Roman Law where it involved 'the formal delivery of a person or property to an individual, typically in accordance with a judicial decision'. While this invokes the idea of relinquished control, the first recorded use with a modern meaning appears much later in the early eighteenth century: 'The Doctor ... made a Forfeit of them, by his too great Addiction to the Bottle, after a very uncourtly manner' (Oxford English Dictionary). This is not to say addiction is a new phenomenon – there are several instances of ancient Egyptian and Greek writings that clearly demonstrate their understanding of the issue. For example, Diodorus and Plutarch noted that 'drink madness is an affection of the body which hath destroyed many kings and noble people' (American Association for the Study and Cure of Inebriety 1893).

By the end of the nineteenth century, physicians were becoming increasingly interested in the scientific study of addiction. The first meeting of what is now the Society for the Study of Addiction was held in 1884 and their scientific ambition required the lay understanding of addiction to be formalised. Early efforts in this direction focused on establishing addiction as a medical disease rather than a moral or spiritual issue. The society defined 'it as a diseased state of the brain and nerve centres characterised by an irresistible impulse to indulge in intoxicating liquors or other narcotics, for the relief these afford, at any peril' (Kerr 1884). Definitions serve a purpose and the necessity of the time was to convince society to treat addiction as a medical problem rather than denounce it as a moral failing.

Definitions in authoritative texts on the subject continued to evolve as knowledge accumulated. However, for a long period, there remained the same theme of addiction involving a state of physiological adaptation to presence of a drug in the body so that absence of the drug leads to physiological dysfunction which is manifest to the sufferer as unpleasant or even life-threatening 'withdrawal symptoms'. An addict was someone who needed to take a drug in order to maintain normal physiological functioning.

For many members of the public and some researchers, this concept of addiction still holds sway. They have an image of the heroin addict suffering stomach cramps, runny nose and shivering or the alcoholic with hands shaking uncontrollably. In some ways, this definition is attractive because it points to a physiological problem with a known or at least discoverable aetiology and mechanism of action. There is a physical abnormality that can be measured objectively and perhaps treated.

The situation has changed considerably in recent years. Nowadays, the term 'addiction' tends to be applied to a syndrome at the centre of which is impaired control over a behaviour to a degree that is causing or could cause significant harm. The fact that there is harm is important because otherwise addiction would be of limited interest. It certainly would not merit spending large sums of public money researching, preventing and treating it. There is impaired control in that an addicted individual feels a compulsion to engage in the activity concerned or else it takes on a priority in his or her life that seems excessive. In many cases, but not always, the addicted individual expresses an apparently sincere desire not to engage in the activity but fails to sustain abstinence.

In this formulation, addiction does not just involve control: there is a syndrome that includes a heterogeneous collection of symptoms. This syndrome and associated diagnostic criteria are based on the alcohol dependence syndrome set out by Edwards and Gross (1976). Thus they still include withdrawal symptoms, cravings and tolerance (reduced drug effect with repeated use), of which more later.

The reason for the change in the way addiction has been conceptualised is that withdrawal symptoms in themselves pose little social threat and are clearly not the main problem. Even where they are unpleasant or dangerous, they are of limited duration and can be treated. By contrast, the compulsion to use drugs or engage in particular behaviours poses a very serious long-term threat to the well-being of sufferers and others and is very difficult to tackle with interventions that are practicable and ethical. It is a much more deserving focus of attention.

Current variation in definitions of addiction

For some researchers, addiction only involves drug-taking behaviour. However, there are strong reasons for extending it to other activities such as gambling. And some would argue that it should be extended further to use of the internet, consumption of palatable foods, purchasing behaviour and sexual behaviours (Padwa and Cunningham 2010). Yet including behaviours other than drug use within the definition causes a problem. It is not a trivial matter to differentiate addiction on the one hand from involuntary tics and obsessive compulsive disorder on the other. Part of the solution seems to be inclusion of the term 'rewarding' in the definition as well as an acknowledgement that the behaviour should be acquired as a result of experience. Thus the definition becomes: 'a syndrome at the centre of which is impaired control over a rewarding behaviour, acquired as a result of engaging in that behaviour'.

Addiction and dependence

It may be useful to distinguish between addiction as a repeated powerful motivation to engage in a rewarding but harmful behaviour and 'physical dependence' as a state of physiological adaptation to a drug which then needs to be taken to prevent adverse withdrawal symptoms. One may even talk about 'psychological dependence' to refer to a state in which an individual, for whatever reason, feels that he or she 'needs' something. But addiction and dependence are often used interchangeably and it is unlikely that we will ever be in a position where there is a strong enough consensus on the definition of and distinction between these terms to arrive at a universally acceptable terminology. Instead, the situation is likely to persist where usage of different terms is led by political or social considerations.

During the 1980s when the American Psychiatric Association (APA) was deciding the classification for DSM-III, there was disagreement between committee members as to which label should be used (O'Brien et al. 2006). Proponents of 'addiction' felt that it conveyed the compulsive nature of drug-taking and distinguished this from 'normal' physical dependence symptoms arising from the routine use of certain medications that may or may not be psychoactive, while those preferring 'dependence' felt it less stigmatising and more easily applicable to all drugs including nicotine and alcohol. The term 'dependence' won by a single vote in one of the final meetings and the APA followed in the footsteps of the WHO which had for similar reasons replaced all reference to the term 'Addiction' with 'Dependence' in 1964.

Fast forward to the present, and it appears that the fifth version of the DSM to be published in 2013 will replace 'Dependence' with 'Addiction' (or at least 'Addictive Disorders'). The re-think has been driven not by a radical re-structuring of the diagnostic criteria – few changes are intended beyond reducing the number of qualifying symptoms that patients are required to have experienced in the past year from three to two and expanding the symptom list to include cravings and several more instances of problematic or harmful use (see www.dsm5.org and Table 2.3 on DSM-IV below). Instead, the critical factor has been the belief of the committee that any harm relating to 'Addiction' stigma has been overshadowed by the reluctance of some clinicians to deliver appropriate medication to patients displaying any signs of tolerance and withdrawal for fear of clinical dependence. Many welcome the change including those involved in the original decision, who now regard it as a 'serious mistake' (O'Brien et al. 2006). Of course, not everyone agrees (Erickson and Wilcox 2006).

Interestingly, in common parlance we tend to use different terminology for different addictions: we usually say 'heroin addiction' not 'heroin dependence' but 'alcohol dependence' not 'alcohol addiction'. With benzodiazepines we tend towards 'dependence' rather than 'addiction'. With nicotine and stimulants we feel about equally comfortable with either term. At the risk of using a language that reads rather strangely, this book will try to use the term 'addiction' to refer to the syndrome at the heart of which is a repeated powerful motivation to engage in a rewarding but harmful behaviour and mostly avoid the term dependence. However, use of language sometimes provides clues to how well underlying concepts fit together and it is worth considering whether the different application of the terms 'dependence' and 'addiction' to different drugs reflects differences in the phenomenology of the problem.

Addiction and intoxication

A position that is no longer seriously advocated is that there must be intoxication for addiction to occur (Robinson and Pritchard 1992). In fact, even at the time the position appeared incompatible with the evidence and was fiercely contested (West 1992; Hughes 1993). Such arguments can be understood by realising they need not be founded on a search for truth; definitions and labels can have far reaching social, political and commercial consequences. Thus in the 1990s it was important to tobacco companies that nicotine not be considered addictive and including intoxication as a defining feature allowed them to make this claim.

The proponents of the intoxication view were arguing that because nicotine is not intoxicating it is not addictive and so smokers were freely risking lung cancer in choosing to smoke – 'because they like it'. This would mitigate the blame attaching to the tobacco industry for promoting and selling the only product in the world, apart from the suicide pill, that is lethal to the user when used exactly as intended by the manufacturer.

Individuals and professional groups are of course at liberty to define addiction in a way that meets their own needs. Some psychologists may feel comfortable with a psychological definition that emphasises the role of decision-making and choice, whereas behavioural pharmacologists may feel more comfortable with one that emphasises learning mechanisms and brain pathways.

Some smokers, who need to feel that they are in control, may prefer to think of addiction in terms that exclude smoking whereas others who need to feel comfortable about the fact that they have tried and failed to stop many times may be attracted to one that includes it. However, at some point we need to agree that a particular definition serves the purposes of research, clinical practice and policy better than others and that is what has happened with the adoption of a version of the Edwards and Gross conceptualisation.

Everyday usage of 'addiction'

It is interesting to see what non-specialists regard as addiction. We asked a number of people with no formal grounding in the field of addiction or behavioural research, but who are thoughtful and intelligent, to say what they thought addiction was. Here are the responses.

NB (Composer of a musical about alcohol dependence): 'Addiction is, amongst many other things, probably as many things as there are addicts. . . . 1. The constant attempt to try and fill a perceived lack of something, real or imagined, 2. A way of never having to say what you really feel . . . the consequence, or maybe the origination, being a physical, emotional and chemical dependence'.

CW (Theatre producer and manager): 'An addiction is something we can't stop doing without some kind of intervention; but then so are breathing and compulsive behaviours . . . perhaps there's a lack of rational justification for the addiction and some sense that the addiction itself continues to "make us do it" (and the judgement that the addiction is "bad"). Do we mix up addictions and compulsions? There seems to be a difference. Are addictions purely chemical and everything else compulsive behaviour? We usually recognise non-physical/chemical components to addictions but at the same time are familiar with an addict's attempts to justify their addiction as part of the addiction itself. Common usage of terms like "physically addictive", "psychologically addictive" and "addictive personality" suggests not only different kinds of addiction but also different attitudes to addiction. It is hard to keep a sense of "good" and "bad for you" out of it. So what am I trying to say? Addiction is something you don't need to do (not something connected to survival) but you can't stop yourself doing (not without help/suffering/effort) and it's somehow self-perpetuating (it becomes a goal in itself). I'm reminded of philosophy classes (what would a philosopher say?), e.g. knowledge = justified, true belief plus a connection between justification and what makes the belief true (to avoid counter-examples) and the ancient Greek concept of akrasia (weakness of the will, or choosing the lesser "good") which is relevant to addiction (as soon as you analyse an example of weakness of the will it disappears because understanding it means it's no longer irrational behaviour and so no longer weakness of the will so is there such a thing?). Perhaps we do addicts a disservice understanding them and so justifying their addictions? We should rather tell them to...'

CC *(Retired nurse)*: 'Addiction is compulsive behaviour in a certain direction. It gives you pleasure. If a person is prone to addiction, if they are not addicted to one thing they will be addicted to something else. It is caused by a genetic susceptibility. The way to tackle addiction is to transfer it to something less harmful and reward them for doing it or put a more powerful motivation in place.'

CD *(Author and actor)*: 'For me, addiction is: security, only noticeable in its absence. A nag in the head. Can say nothing, do nothing, think nothing but "Want a fag". Nothing else will hit the spot, but it doesn't. It's disappointing but the best thing at the same time. And still thinking "The next one will do the trick". A cigarette every half an hour is like having a hug for a dull and miserable life. The alternative is to whine constantly, and who wants to listen to that? So, smoke, smoke, smoke – cheaper than therapy.'

It is remarkable how these off-the-cuff, non-expert views capture much of the discussion that has gone into arriving at the current technical formulation.

Commonly used formal definitions

Table 2.1 shows a range of commonly used definitions of addiction/dependence and comments on how far and in what way they meet or fail to meet a need to include and exclude behaviours that need to be included or excluded.

Arriving at a working definition

There are two further tweaks of wording that are needed to implement what seems to be the intention behind most usage. The conventional formulation talks of 'impaired control'. There is a risk that this might imply specifically that the disorder involves a weakening of self-control rather than an increase in drive to engage in the addictive behaviour. This is an empirical matter and is probably best avoided in the definition of the phenomenon. Additionally the focus on impaired control rather than the force causing the impairment excludes the possibility of addictions with the potential to cause harm where no attempt was (yet) being made to exert control. Therefore, the preferred form of words for this book is:

'Addiction is a chronic condition involving a repeated powerful motivation to engage in a rewarding behaviour, acquired as a result of engaging in that behaviour,

Table 2.1 Commonly used definitions of addiction/dependence

Definition (source)	Comment
Addiction is a primary, chronic disease of brain reward, motivation, memory and related circuitry. Dysfunction in these circuits leads to characteristic biological, psychological, social and spiritual manifestations. This is reflected in the individual pursuing reward and/or relief by substance use and other behaviours. The addiction is characterised by impairment in behavioural control, craving, inability to consistently abstain, and diminished recognition of significant problems with one's behaviours and interpersonal relationships. Like other chronic diseases, addiction can involve cycles of relapse and remission. Without treatment or engagement in recovery activities, addiction is progressive and can result in disability or premature death. (American Society of Addiction Medicine)	This considers addiction as a brain disease which implies that it requires treatment. It neglects environmental and social forces at play, the fact that it involves a continuum and that many individuals 'recover' without treatment.
Compulsive physiological and psychological need for a habit-forming substance or the condition of being habitually or compulsively occupied with or involved in something (The American Heritage Dictionary, 4th edn)	Broadly based but transfers the burden of interpretation on to words such as 'compulsive', 'need' and 'habit'
A physical or psychological need for a habit-forming substance, such as a drug or alcohol. In physical addiction, the body adapts to the substance being used and gradually requires increased amounts to reproduce the effects originally produced by smaller doses. A habitual or compulsive involvement in an activity, such as gambling. (The American Heritage Science Dictionary)	As above but provides a clear definition of 'physical' addiction which represents only a small part of the problem of addiction as currently construed
The condition of being abnormally dependent on some habit, especially compulsive dependency on narcotic drugs (Collins English Dictionary)	Transfers the burden of interpretation to 'abnormal' and 'compulsive'
Addiction is a persistent, compulsive dependence on a behaviour or substance. The term has been partially replaced by the word *dependence* for substance abuse. Addiction has been extended, however, to include mood-altering behaviours or activities. Some researchers speak of two types of addictions: substance addictions (e.g. alcoholism, drug abuse and smoking) and process addictions (e.g. gambling, spending, shopping, eating and sexual activity). There is a growing recognition that many addicts, such as polydrug abusers, are addicted to more than one substance or process. (Gale Encyclopaedia of Medicine)	Brings in the concept of persistence but transfers burden of interpretation to 'compulsive' and 'dependence'

Table 2.1 (*Continued*)

Definition (source)	Comment
A compulsive, uncontrollable dependence on a chemical substance, habit, or practice to such a degree that either the means of obtaining or ceasing use may cause severe emotional, mental or physiologic reactions (Mosby's Medical Dictionary 8th edn)	The use of the term 'uncontrollable' rules out cases where an individual is struggling successfully (for the time being at least) to control the behaviour
(Substance dependence) A preoccupation with and compulsive use of a substance despite recurrent adverse consequences; addiction often involves a loss of control and increased tolerance, and may be associated with a biological predisposition to addiction. (1) A physiologic, physical, or psychological state of dependency on a substance—or pattern of compulsive use, which is characterised by tolerance, craving and a withdrawal syndrome when intake of the substance is reduced or stopped; the most common addictions are to alcohol, caffeine, cocaine, heroin, marijuana, nicotine—the tobacco industry argues that nicotine's addictive properties are unproven, amphetamines. (2) A disorder involving use of opioids wherein there is a loss of control, compulsive use, and continued use despite adverse social, physical, psychological, occupational, or economic consequences. (3) A neurobehavioural syndrome with genetic and environmental influences that results in psychological dependence on the use of substances for their psychic effects; addiction is characterised by compulsive use despite harm. (McGraw-Hill Concise Dictionary of Modern Medicine)	Just deals with substance use and includes a set of features that, while common, are not always present
(Substance dependence) Repeated use of a psychoactive substance or substances, to the extent that the user (referred to as an addict) is periodically or chronically intoxicated, shows a compulsion to take the preferred substance (or substances), has great difficulty in voluntarily ceasing or modifying substance use and exhibits determination to obtain psychoactive substances by almost any means. Typically, tolerance is prominent and a withdrawal syndrome frequently occurs when substance use is interrupted. The life of the addict may be dominated by substance use to the virtual exclusion of all other activities and responsibilities. The term addiction also conveys the sense that such	Includes a detailed description of substance dependence including features that are not always present

(Continued)

Table 2.1 (*Continued*)

Definition (source)	Comment
substance use has a detrimental effect on society, as well as on the individual; when applied to the use of alcohol, it is equivalent to alcoholism. Addiction is a term of long-standing and variable usage. It is regarded by many as a discrete disease entity, a debilitating disorder rooted in the pharmacological effects of the drug, which is remorselessly progressive. From the 1920s to the 1960s, attempts were made to differentiate between addiction and 'habituation,' a less severe form of psychological adaptation. In the 1960s, the World Health Organisation recommended that both terms be abandoned in favour of dependence, which can exist in various degrees of severity. Addiction is not a diagnostic term in ICD-10, but continues to be very widely employed by professionals and the general public alike. (WHO Lexicon of Alcohol and Drug Terms)	
(Substance dependence) When an individual persists in use of alcohol or other drugs despite problems related to use of the substance, substance dependence may be diagnosed. Compulsive and repetitive use may result in tolerance to the effect of the drug and withdrawal symptoms when use is reduced or stopped. (DSM-IV)	Introduces the notion of continued use despite harmful effects

Source: Adapted from West (2013).

that has significant potential for unintended harm. Someone is addicted to something to the extent that they experience this repeated powerful motivation'.

Table 2.2 gives examples of what is included and excluded by this definition. Note that in theory it can cover any behaviour. This offers the possibility that an individual may be regarded as addicted if he or she shows evidence of this condition even though the vast majority of people who engage in the behaviour do not (e.g. shopping, sex etc.). It also allows the possibility that a category of behaviour that at one time may offer little prospect of addiction, may through changes in circumstances or the precise manifestation of the behaviour come to pose a significant addiction problem. This could conceivably happen or have happened with some forms of internet use.

Where does 'craving' fit in?

If the concept of addiction poses difficulties when it comes to achieving consensus, so does the concept of 'craving'. In common parlance, this has a relatively straightforward meaning. It is a subjective feeling of a strong desire to do something. A

Table 2.2 Examples to test a definition of addiction

Scenarios to test definitions of addiction

An individual is addicted who ...

develops a powerful need to drink alcohol in an escalating pattern of consumption

continues to engage in a behaviour to an extent that he or she recognises as harmful despite having tried to stop

regularly experiences a powerful desire to engage in the behaviour

has not smoked cigarettes for 4 weeks but still experiences strong urges to smoke

does not smoke every day but has tried to stop smoking completely and failed several times

drinks alcohol in the mornings to relieve feelings of anxiety

has his/her life dominated by using heroin and obtaining the money to buy heroin

has not drunk alcohol for 3 months but who still gets strong cravings for it

spends hours each day gambling online and stealing to cover the costs

An individual is not addicted who ...

feels a strong motivation to try alcohol but has not yet done so

does not feel a powerful desire to engage in the behaviour in situations when it would normally occur

takes medication every day purely to relieve chronic pain, depression or anxiety

feels a strong motivation to perform excessive hand-washing

has antisocial personality disorder, Tourette's syndrome, bulimia or obsessive compulsive disorder without other behavioural problems

takes a psychoactive drug for the pleasurable experience but does not experience a powerful desire to take the drug when it is not available

gains satisfaction from an activity, and self-consciously decides that the benefits outweigh the costs and this analysis is largely shared by society

drinks heavily but can easily go for several months without drinking

gambles heavily but not to a point where it is causing significant harm

is powerfully motivated to harm others

Source: Adapted from West (2013).

person can say something like, 'I have a craving for chocolate' and someone else knows that this means that the person feels a powerful desire to eat some chocolate. Thus a 'weak craving' is an oxymoron. Someone who craves alcohol will often show all kinds of behaviours, including increased swallowing, increased heart rate, and sweating perhaps. They may become obsessed with thinking about alcohol and perhaps anticipate the pleasure and relief that will come from a large swig of whisky.

So researchers naturally come to think that some or all of these features should become part of the definition of craving. But should they? What was wrong with the original definition accompanied by these other events as interesting correlates of the phenomenon? If we go down the route of adding these other features, we find ourselves in a difficult position that not all those whom we wish to regard as craving, because, for example, they tell us that they badly need a drink, will show all or even some of these other signs. Worse still, craving for different things will manifest itself in different ways and so we can easily end up with different concepts of craving for the different things that people crave.

So in this book, 'craving' refers to the experience of a powerful motivation to engage in a behaviour. It may be reported using words such as 'urge', 'desire' and 'craving' and it is an empirical question as to how it should best be measured for different behaviours in different cultures and in different contexts. Given that it represents a core element of addiction it may well be that measurement of craving can also serve to measure strength of addiction. We will come back to this towards the end of the book.

Diagnosing and measuring addiction

A feature of the definition of addiction that currently prevails is that it is a clinical disorder and in fact it is a disorder of motivation. We also know that it is chronic and in many cases life-threatening. Like most psychiatric disorders, and many physical disorders, it is diagnosed by reference to a set of symptoms rather than an underlying pathology. There is no laboratory test or scan that can be used to say that an individual is suffering from addiction; the symptoms are the sole means of determining whether the disease is present in any one case. But the symptoms are only markers and, for various reasons, an individual may have some symptoms but not others.

There are two main sets of criteria in common use, the World Health Organisation's ICD-10 and the American Psychiatric Association's DSM-IV. Table 2.3 shows how these compare with each other.

Some problems with the DSM and ICD criteria

These diagnostic criteria leave considerable scope for interpretation. For example, how strong does a feeling of desire or urge need to be to count as craving? How severe do effects of withdrawal have to be to count as withdrawal 'symptoms'? How harmful do the consequences have to be for them to count? There are many dimensions to harm and it can be extremely difficult to collapse them into one concept to allow comparison and evaluation (Nutt et al. 2010). The result is that determining whether or not an individual who engages in a behaviour is addicted cannot be specified objectively, but only by reference to judgements made in a clinical interview or by responses that the individual makes on a diagnostic questionnaire.

The arbitrariness is compounded by the specification that only a subset of symptoms is required for the diagnosis to be made. In principle, two 'addicts' could have

Table 2.3 Diagnostic criteria for addiction

___

Diagnostic and Statistical Manual IV (APA 1995)
___
A maladaptive pattern of substance use leading to clinically significant impairment or distress as manifested by three (or more) of the following, occurring at any time in the same 12-month period:

1. Substance is often taken in larger amounts or over longer period than intended
2. Persistent desire or unsuccessful efforts to cut down or control substance use
3. A great deal of time is spent in activities necessary to obtain the substance (e.g. visiting multiple doctors or driving long distances), use the substance (e.g. chain smoking) or recover from its effects
4. Important social, occupational or recreational activities given up or reduced because of substance abuse
5. Continued substance use despite knowledge of having a persistent or recurrent psychological, or physical, problem that is caused or exacerbated by use of the substance
6. Tolerance, as defined by either: need for greater amounts of the substance in order to achieve intoxication or desired effect; or markedly diminished effect with continued use of the same amount
7. Withdrawal, as manifested by either: characteristic withdrawal syndrome for the substance or the same (or closely related) substance is taken to relieve or avoid withdrawal symptoms

International Classification of Diseases 10 (WHO 1992)
___
Three or more of the following must have been experienced or exhibited together at some time during the previous year:

1. A strong desire or sense of compulsion to take the substance
2. Difficulties in controlling substance-taking behaviour in terms of its onset, termination or levels of use
3. A physiological withdrawal state when substance use has ceased or been reduced, as evidenced by: the characteristic withdrawal syndrome for the substance or use of the same (or a closely related) substance with the intention of relieving or avoiding withdrawal symptoms
4. Evidence of tolerance, such that increased doses of the psychoactive substance are required in order to achieve effects originally produced by lower doses
5. Progressive neglect of alternative pleasures or interests because of psychoactive substance use, increased amount of time necessary to obtain or take the substance or to recover from its effects
6. Persisting with substance use despite clear evidence of overtly harmful consequences, depressive mood states consequent to heavy use, or drug-related impairment of cognitive functioning

non-overlapping sets of symptoms. However, this use of 'disjunctive' symptom sets in diagnosis is essential because some of the criteria have little relevance to some types of addictive behaviour. For example, chronic tolerance is marked in the case of alcohol but less so for cocaine. Giving up activities because of the addiction is more relevant to intoxicating drugs such as alcohol than drugs such as nicotine that do not interfere with normal functioning.

Revisions that appear likely in DSM-V may help some of these issues – for example, the expansion of the symptom list to include more concrete examples of what qualifies as problematic or harmful use should help to reduce arbitrary judgments. However, another likely revision – the reduction in the number of qualifying symptoms that patients need to have experienced in the past year from three to two – is likely to exacerbate the problem of non-overlapping symptoms. This suggests that the current diagnostic criteria need further revision beyond those proposed for DSM-V. That is something to which this book returns in the last chapter. It is worth noting at this point, however, that revision of a set of diagnostic criteria and conceptualisations is not something to be undertaken lightly because it creates a disjunction with the past. This affects prevalence estimates as well as estimates of such parameters as heritability. These unavoidable problems of revision must be carefully weighed against any likely benefit (Rounsaville 2002) and are likely to have prevented the sensible proposal to harmonise the similar but distinct DSM and ICD classification systems, whose differences have acted as a barrier to international communication and research (First 2009; Hasin et al. 2006).

Theory and supposition

Let us now turn our attention away from addiction and towards the other term in the title of this book: theory. Kurt Lewin (1951) famously declared that there is nothing so practical as a good theory. This section describes what a theory should be and what makes a good or bad theory. It points out that theories in the field of addiction are rarely tested adequately. This is because the dominant research methodology does not allow it. However, there is an approach that does allow testing of theories and by this method at least some of the theories that have been proposed fail the test. The test is to find somewhere in the real world or the world of experiment a genuine counter-example that conflicts with the theory. This may seem an obvious test but it has been used surprisingly rarely.

What makes a good theory?

Theories are central to science, but they form only a part of it. They are discrete, coherent accounts of a process that are arrived at by a process of inference, provide an explanation for observed phenomena and generate predictions. They consist of statements about the existence of entities and delineate causal interactions between these entities. Much of science does not fall into this category because it consists of disparate observations or is descriptive rather than explanatory. The same is true for the field of addiction. Most of what is known or believed could not be called theories. A good theory should:

- explain a related set of observations;
- generate predictions that can be tested;
- involve no more concepts or elements than are necessary;
- be comprehensible;
- be coherent;
- be internally consistent;
- not be contradicted by observations.

Any number of different theories could be developed and compete for our attention, each good in some ways and not so good in others. So we need to go beyond these principles to decide which theories to use when, how to improve theories and when to replace theories with better ones. If we want theory to progress, we have to have a set of rules for deciding that what we have at the moment is not up to the job and in what way.

Theory development

There are several approaches to theory development (Carlile and Christensen 2004; Lipsey 2004; Dixon-Woods et al. 2011) but ideally it should start with the simplest possible account and set a high threshold for seeking to supersede it. It should ask four questions of the existing body of theory:

- Is it contradicted by observations?
- Does it fail to encompass important relevant observations?
- Does it have more elements than are needed?
- Is it misleading?

The answers to those questions should provide the starting point for modification.

Theory development in the social and behavioural sciences

Unfortunately, the prevailing approach in the field of addiction, like behavioural and social science generally, has been to develop theories with a less than complete analysis of what is already in the literature. In practice, theories of addiction have typically been developed because a researcher has, very understandably, wished to emphasise a particular approach to understanding a set of phenomena, or out of a set of specific observations from which the researcher has wished to generalise.

It is very rare to see direct comparisons between theories, and when these are undertaken they do not usually result in a resolution. The result is that theories in this field tend to take a particular approach to a topic rather than attempting a comprehensive coherent account of the topic, and they frequently (though not always) involve a number of propositions that are not connected in a coherent framework so that any one of them could be false without others being false.

Theories and models

In principle, there is a difference between a 'theory' and a 'model'. A model is a representation of a system, an object or characteristic set of events. It need not explain anything. A theory seeks to explain and predict by proposing the existence or operation of entities that have not been observed. In practice, the two are often used interchangeably and indeed it is sometimes not clear whether the proponents wish their 'account' of addiction to be regarded as one or the other or both. Therefore, this volume considers both theories and models, and hybrids. 'Laws' and 'hypotheses' are also included but coverage is less comprehensive due to the numbers involved. To be clear, a law is a generalisation about how an aspect of nature will behave under a certain set of circumstances, while a hypothesis is yet more specific and provides an individual speculation that is empirically testable.

Test and testability

It was stated earlier that theories in behavioural sciences are rarely tested using a stringent system that would require them to be rejected in favour of better theories. This needs further explanation. There are two reasons for the problem: theories are rarely specified with enough precision to be sure that they could definitely not account for a particular set of observations, and secondly our formal measurement is rarely precise or reliable enough to be sure that we have disproved a prediction from a theory. As Meehl (1978) has pointed out (see box below on p. 28) in behavioural and social science, the result is that theories go out of favour rather than being abandoned, and most researchers seem able to accept that multiple theoretical approaches can be applied. This seems democratic and reasonable but it is not conducive to progress.

The fallibility of scientists

In a lecture about pseudo-science, Richard Feynman described an experiment by Robert Millikan and Harvey Fletcher to measure the charge of an electron with falling oil drops and the subsequent investigation of the phenomenon:

> [they] got an answer which we now know not to be quite right. It's a little bit off, because he had the incorrect value for the viscosity of air. It's interesting to look at the history of measurements of the charge of the electron, after Millikan. If you plot them as a function of time, you find that one is a little bigger than Millikan's, and the next one's a little bit bigger than that, and the next one's a little bit bigger than that, until finally they settle down to a number which is higher. (Feynman 1974)

There was no reason for the discovery to have been so gradual other than for a succession of scientists to have been intimidated by prevailing wisdom. That is, whenever scientists replicated the experiment and got numbers significantly higher than expected, they subjected the result to undue scrutiny and repeated their experiment until they got a number a bit closer to Milikan and Fletcher's. Unfortunately, cases like this abound throughout the history of science and while some can be attributed to honest mistakes others cannot, including the high-profile misconduct of researchers like Cyril Burt and more recently Diederik Stapel. Honest mistakes and misconduct both serve as reminders that science does not exist in a vacuum. When considering why bad theories can be slow to be discredited, it is important to remember that science is conducted by people with the potential to be just as self-interested or intimidated by the establishment as the next person (Pashler and Wagenmakers 2012). By applying the scientific method, employing peer review and demanding transparency, the scientific community hopes to mitigate that potential. However, there remains scope for other measures that would be even more helpful such as the adoption of a publishing and evaluation system that cherished replication as much as novelty.

A new approach is needed

Our approach to testing theories needs to be much more stringent. At present a researcher will claim that a theory is supported because it predicts an association between two variables and indeed a correlation is found of, let us say, 0.30 with a significance level of $p = 0.01$. But is this a good enough test?

Arguably not. Theories can also be tested by looking for and finding counter-examples to the statements they make or the hypotheses they generate. Examining whether a correlation is significant or not often does not provide this opportunity. The correlation may not be significant because of weak measurement or interference from other influences or just sampling error, and it may be significant because of a common confounding variable, common measurement error or sampling error.

One of the clearest examples of this is in 'tests' of a model called the 'Transtheoretical Model' (TTM) of behaviour change (Prochaska and Velicer 1997). This will be described in more detail later, but in essence, the model states that individuals can be classified into 'stages' according to whether they are planning to make the change in some arbitrarily defined timescale or are indeed in the process of making the change or have made the change. The major tests of the model show that individuals who are planning to change or are in the process of change are more likely to have changed when followed up later.

Yet this would be true even if this particular theory were false in all important respects, for example, about the idea that individuals fitted into 'stages'. In fact the association is weak and most individuals fail to show the hypothesised progression, but these are not considered as counter-examples that would lead to the theory being rejected because the theory is not expressed with that level of precision. To date the predictions of the theory have not been compared with a much simpler common model which goes like this:

Desire and intention to make a significant change to a behaviour pattern varies across individuals and within individuals over time. The stronger and more immediate the desire and intention, the greater is the likelihood that environmental triggers will precipitate an attempt at change. Sometimes, individuals take preparatory steps ahead of the attempt at change. The attempt at change itself comes in many different forms including gradual and abrupt. Once the attempt has been initiated, a new set of factors often come into play that make sustaining the change difficult and lapse, then relapse is common. For some types of behaviour change, it becomes easier to maintain the change over time until in many cases it no longer requires an effort of will. But this is not universally true. When relapse occurs, motivation to change is often still high and further attempts are likely.

This does not have the jargon of the TTM and is the implicit model that many people working in behaviour change used prior to the TTM. That model should be tested against this account before being hailed as a breakthrough in behaviour change theory.

Counter-examples and observations of natural behaviour

Many of the counter-examples that can be used to test theories can be found in observation of natural behaviour. It could be argued that we need a radical shift in our approach to the study of behaviour. Rather than assuming that the body of knowledge is what we find from experiments and formal studies with sporadic and unsystematic reference to 'anecdotal evidence', we take as a basic starting point 'observation of nature' and consider formal experiment as a means to help explain this.

Our theories must at the very least account for what we know to be true about behaviour in the real world. Developing elaborate theories about the fine detail of results of experiments that deal with essentially trivial behaviours will not provide us with the advances we seek. Observations of nature can in fact be very powerful for testing theories because of one principle: if just one example of behaviour observed in the real world conflicts with our theory, our theory *must* be wrong.

By these criteria, several dominant theories of behaviour must be wrong because counter-examples abound in the real world. The TTM, already mentioned, is a case in point. It states that people can be categorised into stages based on when they plan to make a change. However, one does not need to undertake extensive surveys to know that large numbers of people do not make plans in that way.

If just one smoker can be found who is thinking that he might try to stop smoking but has not decided definitely (and without being asked) whether it will be in 3 weeks, 3 months or 9 months, he or she contradicts one of the fundamental tenets of the theory. If one smoker can be found who was not thinking about stopping smoking one minute, and then the next minute, because of something he hears or sees, decides never to smoke again without making any plans at all, the theory is surely wrong.

Proponents may argue that this is not a theory about individuals, but then the status of the constructs becomes so ambiguous that the theory loses meaning. How many counter-examples would a theory that is not about individuals need before the theory could be considered wrong?

Another example is the Theory of Planned Behaviour (see Levin 1999). This asserts that behaviours arise from intentions, and intentions arise from a combination of attitudes to the behaviour (a weighted sum of evaluations of the consequences of the behaviour), subjective norms (beliefs about what important other people think about the behaviour weighted by motivation to comply) and perceived control (belief in ability to carry out the behaviour).

In practice, even when the measurements are taken in precisely the manner dictated by the theory, the variables concerned rarely explain more than about 10% of the variance, which is particularly weak in view of the fact that measurement itself *causes* a degree of association and does not simply reflect pre-existing relationships (Ogden 2003; Godin et al. 2008). The variables explain a lot more of the variance in self-reports of behaviours that have already taken place but this could easily be because respondents do not want to make themselves look inconsistent. Does this mean that the theory is correct or incorrect? Proponents of the theory argue that any association that is significant supports the theory but this neglects the fact that most people in the study did not follow the predicted pattern. In fact the theory is contradicted by finding examples of instances in which individuals do not think in the terms defined by the theory; when deciding what to do they do not consider the consequences of their actions but use broader moral or ethical principles.

The weakest form of evidence for a theory

Probably the weakest form of test that researchers apply to theories is captured by the statement: 'X observation is consistent with the theory that Y'. This is such a weak statement it should have no place in anything with aspirations to being a science. To use an extreme example for illustrative purposes: the observation that children put out stockings to be filled with presents at Christmas is consistent with the theory that Father Christmas is real and lives at the North Pole. Why do we use this kind of evidence? It appears that we do so because we want our audience to read more into the term 'consistent' than a literal interpretation warrants. For example, here is an abstract verbatim from a study on nicotine dependence (Mogg et al. 2005):

Rationale: Different theories of addiction make conflicting predictions about whether attentional and approach biases for smoking-related cues are enhanced, or reduced, as a function of the level of nicotine dependence.
Objective: These theoretical views were evaluated by examining cognitive biases in smokers.

Methods: We monitored the eye movements of 41 smokers (predominantly young adults, who smoked from 1 to 40 cigarettes per day) as they completed a visual probe task in which smoking-related and matched control pictures were presented. Participants also completed a stimulus–response compatibility task, which measured the tendency to approach smoking-related cues, and a rating task.

Results: Smokers with lower levels of nicotine dependence showed greater maintained attention and faster approach responses to smoking-related cues. Longer gaze times for smoking cues were associated not only with lower levels of nicotine dependence, but also with higher levels of craving.

Conclusions: Overall, the results seem consistent with an integrated 'incentive-habit' model of addiction.

Choosing this example is not intended to belittle this work from one of the world's leading research groups. It is chosen just to illustrate a very common approach to linking theory to empirical evidence. There is no doubt that the study provided interesting data but arguably the use of the phrase 'consistent with' in the conclusion reveals that in fact the link between theory and data is extremely tenuous.

Meehl's insights into the failure of soft psychology to make progress

The failure of psychology to make progress because of an inappropriate approach to the updating of theories in the light of observation was beautifully described by Meehl some 30 years ago (Meehl 1978). He observed that theories in soft psychology are neither refuted nor corroborated but fade away as people lose interest. There are many intrinsic difficulties with the subject matter that contribute to this. A reliance on 'significance testing' is partly responsible. Significance testing (also known as Neyman Pearson or orthodox statistics) involves the probability of the data being true given a theory or hypothesis, that is, $P(\text{data}|\text{theory})$ and a decisional procedure that ensures results are 'objective' and that long-term error rates of both false positives and negatives are controlled. However, for the purposes of evaluating theory, the $P(\text{theory}|\text{data})$ is clearly more useful. Unfortunately, conditional probabilities cannot be inferred from the inverse. Compare the probability of being dead given decapitation by a lorry with the probability of having been decapitated by a lorry given being dead. Therefore, orthodox statistics do not provide an intuitive means of understanding the likely truth of theory (Dienes 2008, 2011). Instead, researchers are left 'pretending' that there is a relationship if there is a p value of less than 0.05 (or any other value) and not if it does not, and interpreting patterns of p values in terms of relationships that 'exist' or 'do not exist'. Consistency tests that aim to estimate numerical parameters or Bayes factors that indicate degrees of continuous support for hypotheses (Dienes 2011) are much better approaches.

The sensitising role of theory

The preceding analysis has taken a largely Popperian view of theories as statements that are tested against evidence and potentially falsified. Science progresses, it is argued, by a closer and closer approximation to reality in both coverage and content. There is another view. Blumer (1969) argues for the 'sensitising' role of theory: to generate ideas and concepts that help understanding. It could be argued that it is this role that is being fulfilled in theories in psychology.

Thus the role of the Theory of Planned Behaviour, for example, is to alert us to the importance of specific attitudes to a behaviour – our beliefs about what people who matter to us think, and our confidence in being able to successfully complete the action – in determining our intentions to do something. It also emphasises the fact that intentions play an important role in attempts to stop smoking (Norman et al. 1999).

The fact that it fails to consider other important motives, or that in its specific formulation it makes claims about how people combine their motives that are clearly untrue, is less important than the way in which it sensitises us to these ideas.

This is a useful role for theory but if one is willing to propose a theory that even as it is being proposed conflicts with 'big observations' and therefore must be wrong, there is no hope for progress in theory development. In psychology, economics and other behavioural and social sciences, there is a remarkable tolerance for a multitude of theories, many of which overlap considerably, many of which deal with a small part of a system (e.g. the motivational system) that is in fact integrated and many of which are contradicted by big observations.

When on occasions a researcher seeks to compete one theory against another (see Farkas et al. 1996), it is considered almost impolite and is rarely if ever successful because the proponents of the losing theory can always find ways to claim that the competition was unfair or as a last resort that their theory is basically correct and can be modified to take account of apparently conflicting evidence rather than be abandoned.

We can summarise the process of theory generation currently in operation as follows: a researcher has an insight which he or she believes is novel and has the intellectual capability and motivation to turn it into a theory; he or she does this with insufficient regard to other theories or big observations that would mean that the theory as stated must be incorrect even though the basic idea is useful; the ideas in the theory capture the imagination and appeal to a following who then start to use it even though it has not been rigorously tested against competing theories. Such theories play a useful sensitising role for the ideas being presented but at the expense of neglect of other ideas that are as or more important when considering the behaviour in question.

Perhaps one should not underestimate the importance of establishing a personal reputation or even financial reward in this process. It is easy to forget that researchers, just like anyone else, have personal motives for career advancement and the plaudits of our colleagues.

For theory development to proceed, what is needed is a much fuller analysis of what problems the proposed theory addresses and a recognition that, while the proposed theory may make statements that cannot currently be tested, it absolutely must not be contradicted by observations that are already available.

'Big observations' in the field of addiction

We close this chapter with consideration of some major observations that any comprehensive theory of addiction needs to be able to accommodate.

A comprehensive theory of addiction has at the very least to account for what we know about the phenomenon, and we know a great deal. It has to account for the diversity of the experience of addiction, the social and economic data relating to addiction and major findings from the field of neuroscience. Throughout this book, we will try to draw attention to observations and systematic research that bear on the development of theory, but we will begin with a brief summary of some of the big questions.

Some big questions

(1) *Why are some drugs and activities more addictive than others?*

It has been estimated that at the start of the twenty-first century, there are 230 million people—or 5% of the world's population—using illicit drugs (primarily opium, heroin, cocaine, stimulants and cannabis) of whom some 27 million are suffering from a 'drug use disorder'. A further 76 million are suffering from alcohol use disorders and 1150 million people use tobacco of whom a majority could probably be classified as dependent (see www.who.int/substance_abuse/facts/en/ and United Nations Office on Drugs and Crime 2012).

All addictive drugs act directly on the central nervous system. Most are rewarding in the sense that a substantial proportion of users report enjoying their effects and some are only rewarding in the sense that they relieve unpleasant feelings. Even in those that provide enjoyment, the degree to which they are addictive is not directly correlated with the amount of enjoyment that users obtain from them, nor the strength of their other subjective effects (e.g. the extent of intoxication).

Nicotine from cigarettes produces modest effects and mild enjoyment but is apparently more addictive than cannabis, alcohol or cocaine. Reported enjoyment of smoking only predicts whether a smoker tries to quit but not whether they are successful (Fidler and West 2011). Some addictive drugs lead to physiological adaptation so that the body does not function properly when they are removed. But there are many drugs to which the body adapts so that sudden withdrawal leads to unwanted withdrawal symptoms that are not addictive. Addictive activities that do not involve drug-taking are also rewarding in the broad sense, at least to some people, but not every rewarding activity is addictive.

(2) *Why does addiction take repeated exposures to develop but then remain roughly at the same level with further exposure?*

It can take months or years from the initial sampling of an activity for addiction to develop (e.g. Robinson et al. 2004; Vitaro et al. 2004; Fidler et al. 2006; Wanner et al. 2006). In some cases, the activity is sampled and then not tried again for some time. Then there appears to be a period that can be just a few months or several years while the severity of dependence increases. After that time, there is no evidence of an increase. It should also be noted that the positive experience that addicts obtain from their drug is never abolished through habituation; even long-term heavy users of a drug, for example, obtain pleasurable sensations from it.

(3) *Why are some individuals, strata in society, ethnic groups and cultures more susceptible to addictions than others?*

Prevalence of almost all recognised addictions is higher in men than women but this is subject to cultural and temporal variation (e.g. Pomerleau et al. 1993; Burt et al. 2000; Zilberman et al. 2003). These differences in prevalence may be related to the gender differences present in all phases of drug abuse, including initiation, escalation of use, addiction and relapse following abstinence (Becker and Hu 2008). In the case of most addictive behaviours, prevalence is also associated with economic deprivation. There are also substantial cultural and regional variations. At an individual level, onset of most addictions is more likely in people who show greater propensity to antisocial behaviour as well as anxiety and depression. Being subject to physical or sexual abuse as a child is strongly linked to development of addiction to illicit drugs and alcohol (see e.g. Wilsnack et al. 1997; Marcenko et al. 2000; Langeland et al. 2003).

(4) *Why are many addicts able to stop engaging in an activity to which they have been addicted but very few are able to maintain a pattern of non-addicted use?*

A large proportion of individuals addicted to alcohol, heroin, cocaine, nicotine and gambling appear eventually to stop engaging in the activity (Granfield and Cloud 2001; Russell et al. 2001; Klingemann and Carter-Sobell 2007). In many cases, this seems to occur without formal treatment but usually depends on the availability of psychological and social capital (Bischof et al. 2001; Laudet and White 2008). On the other hand, for individuals who have developed an addicted pattern of use, the prospect of achieving a stable pattern of non-addicted use is slim. This is true for smoking (Hajek et al. 1995) and alcohol (Mann et al. 2005).

(5) *Why are withdrawal symptoms not strongly related to failure to maintain abstinence?*

Some addictive drugs such as heroin and alcohol have a very clear withdrawal syndrome involving unpleasant physical symptoms (Hughes et al. 1994). Withdrawal from other drugs such as nicotine clearly leads to a well-defined set of psychological symptoms and some minor physical symptoms. With some drugs such as amphetamine it is less clear that there is a distinct syndrome but mood disturbance is common. But how important are these to the pattern of compulsive use observed? The evidence suggests that the relationship is modest at best (see e.g. Patten and Martin 1996).

(6) Why do some situations increase the likelihood of relapse when people are trying to stop the addictive activity?

Unpleasant events, periods when there is a lack of interesting things to do, situations and stimuli that have previously been associated with the activity and the sight of someone else engaging in the activity all increase the likelihood of relapse (e.g. Annis 1990).

(7) Why are some interventions and treatments for addiction more successful than others?

What we know about effective treatment for addiction can be summed up relatively easily: we know surprisingly little (Lingford-Hughes et al. 2012).

With heroin addiction, we know that the supervised long-term substitution of methadone or buprenorphine can reduce or in some cases eliminate heroin use. We do not know whether or not psychological support such as counselling helps to reduce or eliminate heroin use. Neither do we know whether or not the use of a gradually diminishing dose of methadone or other drugs helps a heroin user to become completely drug free.

With alcohol addiction, we know that a programme of psychological support of some kind (we do not know what) can increase the ability of alcoholics to remain abstinent for months or even years. We also know that using either acamprosate or naltrexone can help.

With nicotine addiction, we know that a relatively brief programme of psychological support lasting for about 6 weeks increases the ability of smokers to remain abstinent for at least 12 months. It is not clear exactly what constitutes effective support but certain techniques may be more helpful than others, such as showing smokers their expired-air carbon monoxide readings to boost motivation to stop. The effect of support most typically used is not large: between 1 in 20 and 1 in 10 smokers stop smoking who would not otherwise have done. We also know that a variety of different drugs can each increase the number who stop successfully, including the various forms of nicotine replacement therapy (NRT) – such as gum, skin patch and lozenge – the nicotinic receptor agonists varenicline and cytosine, and the antidepressants bupropion and nortriptyline. The most effective is either varenicline or a combination of an NRT patch plus a faster-acting form, such as the gum. Putting psychological support and one of these drugs together it seems that as many as 10–15% of addicted smokers can be helped to stop for at least 12 months over and above those who could have stopped anyway.

(8) *Why do different addictive drugs follow particular consumption distributions in the population?*

Alcohol has a pattern with a small proportion of total abstainers (in drinking cultures), together with a unimodal (with one peak) distribution with most of the population drinking at a level that is not harmful but a 'tail' that extends into very high and damaging levels of consumption. Heroin is used by only a very small minority of the population (probably less than 1% of the population in the United States). These patterns, and patterns of use of other drugs, are discussed later in this chapter.

(9) *Why do different addictive drugs show different temporal patterns of use?*

Alcohol is mostly used in drinking sessions that occur during leisure time; these sessions are often terminated at or below moderate levels of intoxication but they are sometimes continued until a high level of intoxication is reached. For some individuals, these 'binges' are frequent but still limited to leisure time. Some individuals drink most of the day at a level that causes intoxication. Smoking patterns tend to follow a pattern that reflects restrictions. Where it is permitted at all times and can be afforded easily, it tends to occur at regular intervals throughout the day, but where there are restrictions naturally it clusters around certain times and places. These patterns and temporal patterns of usage of other drugs are considered in more detail later.

The natural history of addiction in individuals

The development of addiction follows many different trajectories but there are some commonalities. An activity is sampled first of all, often with no particular intention to make it a regular thing. The individual is curious to see what it is like and unafraid that just sampling the activity will lead to serious lasting harm. This lack of fear may be because the individual does not believe that sampling the activity will lead to harm, or it may be because the person does not mind particularly about the harm that it could lead to or it may be because the individual does not give the future any particular thought.

Initially, the activity occurs at a relatively low rate and is linked to particular situations or particular times. The individual will report that the behaviour is enjoyable or serves some particular purpose. Then it becomes more frequent and the individual will seek out more opportunities to engage in it. This may mean giving up other activities. It may also mean engaging in additional activities to support the behaviour in question.

The enjoyment of the activity may or may not change during this period, but a sense of wanting to engage in the activity or even 'needing' to engage in it will develop. This does not necessarily occur at all times, but may be tied to situations or times when there is seen to be an opportunity to engage in the behaviour. If the activity cannot be engaged in, the individual will often experience unpleasant effects. In the case of some drug addictions, these are generally a combination of adverse mood and physical symptoms.

At some point, the individual may notice (or have it drawn to his or her attention) that the behaviour is causing problems, and may seek to reduce its frequency or stop it altogether. This results in an increase in feelings of need to engage in the activity that has to be countered by restraint. In most cases, the restraint is insufficient to prevent a 'lapse' in which the behaviour re-occurs. This lapse then usually turns within a short period into a 'relapse' where the individual resumes his or her activity at approximately the same rate as before. The individual, feeling that he or she is unable to exercise restraint, will sometimes seek help with doing so. With the benefit of this help, the individual stands a better chance of maintaining abstinence, though relapse still occurs in the majority of cases. The longer an individual, with or without help, is able to maintain abstinence, the greater his or her likelihood of continuing to maintain it indefinitely.

More on the addictive potential of drugs and activities

Addiction occurs mostly to the activity of taking particular drugs, but it can also occur to other activities, most notably gambling. Drugs that cause addiction in a significant number of users are typically those that give an experience of pleasure or reduce feelings of anxiety. Table 2.4 gives a list of activities or consumables that at least some researchers consider are addictive to *some people* (see e.g. Bruinsma and Taren 1999; Irons and Schneider 1997; Holden 2001; Padwa and Cunningham 2010; Potenza 2001). It offers a possible view on the level of 'addictive potential' of these drugs or activities. In some cases, as with nicotine and heroin, this view is not controversial. In other cases, such as shopping and eating tasty food, views legitimately differ with regard to the propositions that they have moderate addictive potential to none at all.

For the United States, the National Comorbidity Survey provided estimates of dependence potential of some drugs using a national sample aged 15–54 years (Warner et al. 1995). The survey tallied lifetime prevalence of drug addiction using DSM-IIIR criteria and it also examined 'ever use'. Tobacco dependence was by far the most prevalent of drug dependencies: among ever users (used at least once in a lifetime), 32% of tobacco users were dependent compared with 23% of heroin users, 17% of cocaine users and 15% of alcohol users. These percentages are based on those who ever used each drug for a non-medical purpose. In 2007, Louisa Degenhardt et al. undertook a similar exercise, excluding tobacco, with broadly similar results (Degenhardt et al. 2007).

Table 2.5 shows rough estimates of ever users (by self-report) and use in the past month of illicit drugs in the United Kingdom in 2000. It also shows the approximate costs of regular monthly use. The percentage of users in the past month gives a possible upper estimate of the propensity of a drug to elicit regular use and possibly addictive use. What is noteworthy is that most of the figures are broadly in line with figures cited above from the United States.

Table 2.4 Drugs and activities that at least some people have seriously claimed to have addictive potential

Drug/activity	Plausible estimate of 'addictive potential' (proportion of ever users who become addicted)
Those with at least some usable data	
Heroin	High
Methadone	High
Nicotine	High
Amphetamines	Moderate
Ecstasy	Moderate
Cocaine	Moderate
Alcohol	Moderate
Marijuana	Moderate
Benzodiazepines	Moderate
Gambling	Low
Those with little usable data	
Inactivity	Moderate
Tasty food	Moderate
Barbiturates	Low
Inhalants	Low
Gammahydroxybutyrate (GHB)	Low
Steroids	Low
Stealing	Low
Violence	Low
Diving	Low
Surfing	Low
Fast driving	Low
Exercise	Very low
Sexual behaviours	Very low
Using the internet	Very low
Playing computer games	Very low
Chocolate	Very low
Self-harm	Very low
Caffeine	Very low
Watching TV	Very low
Work	Very low
Shopping	Very low

Addictive potential in this case refers to the proportion of ever users who develop an addictive pattern of use at some point in their lives. At best only rough estimates are possible. High, >20%; moderate, 10–20%; low, 5–10%; very low, <5%. This is presented in a simplistic version that does not take account of mode of administration of drugs or cultural context. The purpose is simply to make concrete the idea that activities and drugs may differ in addictive potential.

Table 2.5 Use, prevalence and cost of addictions to illicit drugs in the United Kingdom in 2001

Drug	Percentage of population who are ever users	Use in past month (%)	Percentage of ever users who used in past month	Approximate monthly cost of regular use (£)
Cannabis	8.0	2.5	31	85
Amphetamine	4.0	0.3	7.5	100
Cocaine	2.0	0.4	20	160
Crack	0.3	0.1	33	450
Heroin	0.3	0.1	33	450
Ecstasy	2.0	0.4	20	40

Source: Data derived from Atha (2004).

The major anomalies are ecstasy and cannabis in which other evidence shows that regular use is only a fraction of the figure for use in the past month, probably reflecting the lifestyle of the users. What is clear is that, even with the most addictive drugs, only a minority of people who try them develop anything that could be called chronic addiction.

We should not make too much of these kinds of quantitative estimates. It is clear that all the important parameters can be influenced by social and cultural factors as well as the purity and mode of administration of the drugs themselves (see e.g. Degenhardt et al. 2007 and Giovino et al. 2012). However, they do tell us what is *possible* in particular social climates in which it is known that addiction does occur.

Recapitulation

This chapter has attempted to set the scene for the development of a theory of addiction by exploring the changing definition of addiction, issues in the criteria used to diagnose addiction, what makes a good theory, how evidence has been and should be used in the development of theories and some important observations about addiction that need to be accommodated by any comprehensive theory. Now it is time to begin the journey to a theory that is sufficiently broad to account for the phenomenon.

References

American Association for the Study and Cure of Inebriety (1893) The disease of inebriety from alcohol, opium and other narcotic drugs, its etiology, pathology, treatment and medico-legal relations. E. B. Treat Publisher, New York.

Annis, H.M. (1990) Relapse to substance abuse: empirical findings within a cognitive—social learning approach. *J Psychoactive Drugs* 22(2): 117–124.

APA (1995) *Diagnostic and Statistical Manual of Mental Disorders*, 4th edn. American Psychiatric Association, Washington, DC.

Atha, M. (2004) Taxing the UK drugs market. Independent Drug Monitoring Unit, Wigan, UK.

Becker, J.B. and Hu, M. (2008) Sex differences in drug abuse. *Front Neuroendocrinol* 29(1): 36–47.

Bischof, G., Rumpf, H.J., Hapke, U., Meyer, C. and John, U. (2001) Factors influencing remission from alcohol dependence without formal help in a representative population sample. *Addiction* 96(9): 1327–1336.

Blumer, H. (1969) *Symbolic Interactionism: Perspective and Method*. Prentice-Hall, Englewood Cliffs, NJ.

Bruinsma, K. and Taren, D.L. (1999) Chocolate: food or drug? *J Am Diet Assoc* 99(10): 1249–1256.

Burt, R.D., Dinh, K.T. Peterson, A.V. Jr and Sarason, I.G. (2000) Predicting adolescent smoking: a prospective study of personality variables. *Prev Med* 30(2): 115–125.

Carlile, P.R. and Christensen, C.M. (2004) The cycles of theory building in management research. Harvard Business School Working Paper No. 05–057. Harvard Business School, Boston.

Degenhardt, L., Chiu, W.T., Sampson, N., Kessler, R.C. and Anthony, J.C. (2007) Epidemiological patterns of extra-medical drug use in the United States: evidence from the National Comorbidity Survey Replication, 2001–2003. *Drug Alcohol Depend* 90(2–3): 210–223.

Dienes, Z. (2008) *Understanding Psychology as a Science: An Introduction to Scientific and Statistical Inference*. Palgrave Macmillan, Hampshire, UK.

Dienes, Z. (2011) Bayesian versus orthodox statistics: which side are you on? *Perspect Psychol Sci* 6(3): 274–290.

Dixon-Woods, M., Bosk, C.L., Aveling, E.L., Goeschel, C.A. and Pronovost, P.J. (2011) Explaining Michigan: developing an ex post theory of a quality improvement program. *Milbank Q* 89(2): 167–205.

Edwards, G. and Gross, M.M. (1976) Alcohol dependence: provisional description of a clinical syndrome. *Br Med J* 1(6017): 1058–1061.

Erickson, C.K. and Wilcox, R.E. (2006) Please, Not "Addiction" in DSM-V. *Am J Psychiatry* 163(11): 2015–2016; author reply 2016–2017.

Farkas, A.J., Pierce, J.P., Zhu, S.H., et al. (1996) Addiction versus stages of change models in predicting smoking cessation. *Addiction* 91(9): 1271–1280; discussion 1281–1292.

Feynman, R.P. (1974) Cargo cult science. *Eng Sci* 10–13.

Fidler, J.A., Wardle, J., Henning Brodersen, N., Jarvis, M.J. and West, R. (2006) Vulnerability to smoking after trying a single cigarette can lie dormant for three years or more. *Tob Control* 15(3): 205–209.

Fidler, J.A. and West, R. (2011) Enjoyment of smoking and urges to smoke as predictors of attempts and success of attempts to stop smoking: a longitudinal study. *Drug Alcohol Depend* 115(1–2): 30–34.

First, M.B. (2009) Harmonisation of ICD–11 and DSM–V: opportunities and challenges. *Brit J Psychiatry* 195(5): 382–390.

Giovino, G.A., Mirza, S.A., Samet, J.M., et al. (2012) Tobacco use in 3 billion individuals from 16 countries: an analysis of nationally representative cross-sectional household surveys. *Lancet* 380(9842): 668–679.

Godin, G., Sheeran, P., Conner, M. and Germain, M. (2008) Asking questions changes behavior: mere measurement effects on frequency of blood donation. *Health Psychol* 27(2): 179–184.

Granfield, R. and Cloud, W. (2001) Social context and 'natural recovery': the role of social capital in the resolution of drug-associated problems. *Subst Use Misuse* 36(11): 1543–1570.

Hajek, P., West, R. and Wilson, J. (1995) Regular smokers, lifetime very light smokers, and reduced smokers: comparison of psychosocial and smoking characteristics in women. *Health Psychol* 14(3): 195–201.

Hasin, D., Hatzenbuehler, M.L., Keyes, K. and Ogburn, E. (2006) Substance use disorders: Diagnostic and Statistical Manual of Mental Disorders, fourth edition (DSM-IV) and International Classification of Diseases, tenth edition (ICD-10). *Addiction* 101: 59–75.

Holden, C. (2001) 'Behavioral' addictions: do they exist? *Science* 294(5544): 980–982.

Hughes, J. (1993) Smoking is a drug dependence: a reply to Robinson and Pritchard. *Psychopharmacology* 113(2): 282–283.

Hughes, J.R., Higgins, S.T. and Bickel, W.K. (1994) Nicotine withdrawal versus other drug withdrawal syndromes: similarities and dissimilarities. *Addiction* 89(11): 1461–1470.

Irons, R. and Schneider, J.P. (1997) When is domestic violence a hidden face of addiction? *J Psychoactive Drugs* 29(4): 337–344.

Kerr, N. (1884) President's Inaugural Address. *Proceedings of the Society for the Study and Cure of Inebriety.* 1(1): 2–17.

Klingemann, H. and Carter-Sobell, L. (2007) *Promoting Self-change from Addictive Behaviors: Practical Implications for Policy, Prevention, and Treatment.* Springer, New York.

Langeland, W., Draijer, N. and van den Brink, W. (2003) Assessment of lifetime physical and sexual abuse in treated alcoholics. Validity of the addiction severity index. *Addict Behav* 28(5): 871–881.

Laudet, A.B. and White, W.L. (2008) Recovery capital as prospective predictor of sustained recovery, life satisfaction, and stress among former poly-substance users. *Subst Use Misuse* 43(1): 27–54.

Levin, P.F. (1999) Test of the Fishbein and Ajzen models as predictors of health care workers' glove use. *Res Nurs Health* 22(4): 295–307.

Lewin, K. (1951) *Field theory in social science: Selected theoretical papers* (ed. D. Cartwright). Harper & Row, New York.

Lingford-Hughes, A., Welch, S., Peters, L., Nutt, D., et al. (2012) BAP updated guidelines: evidence-based guidelines for the pharmacological management of substance abuse, harmful use, addiction and comorbidity: recommendations from BAP. *J Psychopharmacol* 26(7): 899–952.

Lipsey, M.W. (2004) Theory as method: small theories of treatments. *New directions for program evaluation* 1993(57): 5–38.

Mann, K., Schafer, D., Längle, G., Ackermann, K. and Croissant, B. (2005) The long-term course of alcoholism, 5, 10 and 16 years after treatment. *Addiction* 100(6): 797–805.

Marcenko, M.O., Kemp, S.P. and Larson, N.C. (2000) Childhood experiences of abuse, later substance use, and parenting outcomes among low-income mothers. *Am J Orthopsychiatry* 70(3): 316–326.

Meehl, P.E. (1978) Theoretical risks and tabular asterisks: Sir Karl, Sir Ronald, and the slow progress of soft psychology. *J Consult Clin Psychol* 46: 806–834.

Mogg, K., Field, M. and Bradley, B.P. (2005) Attentional and approach biases for smoking cues in smokers: an investigation of competing theoretical views of addiction. *Psychopharmacology* 5: 5.

Norman, P., Conner, M. and Bell, R. (1999) The theory of planned behavior and smoking cessation. *Health Psychol* 18(1): 89–94.

Nutt, D.J., King, L.A. and Phillips, L.D. (2010) Drug harms in the UK: a multicriteria decision analysis. *Lancet* 376(9752): 1558–1565.

O'Brien, C.P., Volkow, N. and Li, T.K. (2006) What's in a word? Addiction versus dependence in DSM-V. *Am J Psychiatry* 163(5): 764–765.

Ogden, J. (2003) Some problems with social cognition models: a pragmatic and conceptual analysis. *Health Psychol* 22(4): 424–428.

Padwa, H. and Cunningham, J. (2010) *Addiction: A Reference Encyclopedia*. ABC-CLIO, Santa Barbara, CA.

Pashler, H. and Wagenmakers, E.J. (2012) Editors' Introduction to the Special Section on Replicability in Psychological Science: a crisis of confidence?. *Perspect Psychol Sci* 7(6): 528–530.

Patten, C. and Martin, J. (1996) Does nicotine withdrawal affect smoking cessation? Clinical and theoretical issues. *Ann Behav Med* 18(3): 190–200.

Pomerleau, O.F., Collins, A.C., Shiffman, S. and Pomerleau, C.S. (1993) Why some people smoke and others do not: new perspectives. *J Consult Clin Psychol* 61(5): 723–731.

Potenza, M.N. (2001) The neurobiology of pathological gambling. *Semin Clin Neuropsychiatry* 6(3): 217–226.

Prochaska, J.O. and Velicer, W.F. (1997) The transtheoretical model of health behavior change. *Am J Health Promot* 12(1): 38–48.

Robinson, J.H. and Pritchard, W.S. (1992) The role of nicotine in tobacco use. *Psychopharmacology (Berl)* 108(4): 397–407.

Robinson, M.L., Berlin, I. and Moolchan, E.T. (2004) Tobacco smoking trajectory and associated ethnic differences among adolescent smokers seeking cessation treatment. *J Adolesc Health* 35(3): 217–224.

Rounsaville, B.J. (2002) Experience with ICD-10/DSM-IV substance use disorders. *Psychopathology* 35(2–3): 82–88.

Russell, M., Peirce, R.S., Chan, A.W., Wieczorek, W.F., Moscato, B.S. and Nochajski, T.H. (2001) Natural recovery in a community-based sample of alcoholics: study design and descriptive data. *Subst Use Misuse* 36(11): 1417–1441.

United Nations Office on Drugs and Crime (2012) *World Drug Report*. Geneva, United Nations.

Vitaro, F., Wanner, B., Ladouceur, R., Brendgen, M. and Tremblay, R.E. (2004) Trajectories of gambling during adolescence. *J Gambl Stud* 20(1): 47–69.

Wanner, B., Vitaro, F., Ladouceur, R., Brendgen, M. and Tremblay, R.E. (2006) Joint trajectories of gambling, alcohol and marijuana use during adolescence: a person- and variable-centered developmental approach. *Addict Behav* 31(4): 566–580.

Warner, L.A., Kessler, R.C., Hughes, M., Anthony, J.C. and Nelson, C.B. (1995) Prevalence and correlates of drug use and dependence in the United States. Results from the national comorbidity survey. *Arch Gen Psychiatry* 52: 219–229.

West, R. (1992) Nicotine addiction: a re-analysis of the arguments. *Psychopharmacology* 108(4): 408–410.

West, R. (2013) Models of Addiction. European Monitoring Centre for Drugs and Drug Addiction, Lisbon, Portugal.

WHO (1992) *International Classification of Diseases and Related Health Problems, Tenth Revision (ICD-10)*. World Health Organisation, Geneva, Switzerland.

Wilsnack, S.C., Vogeltanz, N.D. Klassen, A.D. and Harris, T.R. (1997) Childhood sexual abuse and women's substance abuse: national survey findings. *J Stud Alcohol* 58(3): 264–271.

Zilberman, M., Tavares, H. and el-Guebaly, N. (2003) Gender similarities and differences: the prevalence and course of alcohol- and other substance-related disorders. *J Addict Dis* 22(4): 61–74.

Chapter 3
BEGINNING THE JOURNEY: ADDICTION AS CHOICE

This chapter starts the journey to the development of a comprehensive theory of addiction. It begins with the simplest common-sense model of rational, informed choice with stable preferences, moves on to a model of choice with unstable preferences, and then considers ways in which the choice might be irrational. Regarding addiction as a choice process goes a surprisingly long way towards explaining the major phenomena and most theories of addiction, and attempts at combating addiction derive from this approach. However, we have to conclude at the end of the chapter that addiction cannot be exclusively construed in terms of choices.

Addiction as a reflective choice

Having established in the previous chapter broadly what it is we are talking about, let us now start our journey of trying to understand it. The most obvious starting point is a reflective choice model of behaviour. Reflective choice involves the self-conscious analysis of the options and a decision to enact one of those options. The choice may be rational or biased but it always involves an explicit consideration of the options. The Rational Informed Stable Choice (RISC) is the most straightforward version of this model.

Addiction as cost–benefit analysis

Under this model, we do things because we expect them to confer benefits and we know about and are willing to accept the adverse consequences. For most of us, this is the default model for explaining our own behaviour and that of other people. It provides the starting point for our thinking. Under the most extreme version of this theory, there is no abnormality in the mental functioning of the addict, no disorder: there only appears to be. When we see a heroin addict living in squalor and suffering ill health, we wrongly assume that this person would prefer not to live like this and only does so because he or she has lost control over the activity.

Theory of Addiction, Second Edition. Robert West and Jamie Brown.
© 2013 John Wiley & Sons, Ltd. Published 2013 by John Wiley & Sons, Ltd.

The importance of the addict's eye view

Under this view, it may be that the addict would prefer to live differently, but *among the options that he or she sees as actually open to him or her* – this is judged to be the best on offer at the time. When we see the alcoholic sleeping on the street, living a life of degradation in a drink-fuelled haze with the likelihood of an early death, it is wrong to assume that he or she does so because he or she cannot stop drinking. This life may be preferable to his or her own life without alcohol. When we see smokers puffing on a cigarette in the cold outside the back door of their office building, risking lung cancer, heart disease and chronic bronchitis, it is wrong to believe that they do so because they cannot stop. Under an RISC model, they prefer the life of a smoker to the alternative that is open to them – their own life as a non-smoker.

The RISC theory: one addict's eye view

All things considered, I prefer my life as a [drinker/smoker/heroin user/gambler/ tranquilliser user/crack user] because it is better than my life would be if I stopped. This is because it [gives me pleasure/makes me feel better/is part of who I am/helps me to cope with life/helps me do things I need to do]. I realise that [it is doing me harm/might do me harm in the future/is doing harm to people I care about/may make people I care about unhappy]. But for me the benefits outweigh the costs. This may change if my situation changes so that, for example, it becomes clear that what was once just a possibility of harm (such as getting heart disease) becomes more likely. On the other hand, I know that my activity [is causing problems for myself/is causing problems for other people/is viewed as morally wrong] so it serves me to present the activity as being outside my control.

Numerous qualitative studies have revealed that aspects of the above story are often cited by people explaining their addictive behaviour. For example, below are two excerpts from interviews with opiate addicts conducted by McAuliffe and Gordon (1974) in Baltimore:

Respondent: I like being high.
Interviewer: What do you like about being high?
R: I like the rush when you fire and I like the nod.
I: Why do you like being high?
R: It's just like when people like to get drunk, you know, they do it because they feel good.
I: What do you mean, "They feel good"?
R: They just feel good, that's all. Just like most people like to ball [have intercourse with] a girl to get the climax because it feels good.
I: So, when you're high, when you say you feel good, what's that mean to you?
R: I'm happy and content.
I: Anything else?
R: No, just satisfied.

I: When you fire [inject opiates], are you usually just trying to feel normal, or are you firing to get high in a way that makes you feel *better* than normal?
R: I think I am firing to get high and feel better than normal.

> **I:** How many caps of good smack [heroin] do you need a day to just keep your sickness away? That is, just enough for you to feel normal all day?
> **R:** Right now I need four all day to keep me going. I could space them but I don't like it. I did two and one-half this morning, and that will hold me until late tonight.
> **I:** Then you'll do two more?
> **R:** Yeah, I'll do two, maybe more.
> **I:** Suppose you had twice that many, and it was the same good stuff, how many would you cook up and fire at one time, assuming that you have money to cop [buy drugs] for the next day ? Suppose you had eight?
> **R:** I'd do all of them. Not for one shot though. I'd throw in [to the cooker] about three.
> **R:** Why would you fire that many?
> **R:** To get high.

When we see the gambler who has lost his or her family and is living in debt to loan sharks but keeps returning to the betting shop in the hope of a big win that when it comes just provides more stake money, it is wrong to assume that there is something wrong with him or her. The behaviour seems to be out of control but according to an RISC analysis, he or she prefers to live this way than what for him or her would be the alternatives.

'Do you want to stop?'

According to this view, it is misleading to ask the smoker or the alcoholic if they want to stop smoking and to use a contradiction between their responses and their behaviour as evidence of addiction. The smoker may well say that he or she wants to stop smoking, just as he or she may say that he or she would like to be a multimillionaire. There are lots of things we would like. The real question is, 'Does the prospect of becoming a non-smoker and all that this entails appeal to you more than continuing, for the time being, your life as a smoker?' If the smoker says 'Yes' and continues to smoke, there would be at least a prima facie case against the RISC model.

Addiction is a matter of perspective

According to this model, the concept of addiction is an illusion that stems from the failure of perspective on the part of onlookers. We see the life the addict leads and we imagine a life that would be so much better if the person were not engaging so frequently in the addictive behaviour.

However, we forget that the alternative life we imagine for the addict is not the alternative life the addict imagines for himself or herself. The pleasure or escape that the addict obtains from a drug is worth whatever short- and long-term costs there might be for that individual. If a drug is particularly pleasurable for an individual, it could be worth the risk of an early grave. Even if a drug is not particularly pleasurable, if the addict's emotional state or life circumstances as an ex-drug user are bleak and unhappy, it would be quite rational to choose to remain a user.

Rational addiction theories

There are a number of theories that fall within the Rational Choice model of addiction (see Vuchinich and Heather 2003). Box 3.1 gives an interesting example which highlights the observation, undoubtedly valid, that addiction is a social construct that serves a particular purpose for particular individuals at particular times. People may label themselves as addicted on one occasion and not on another depending on the benefits or costs of attaching these labels. However, it only highlights one feature of the application of the label 'addiction' and if it were proposed as a theory of addiction would fall foul of strong contradictory evidence as discussed later.

Box 3.1 The myth of addiction

According to Davies (1997), addiction is a myth or legend similar to 'possession' that serves particular functions for society. Davies notes that the language that addicts use to describe their behaviour varies depending on the person to whom they are talking. If they are talking to health workers or the police, they use the language of addiction; their behaviour is out of control and they cannot help themselves.

In this way they minimise blame and punishment and maximise their chances of forgiveness, understanding and help. When so-called addicts talk to their peers, they use a different kind of language that would be hard to distinguish from the language they use to talk about other behaviours such as shopping. They are exercising preferences that are understandable and rational given the kinds of people they are and the circumstances in which they live.

Attributing drug taking or other damaging excesses to addiction also serves the needs of people other than the addict. It serves the needs of those in the professions whose living depends on treating addicts as though they were ill. It serves the emotional needs of families of addicts who find it difficult to accept that someone they care for is behaving in a way that is harming themselves and others and otherwise would be morally wrong. It serves the needs of politicians and pundits who prefer not to make moralistic judgements about people. Similar arguments centring around the 'myth of addiction' are well rehearsed and continue to inspire a fairly devoted following (Szasz 1972; Room 1983; Fingarette 1988; Fitzpartick 2003; Heyman 2009; Schaler 1999).

Issues and evaluation
This theory highlights an important feature of addiction that is easily over-looked: that the terminology used serves a function for the user. In this case, attributing certain activities to addiction enables the addict or other members

of society to meet their physical or emotional needs regarding help and understanding rather than blame and personal responsibility. However, denial of the reality of the phenomena of addiction, including the feelings of craving and compulsion are contradicted by observation. Measures of nicotine dependence, such as the severity of urges to smoke, predict the likelihood of an ex-smoker relapsing where self-reports of enjoyment or motivation to quit fail. These phenomena are not myths and denial of these phenomena similarly serve functions for tobacco industry apologists and public health advocates whose careers have been built on interventions that assume rational choice.

The RISC model can perhaps explain why drugs such as heroin and cocaine have a strong addictive potential: it is just that they are very pleasurable. It can explain why heroin use is so much less common than, say, marijuana use: it may be partly because of the greater severity of legal sanctions but is also explained by a greater fear of the adverse consequences – most people see heroin as a dangerous drug that they do not even want to try. It can explain why some people are more susceptible to heroin addiction: perhaps they place greater value on immediate pleasure or their lives without heroin are more bleak and meaningless.

It can perhaps explain why activities such as smoking that are only mildly pleasurable appear to be addictive: while young the prospect of possible death and illness in the distant future is not a sufficient deterrent to overcome the enjoyment experienced in the present; when old and infirm there is no reason to stop smoking because the damage is already done. Thus, the costs of smoking are not judged to be particularly great early on, and later on it is too late to do anything about it.

Economists have developed a number of models that attempt to explain addiction as a societal phenomenon. These models are typically choice models and stem from a fundamental precept of economic theory, that at a population level, consumer choices can be understood in terms of maximising 'utilities'. That is, consumers will expend resources according to their judgements about benefits to them of the goods they are acquiring.

One of the most widely cited economic models of addiction is the Theory of Rational Addiction by Becker and Murphy (Box 3.2). This develops a number of equations relating to the consumption of addictive 'goods' on the assumption that addicts are making rational choices with stable preferences. This model appears to be contradicted by observations at both the individual and population level.

Box 3.2   Vaguely right or precisely wrong? The Theory of Rational Addiction

Becker and Murphy (1988) have proposed an economic model of addiction that is based on the idea of stable rational preferences. Rationality is defined as a 'consistent plan to maximise utility over time' (p. 675).

Utilities

Utility is a term that economists use to quantify benefits or losses as the person concerned sees them. It is different for different individuals and not the same thing as objective value. For example, $100 will have a different utility for a beggar than for a millionaire and even for the millionaire will have a different utility when taken off the price of a house as when deducted from the price of a hi-fi. Utility provides a single dimension on which to compare things that are very different – which is of course necessary when making choices. For example, when deciding to spend a windfall on a yacht or a house, we have to convert the various desirable attributes of each to a single scale so that they can be weighed against each other: that scale is utility.

Addictive 'goods'

In the Theory of Rational Addiction (TRA), addiction is manifest as an increase in consumption of a 'good' (as in 'goods', e.g. drugs, gambling or anything that costs resources) as a result of past consumption. Thus an increase in the present consumption leads to an increase in the future consumption.

The model is supposedly able to explain patterns of consumption that include bingeing and temporary and permanent abstention. According to this theory, addiction is a term that can be applied to a wide range of 'goods' such as gambling, watching TV, sex and other people. In addictions to things that cost money, it predicts that addicts will respond more strongly to permanent than temporary price changes and that increased tension precipitates addiction.

Harmful and beneficial addictions

The theory makes a distinction between 'harmful' and 'beneficial' addictions. Addiction to heroin and alcohol are harmful, whereas addiction to religion and jogging are beneficial. The difference between the two appears to lie in the effect of consumption on an individual's 'stock' of capital – resources.

Addicts look ahead and maximise utilities

According to this theory, addicts are mostly rational consumers who look ahead and behave in a way that maximises preferences that they hold and that remain stable over time. This seems at odds with the observation that preferences change over time with mood and time since last partaking of the goods, but the proponents of the theory argue that it is not. They also claim that what lies at the heart of addiction is an 'unstable steady state'.

This sounds like a contradiction in terms, an oxymoron, but it is not. An unstable steady state is one in which the behaviour changes over time as a function of underlying conditions (expressed as parameters in their equations – see 'The dynamics of addiction' below) that remain stable.

What makes a 'good' addictive?

So to the mechanism: the first thing to note is that the theory is expressed as a set of equations relating variables that are drawn from market economics but which are used to represent psychological variables: stock, consumption, depreciation, and so on. This makes it difficult to interpret because the concepts are similar to but not the same as those that we generally use when thinking about behaviour; on the other hand, they are not strictly economic variables either. This allows the theory to get away with some questionable assumptions on the one hand and to state some truisms as though they were genuine insights on the other.

So what follows is an attempt to translate the theory into language a non-economist can understand. According to the TRA, addiction arises from an interaction between individuals and goods. Individuals are generally more susceptible to harmful addictions to the extent that they disregard future consequences of their actions. They are more susceptible to beneficial addictions to the extent that they are more future-oriented. Goods are addictive for individuals to the extent that, for those individuals, they are reinforcing and they induce tolerance.

Goods are reinforcing for an individual if each time they are used they increase the likelihood that they will be used again. This is akin to the psychological notion of positive reinforcement: giving a hungry rat food if it presses a lever increases the likelihood of the rat pressing the lever again, and the rate of pressing will increase with each repetition of the sequence. The food is a positive reinforcer. However, the description by the TRA is much simpler and falls short of an adequate depiction of how rewards affect behaviour.

Tolerance represents a reduction in the utility of a good as a result of consumption. It is akin to, but again a much simplified version of, the concept of pharmacological tolerance in which there is physiological adaptation to ingestion of a drug so that it has less of an effect with repeated use. In reality, tolerance occurs to both unpleasant and sought-after effects of some drugs and for other drugs it seems to occur primarily to the unpleasant effects. In fact, in the case of stimulants such as cocaine, the rewarding effect of the drug appears to increase with repeated use.

Individual differences
Individuals differ, not only in their propensity to reinforcement and tolerance, but also in the resources (e.g. income) at their disposal to participate in the activity and how the activity affects these. One individual will be able to get drunk on a regular basis without damaging his or her livelihood while another will not. The non-economic costs of the activity will also differ; an individual who suffers severe hangovers after relatively light drinking will be less inclined to drink heavily.

The dynamics of addiction
Depending on the values of the various parameters that are plugged into the equations, an individual may exhibit an increase in consumption that then

stabilises, a continuing increase followed by abrupt cessation, cycling through consumption and abstinence, bingeing or merely brief flirtation with the activity followed by no further use. Drugs that are highly addictive are characterised by parameters that mostly lead to either high levels of consumption or complete abstinence.

Nicotine would seem to be such a drug. Becker and Murphy (1988) state that cocaine follows this pattern as well but actually that is not the case; most cocaine use is at a relatively low level (Gossop et al. 1994; Shearer et al. 2007). Drugs that have relatively low addictive potential have parameters resulting in a unimodal distribution (with a single peak) that is below the level for harmful use but with a tail that includes very high levels of consumption that are harmful. According to the theory, looking at the consumption patterns of individuals, those that are addicted typically show the bimodal (all or nothing) pattern of consumption.

The theory argues that older people should be 'rationally myopic' in that they have less time to live and therefore should be less concerned about the future. This illustrates rather nicely the difficulty in arriving at unequivocal, testable predictions in this area. It is obviously extremely rare for people to develop addictions in old age but this can then be explained by life circumstances and opportunity.

Theory predictions
The forward-looking nature of addicts specified by the theory predicts that just the *announcement* of a future price increase should change current consumption. On this prediction, the theory appears supported by evidence that US monthly cigarette consumption is affected by state excise tax increases that have been legislatively enacted but not yet enforced (Gruber and Koszegi 2001). However, the theory also predicts that a price increase will have a small initial effect on consumption but this will grow with time until a new steady state is reached. This appears to be contradicted by the evidence but then it all depends on the timescale over which one is looking and of course there will be some specific factors that will be important. The effect of price on cigarette consumption appears to be immediate and similar observations have been made for alcohol and heroin. However, the theory can always claim that the effect is progressive but over a relatively short timescale or that other factors also come into play.

The theory predicts that for individuals, an addictive pattern of consumption will be triggered by stressful life events. This is because the overall utility of the individual will be reduced and the marginal utility from consuming the addictive good relative to it will be greater.

One controversial postulate of the theory is that addicts are happier than they would be without their drug or addictive activity. It is argued that the reason that addicts generally appear to be more distressed than non-addicts is that distress has led them to addiction and keeps them in it. Again, this appears to be contradicted by studies with smokers, for example, which show that well-being does not diminish when they stop. If anything, the happiness of smokers appears to improve after quitting (Shahab and West 2012). But again, the conflicting observations can be explained away in terms of measures that are used or other confounding variables.

This is an economic theory and so deals with a conceptualisation of addiction that is different from that of the clinician, behavioural scientist or even member of the lay public. It deals with 'consumption' of a 'good'. Its explanatory concepts are also somewhat different from those that most of us would understand, though in some cases they are presented as variants of psychological concepts such as 'reinforcement' and 'tension'.

Issues and evaluation
The theory makes a lot of assumptions and allows itself a great deal of latitude in explaining patterns of consumption that the proponents believe to occur, but except in the most general of terms, the patterns of consumption observed are not those that the model predicts. In attempting to derive a mathematical description of consumption, the theory fails to do justice to the complexity of the phenomenon and calls to mind the old adage that economists prefer to be precisely wrong rather than vaguely right.

Probably its most useful insight is that, when addicts say they want to stop using a drug or whatever, they do not necessarily mean that they would prefer their own life without drugs and they do not necessarily mean that they would like it to happen in the immediate future.

Self-medication and choice

We noted earlier that there are strong associations between drug use in particular and psychological problems, and that so-called addicts may be taking drugs as a means of coping with or ameliorating adverse life experiences. This approach has found its clearest expression in the Self-medication Model of addiction (Box 3.3).

This model has been proposed by many people in many forms. In one form, it proposes that drug taking involves a cost–benefit analysis in which the benefits of the drug outweigh the costs. Apart from problems of mood disorder, we can expand this approach to any psychological deficits. For example, it has been proposed that smokers may smoke, at least partly, in order to combat problems they have in maintaining attention. It is argued that nicotine in particular helps with sustained attention (Warburton 1985, 1992). Related to this it has also been argued that smokers may have an underlying deficit in 'sensory gating' – tuning out irrelevant stimuli – and that nicotine helps to correct this disorder. In fact there is disagreement about the supposed beneficial effects of nicotine (West 1993) but that does not alter the fact that at least some researchers have claimed that it plays a role in why some people choose to smoke.

Box 3.3 The Self-medication Model of addiction

The Self-medication Model of addiction seeks to explain the development of addiction and individual differences in susceptibility to it. It proposes that individuals intentionally use drugs to treat psychological symptoms from which they suffer (e.g. Gelkopf et al. 2002).

Drugs as rational coping mechanisms

The Self-medication Model of addictive disorders derives from clinical observations and surveys of addicted individuals showing that they are predisposed to addiction if they suffer from unpleasant affective states and psychiatric disorders (Khantzian 1997; Farrell et al. 2001). The model proposes that the particular drug an addict uses is not decided upon at random but is one that helps with the particular problem or problems that the person is struggling with. Therefore, initiation of drug use and the choice of drug are based on the drug effect sought by the individual. Drugs may be chosen because they alleviate feelings of anxiety, help to control aggressive impulses, help to cope with psychotic symptoms and so on (Buckley 1998).

The model need not be limited to diagnosable psychological disorders. In principle it can be extended to any level and form of psychological need, however caused. For example, it could apply to anxiety and depression resulting from life circumstances. In a further variant of the model, the drug or activity may not even make things better – they need only be judged to do so by the person concerned.

Drug use and stress relief

For example, most smokers will cite 'stress relief' as a major motivating factor and yet current smokers report higher levels of stress than never smokers or even ex-smokers. Moreover, when smokers stop, their stress levels actually decrease and when they relapse they go up again (Cohen and Lichtenstein 1990). It is possible that each cigarette has an acute effect on stress, possibly because it relieves withdrawal symptoms that arise when the smoker cannot smoke, but there is a chronic effect in increasing stress (Parrott 1998).

Something similar may happen with alcohol. Acute intoxication without doubt can help people to 'forget their troubles', calm fears and ease pain. However, once the effect has worn off, there may be a rebound increase in anxiety. Moreover, repeated intoxication has an adverse effect on the life of the drinker which leads to increased stress and anxiety.

Combating the side effects of other drugs

In a further development of the model, it has been proposed that some drugs may serve a purpose in alleviating the side effects of drugs that are used to treat psychiatric disorder. This is particularly so for smoking, in which, for example, the effect of nicotine in increasing dopamine release at certain nerve terminals has been argued to help with the side effect of neuroleptic drugs (Poirier et al. 2002).

Possible mechanisms
The Self-medication Model in its most general form covers short-term situational as well as chronic, environmental, short-term state and long-term trait problems that might be ameliorated by addictive drugs. Possible mechanisms and brain pathways underpinning self-medication effects have been proposed (Kassel et al. 2003).

Issues and evaluation
In its basic form, the Self-medication Model requires that psychological disorders predate drug use and this is often though not always the case. The model cannot explain the many cases of addiction where there is no underlying pathology. Neither can it explain drug use in situations where there are no psychological problems to be overcome. The model also fails to account for the extensive evidence of biological and psychological changes that occur with chronic drug use that appear to underpin compulsion.

Overall, the Self-medication Model fits well with a choice theory and can explain some of the phenomena of addiction but by no means all. Therefore, a synthetic theory of addiction should probably include the concept.

The issue of informed choice and future orientation

The view that many people who are classified as addicts are highly motivated by problems that they have in their lives seems inescapable. However, as a comprehensive model of addiction, it is contradicted by the fact that many addicts show no evidence of underlying problems apart from their addiction. Thus, the model should contribute to a comprehensive theory but cannot be one in itself.

Let us return to the basic concept of informed choice and addiction. According to this type of theory, when first introduced to a potentially addictive behaviour, addicts-to-be look at their current situation and at their future and what they think the activity or drug has to offer; they know about the risks of sampling an activity or drug and they are willing to take that risk. Once they have sampled the wares and they have a better idea of what it entails and what it delivers, their preferences are adjusted accordingly.

At all times these people are engaging in a process of weighing up costs and benefits. In some cases, they decide that the costs outweigh the benefits and they change their pattern of behaviour or stop it altogether. This theory involves 'choice' because addicts are aware of and deliberately select from a number of options. It is informed because they are aware of all the relevant information about risks and benefits. It involves rationality because the process by which the information is used to arrive at a decision is one that maximises the chances of arriving at what for that person is the best outcome.

Under this model, the addict is aware at the outset that he or she might become addicted and is willing to take the risk. In the beginning, the advantages of sampling the activity might be pleasant sensations, social approval or escape from mental or physical pain. The risks are those of becoming addicted, and the physical and social harm that the activity might cause. This may include shame or embarrassment at being someone who gambles, smokes, takes heroin or whatever. Since we are still assuming that the individual is well informed, we presume that he or she has made a realistic appraisal of the likelihood of each of the various outcomes. However, as time goes on, the best appraisal of those likelihoods can change.

For example, someone who begins to use heroin may start with a view that the chances of becoming a compulsive injecting user are less than 50%. However, after having smoked heroin for a few months, the person may notice that the consumption is escalating and reappraise the risk of becoming an addict. That in itself would not constitute a change in preference but for many people the more imminent prospect of something bad happening will lead to a re-evaluation of exactly how bad it is. For some users, that prospect would be very unwelcome, so much so that they may choose to exercise restraint or even stop using altogether to avoid it. In other cases, the prospect of becoming an addict may not be a sufficient deterrent because the benefits of the drug are so great or the prospect of being an addict, given their life circumstances, is not of great concern.

In another example, a smoker may start smoking aware of and willing to accept the risks of illness and death in middle or old age. As the years pass, he or she may continue to feel in good health and come to believe that he or she will escape the major ill-effects of smoking so that the motivation to stop actually reduces. Then he or she may be diagnosed with lung cancer and still not stop because he or she believes that there is insufficient prospect of recovery to make it worthwhile.

What is rational choice?

It is worth reflecting some more on what rational choice actually is. It does not have to be sensible or adaptive. It only has to result from a weighing up of the costs and benefits as the decision-maker sees them. So it is rational, if often unwise, for a person to choose short-term gain over a possible longer-term pain. A young person with a short time-horizon may simply not care about life after 30. In the throes of an alcohol binge, an individual may not even care about the prospect of a hangover the following day. These are unwise choices but they are not irrational.

Habituation and withdrawal symptoms

Some, or possibly all, addictive activities appear to involve some kind of short- and/or long-term habituation and this might contribute to escalation of the activity and continued engagement in the activity. Postulating such a process is compatible with a Rational Choice Theory of addiction. The addict chooses to escalate the 'dose' because of a stable preference for a particular effect and continues to engage in the activity because of a choice to avoid or escape from withdrawal symptoms. Drug withdrawal, defined as a combination of signs and symptoms paired with abstinence, differs in manifestation across drug types in terms of magnitude, type and persistence.

For example, with opioid withdrawal, symptoms experienced upon cessation include nausea, lacrimation, perspiration, tremor, restlessness and yawning. Nicotine withdrawal symptoms include depressed mood, poor concentration, restlessness, increased appetite and irritability. The link between habituation and withdrawal symptoms has been elaborated in an important theory of addiction: the Opponent Process Theory (see Box 3.4). The theory could have been placed almost anywhere in this book but it is placed here because it is compatible with a choice in which addicts consciously decide to continue to use a drug to avoid withdrawal symptoms.

Box 3.4 Opponent Process Theory

The drug reward process from repetitive drug use is upset by opponent processes that have a homeostatic function following drug euphoria to restore baseline levels. This leads to a reduction in the effect of the drug and withdrawal symptoms during abstinence.

The Opponent Process Model (Solomon and Corbit 1973, 1974; Solomon 1980) describes the positive and negative affective processes that underlie addiction. It proposes that internal reward processes are distorted by drug use and that drug-induced increases in reward threshold result in compulsive drug self-administration.

Maintenance of hedonic balance

The core tenet of the Opponent Process Model is that our central nervous system works to maintain hedonic balance. According to the theory, the primary 'a-process' for the hedonic drug effect is aroused by a stimulus. An 'opponent loop' generates a secondary 'b-process', which has an opposite effect to the hedonia aroused by the input. The loop generating the b-process is activated once a hedonic experience follows input. The b-process has a relatively slow build-up and decline (Figure 3.1).

The a- and b-processes combine to create the experienced hedonic state. The initial experience dominated by the a-process is labelled the A-state and the subsequent experience in which the b-process dominates is the B-state. Figure 3.1 shows the sequence of the peak primary reaction A, adaptation, steady level, after-reaction B and the decay of B.

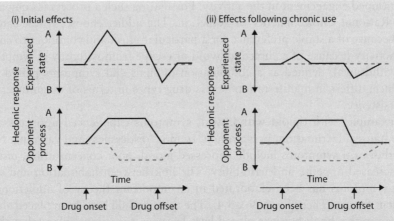

Figure 3.1 A simplified view of the Opponent Process Model of addiction. The affective (hedonic or emotional) response to a stimulus (such as a drug) is the underlying a-process, which elicits the opponent b-process. These processes add together to create the pleasant A-state followed by an unpleasant B-state. On first use the pleasant A-state is large, followed by a small B-state (see i). With repeated drug use, the b-process increases in magnitude and duration, leading to an experience dominated by the unpleasant symptoms associated with withdrawal (see ii).

The opponent b-process is activated indirectly via the activation of the a-process. It has an evocation threshold, a latency or recruitment time. Under certain conditions, the opponent process can be activated by events in memory and as a consequence of Pavlovian conditioning.

The temporal patterning of hedonic states
Thus according to the Opponent Process Model, the temporal pattern of affective states caused by a stimulus has five distinctive features:

- The peak of primary hedonic process state precipitated by stimulus onset.
- A period of hedonic or affective adaptation during which the intensity of hedonic state declines, even though stimulus intensity is maintained.
- A steady level of the hedonic process which continues as long as stimulus intensity is maintained.
- A peak of affective after-reaction, which quickly follows stimulus termination and whose quality is hedonically different from that of the primary hedonic state.
- Decay of the after-state.

Effect of drug use on the opponent process
The opponent process is strengthened by drug use and weakened by disuse, although the primary affective process is not affected by use. A b-process will

acquire more power if frequently elicited. It will show a shorter latency of response to the a-process, a quicker rise, a higher asymptote and a longer decay time. In contrast, an a-process is a relatively stable, unconditioned reaction. Disuse weakens the b-process and it should return to its original magnitude whenever the a-process has not occurred for long time. Thus over time:

- The peak of A′ (the prime denotes the situation after extended drug use) will be less intense because the latency of the b-process is decreased and its intensity increased.
- The steady level of A′ (a–b) during maintained stimulation will be close to baseline and even below that in some cases.
- The peak of B′ should be more intense and long lasting.

Aversive states, manifesting themselves after the sudden termination of pleasurable inputs, become more intense with repeated experiences. Mild desire later becomes abstinence agony and intense craving. In addition, after many repetitions, the steady level of pleasure produced by the continued presence of pleasurable stimulus input has decreased.

It is proposed that prolonged activity of an opponent process system, whether it be pleasurable or aversive, may cause psychological 'stress' in the sense that many physiological resources may be required in order to keep the opponent process strong.

Opponent processes and behavioural disorders

It is expected that a constant demand might lead to the exhaustion of a particular overworked opponent process system or to the debilitation of other defence systems. Theories of mental disease, psychosomatic disease and behavioural disorders usually emphasise that aversive stimuli lead to stress, stress is aversive and both cause emotional disorders, psychosomatic illness and behavioural malfunctions. The Opponent Process Model takes a different view. In this view, stress caused by aversive stimulation is only part of the story. There are behavioural disorders caused by lasting, repeated and intense b-processes in general.

Pleasurable and aversive A-states

The theory argues that A-states may be pleasurable or aversive and the corresponding B-state is the reaction to that and has the opposite hedonic value. Motivational systems involving pleasurable A-states and aversive A-states are similar. In both cases, the onset, maintenance and termination of the stimulus results in a certain amount of pleasure and a certain amount of displeasure. They mainly differ in terms of whether pleasure or displeasure comes first.

In the case of pleasurable A-states, it is proposed that the subsequent aversive B-state functions as a drive that energises behaviour and that the pleasurable

A-states reward these behaviours. Electrical self-stimulation of rewarding brain sites, chemical self-stimulation with opiates and love relationships are argued to work in this way.

Variability in activation of opponent processes

Not all stimuli result in an opponent process. A non-opposed system would manifest no peak of the A-state, no adaptation and no appearance of a B-state after stimulus termination. It is argued that the hedonic state engendered by marijuana could be an example. As a chemical stimulus it precipitates a pleasurable A-state. However, there is no reported peak or adaptation nor are there supposedly aversive withdrawal symptoms or craving (though this now appears not to be true). Nausea is possibly an aversive A-state without a B-component state.

There are argued to be wide variations in the strengths and variations of b-processes after repeated elicitations. Taste cravings as b-processes, for example, may last a few minutes; exhilaration following exercise on the other hand can last somewhat longer. Craving following withdrawal from opiates, alcohol or barbiturates can last for months.

The example of opiate use

Opiate use is given as a classic case of the operation of opponent processes. In the initial stages of opiate use, the user experiences an intense pleasurable feeling, described as a 'rush', immediately after the opiate injection. The rush is then accompanied by a period of euphoria, but of reduced intensity. Later on, the individual experiences aversive withdrawal symptoms, together with a feeling of craving. Over several weeks, with repeated doses, the A-state begins to weaken, and at the same time, the B-state intensifies and takes longer to return to baseline. The A-state becomes a state of just normal functioning as opposed to the experience of euphoric sensations. The B-state becomes more extreme and longer in duration.

The development of addiction

It is proposed that repeated use of some drugs is responsible for people finding themselves craving a substance which previously held little interest, and the model is argued to explain opiate, alcohol, barbiturate, amphetamine and nicotine addiction. In these cases:

- The B-state lasts a long time.
- The acquired B-state is highly aversive.
- The elicitation of the A-state is effective in causing rapid alleviation of the B-state.
- The user learns to use the drug which elicits the A-state in order to remove the B-state.

Addiction will not occur (even if A and B are experienced repetitively) if the properties of affective response to a drug are such that B regresses to baseline quickly – another dose is never needed to remove the effects of the aversive B-state as it quickly disappears anyway.

If the b-process is strengthened through repetition, withdrawal can be reinstated by a small dose of the drug. In the case of longer-term abstinence from the drug, the b-process decays but it is argued that the system may not return to normal and that there is always a vulnerability to relapse (Weiss et al. 2001).

Possible mechanisms

Suggestions for neural circuitry in relation to the opponent process model have included the suggestion that the positive a-process is caused by activation of mesolimbic dopamine projections to the nucleus accumbens and amygdala that mediate positive reinforcement and the b-process involves down-regulation in the mesolimbic dopamine system (Weiss et al. 2001).

Extensions of the model

The model has been extended and developed to account for complex temporal variations in the rewarding properties of stimuli. It has been proposed, for example, that a single drug administration may create a temporary decrease in reward threshold (Koob and Le Moal 1997). A second administration of the drug may produce an increased euphoric effect. This can lead to repeated drug use prior to onset of addiction. After further repetitions, internal processes oppose the drug-induced reduction in reward threshold, restoring its original pre-drug state.

Koob and Le Moal (1997) propose a 'spiralling distress' concept in which initial drug use reduces reward threshold making future use more likely. Then subsequent increases in reward threshold mean that periods when the drug is not available are accompanied by increasing levels of negative affect and greater emotional distress.

Koob and colleagues (Koob and Le Moal 1997; Koob et al. 1997) have also suggested that repeated drug use activates an additional b-process via the hypothalamic–pituitary axis stress system, causing release of corticotrophin-releasing factor in the amygdala region as well as other stress responses. Under this view, it is hypothesised that an individual progresses into an addictive state of drug use if the addict originally began drug taking for the positive hedonic effects, which eventually progress into a predominantly negative hedonic state.

A further development of the model has been proposed in which it is argued that the b-process arises from Pavlovian conditioning. Siegel (1988) proposed a conditioning model based on the Opponent Process Theory. In that model, the stimuli that accompany drug-taking trigger the opponent process by virtue of being associated with the drug effect. This derives from the observation that the experience of drug withdrawal in humans and other animals is more severe in the presence of stimuli that accompanied the drug experience.

Opponent processes, choice and instrumental learning
Note that although we have positioned the model in the part of the book that deals with rational choice, many proponents of the model would argue that it fits better within a later section dealing with instrumental learning. However, the model is in principle agnostic as to whether the distress that is presumed to motivate drug-seeking behaviour involves conscious choice or an automatic cue–response process.

Issues and evaluation
The model has considerable explanatory power that goes well beyond explanation of drug dependence. For example, it can explain acquired tastes (where the initial experience of something is unpleasant but apparently by virtue of that unpleasantness it then becomes much sought after). It can explain the dynamics of the hedonic experience in both the short and long term in response to drugs as diverse as cocaine and alcohol.

On the other hand, it remains highly speculative and its flexibility, in terms of allowing very different parameters with different drugs and other stimuli, makes it difficult to test as a general concept.

Perhaps the major limitation is not with this particular theory but with its use as the dominant theory underpinning drug dependence. Although the suggestion that addiction is motivated primarily by avoidance of distress makes intuitive sense, it seems unlikely that it is the only or even a major cause of addictive patterns of drug-seeking behaviour. There are just too many counter-examples.

In the realms of animal research, there are many observations that cause difficulties for the theory. For example, Stewart and Wise (1992) conducted experiments in which rats were trained to respond for heroin infusions. The animals were then subjected to a period in which the drug was not administered. This was followed by a number of different experimental manipulations. In one of these, the a-process was activated by giving the rats a small injection of their drug prior to the test (priming injection). In the other condition, the b-process was activated by administration of naltrexone, which is an opioid antagonist drug that blocks opioid receptors in the brain and has the potential to induce withdrawal symptoms in individuals who are heroin dependent. Precipitated withdrawal, it is argued, represents a b-process and is expected to be the most powerful cause for reactivating drug-seeking behaviour. A priming drug injection turned out to be far more effective at reinstating drug-seeking than naltrexone administration.

Besides this, the timing of withdrawal states and relapse in humans and reinstatement of drug use in animals do not match up well. To account for this, a b-process has been proposed that decays slowly after long periods of abstinence.

It has also been suggested that associative conditioning causes predictive drug cues to elicit conditioned tolerance and continued withdrawal essentially as conditioned b-processes. However, many human addicts report cues that often fail to elicit conditioned withdrawal. In addition, drug cues often elicit quite different effects such as conditioned feelings of a drug high (a-process) or feelings of drug craving by themselves.

The Opponent Process Model offers some intriguing possibilities but is only one of a number of possible ways in which individuals may become habituated to the effects of drugs or other rewarding experiences. Some of these mechanisms may lead to onset of adverse withdrawal symptoms when the drug or experience is not available.

For example, Peper (2004a, 2004b) has provided a very full conceptual and mathematical account of the process of development of tolerance to drugs which is purported to explain many of the features observed in animals and humans. A detailed examination and critique of this new model is beyond the scope of this book. The point we wish to make here is only that a synthetic model of addiction needs to be able to accommodate such detailed models but at this stage must be agnostic on the precise details until more is known.

Opponent process theory is one example of a theory about how an individual comes to suffer negative consequences of drug use that then go on to drive further use. We have already alluded to the possibility, even likelihood, that in at least some cases an individual's personal characteristics or circumstances create unpleasant experiences that an addictive drug can be perceived as helping with. These include depression, anxiety and possibly boredom.

One problem that is not so obvious is that of difficulties with intimacy (Keane 2004). It is argued that individuals with particular problems with intimacy in personal relationships may have their needs met by an intense intimate relationship with a drug. This certainly fits with some observations about addiction such as the fact that experience of abuse as a child predisposes to addiction to drugs such as alcohol and heroin (e.g. Marcenko et al. 2000).

Policy implications of a Rational Addiction Theory

The policy implications of a Rational Informed Choice Theory of addiction tend towards a libertarian view that individuals should be left to make (and suffer the consequences of) their decisions without state interference. This view is typified by the law professor Viscusi who argues that the present adversarial approach to tobacco control is misplaced – we should present the information and let smokers decide (Viscusi 1998).

In the case of addictions in which harm is caused to others, this should be dealt with by the criminal justice system. Although proponents of this approach may recognise that use of an addictive drug leads to withdrawal symptoms, the addict was aware of this at the outset and should be held accountable for his or her earlier decision to experiment with the drug in spite of this. It might even be argued that offering treatment to reduce the severity of the effects of addictions is counter-productive because it shifts the balance of preference in favour of uptake and continuation.

Irrational, ill-informed choice and unstable preferences

The Rational Informed Choice Model cannot account for the fact that many addicts choose to exercise restraint and in many cases go to great lengths and expend time, effort and money to achieve this, and yet still fail. Many addicts also regret having started down the road that has led them to this state. However, a Rational Choice Model can still be entertained if one assumes that the addicts' preferences change over time, and particularly between the time when a decision is made to restrain use and when that restraint has been exercised for a while. We also have to postulate that the addict is not very good at predicting what the consequences of trying to exercise restraint would be. If they were good at predicting it and were acting rationally, they would only try it when they were going to succeed.

The idea that addicts are fully able to predict their future reactions and that their preferences do not change was always going to be unrealistic. We are ill-informed about many other aspects of our lives and reactions and we also change our minds about things. Introducing unstable preferences clearly goes a long way to explaining why addiction develops and why attempts to restrain the activity fail: the preferences change.

Rational ill-informed choice with unstable preferences: an addict's eye view

Time 1 (while still partaking)
I want to stop being a [drinker/smoker/heroin user/gambler/tranquilliser user/crack user]. This is because although it [gives me pleasure/makes me feel better/is part of who I am/helps me to cope with life/helps me do things I need to do], I realise that it [is doing me harm/might do me harm in the future/is doing harm to people I care about/may make people I care about unhappy].

Time 2 (during an attempt to exercise restraint or abstain completely)
I want to go back to my old ways because [I miss the benefits/I do not want to put up with the unpleasant consequences of abstinence].

How well informed are addicts?

There is in fact evidence that addicts are ill-informed. For example, smokers greatly overestimate the likelihood that they would be able to stop if they tried. They are

also often unaware of the full range of adverse health effects of smok
have the view that they will escape the unpleasantness of old age if the
from smoking. In fact, smokers spend more of their shortened lives in disaʋ...
pain as a result of chronic smoking-related diseases. In effect, smoking brings old
age on early – not just death. It is also the case that many alcoholics underestimate
the adverse health consequences of their alcohol use and even deny that they have
a problem.

Allowing for those who engage in addictive behaviours to misjudge the consequences of their actions greatly eases the task of explaining what is going on. It is
possible that addiction arises because, while the immediate effects of the activity
are known, the longer-term risks are not accurately judged. This may occur because
the addict is not aware of the information or even because the addict's awareness
is biased by emotional needs.

Ignorance and education

It would be tempting to assert that lack of information about addictive behaviours
helps to explain a higher prevalence among those in society who are less well
educated. However, this does not work. In the case of smoking, for example, in
countries such as the United Kingdom where there is a strong association with
educational level, there is no difference between more and less well-educated
smokers in their desire to stop or indeed in the frequency of their attempts
to stop. Also, there are countries where smoking prevalence is as high among
doctors who are fully aware of the health risks as among other members of
the population.

A great deal of the effort that goes into preventing and even treating addiction
seems to assume that it is partly caused by lack of knowledge. It is presumed
that providing more information on the harmful effects of addictive behaviours
can influence people to exercise restraint. This is not as easy an assumption to
test as might be imagined. We pointed out earlier that on the face of it there is
no evidence that people who are better informed are more motivated to exercise
restraint. However, things are more complicated than that.

First of all, the studies are typically carried out in a society that is saturated with
information about the harmful effects of addictive behaviours. One would have
to have lived in a cave all one's life not to have heard that excessive alcohol consumption can lead to an early grave. If just about everyone is aware of the harmful
effects of an addictive activity, there is obviously minimal scope for showing that
lack of knowledge is contributing to addiction.

Secondly, it is entirely possible that our measurement of how well informed
addicts are is not up to the job. Information is not a simple quantity of which
we have more or less. It consists of discrete items, some of which may affect our
choice while others do not. Moreover, what affects our choices may be different
for different people. For some people, showing them what they really look like
when they are drunk or smoke may be more important than others for whom the
prospect of disability in later life may be more motivating.

Expectancies and addiction

The idea that beliefs about the consequences of an activity, which may or may not be accurate, may contribute to addiction that has been extensively explored in what are known as Expectancy Theories (Box 3.5).

Box 3.5 Expectancy Theories

'Expectancies' about the costs and benefits of an addictive activity are assumed to contribute to excessive use. These may be inaccurate. There is interest specifically in how far addicted individuals differ from non-addicted individuals in expectancies about the positive versus negative effects of the activity. Expectancies may involve more than beliefs. They may be 'memory templates' of the rewarding value of the addictive behaviour.

Expectancy Theories view drug use that escalates into addiction as being a result of the expectations an individual holds regarding the costs and benefits of the activity. Using alcohol consumption as an example, Expectancy Theories propose that the level of alcohol consumption is related to how much the person expects it will deliver a desired effect.

Positive and negative expectancies

It has been found that extent of drinking is positively correlated with positive expectancies and inversely associated with negative expectancies (Christiansen and Goldman 1983; Brown et al. 1987; Reich et al. 2004). Heavier drinkers report more positive expectancies than lighter drinkers (Southwick et al. 1981) and heavier drinking has been found to be associated with expectations of social and physical pleasure, social assertion, tension reduction, greater sociability and enhanced cognitive and motor functioning (Brown 1985).

Alcoholics and non-problem drinkers have also been found to differ on measurements of global positive changes, sexual arousal, physical and social pressure, assertiveness, tension reduction and arousal aggression (Connors et al. 1986). Expectancies may be more consistently associated with quantity than frequency of drinking (Chen et al. 1994). Even when demographic variables that are known to contribute to drinking are accounted for (e.g. age and gender), expectancies have been found to be associated with drinking versus not drinking and with quantity of drinking (Mooney et al. 1987). However, the proportion of variance explained by expectancies is typically low: in the Mooney study, it was 6% for drinking versus not drinking and 15% for quantity of drinking.

Alcohol expectancies have also been found to predict self-reported alcohol consumption in adolescents (Christiansen et al. 1989). The strongest predictors of behaviour are argued to be beliefs and expectancies that relate to specific actions. For example, 'I will not drink alcohol at all (single behaviour) this week (time specific)'. Expectancy Theories have also been applied to the outcome of attempts to control addictive behaviours. For example, Brown (1985) found that higher positive outcome expectancies were associated with decreased likelihood of achieving a year's abstinence and with treatment compliance.

It has been reported that in some populations, men have stronger positive and weaker negative expectancies than women. In one study, men had higher levels of expectancy for tension reduction, social facilitation, activity enhancement and performance enhancement (Sher et al. 1996).

Self-efficacy expectancies

'Self-efficacy' expectations are particular kinds of beliefs that are postulated to reflect individuals' beliefs in their ability to perform certain behaviours, that is, smokers would be more motivated to quit smoking if they thought that they would be able to do it successfully. Generalised self-efficacy beliefs refer to the belief that an individual can cope with the demands of everyday life across a broad range of behaviours.

Expectancies may be more than beliefs

Some Expectancy Theories consider the core construct as much more than simple beliefs. Goldman and Darkes (2004) have argued that expectancies are part of the memory structures that organise input to the central nervous system and guide behaviour. Expectancies are also regarded as having a moderating function, for example in moderating the role of stress in alcohol consumption. Goldman and Darkes suggest that expectancies are the pathway through which genetic predisposition, social and cultural information, affective state, personality and so on influence drug use and abuse.

Brandon et al. (2004) have argued that in considering the quantity of information that must be processed and the required speed of processing for large amounts of information, the expectancy-based control systems are 'automatic', functioning through parallel processes that operate outside of conscious awareness.

Rather et al. (1992) have used the application of a mathematical information processing model to propose that affect (or expectancy) can be mapped within a two-dimensional model (e.g. arousal and valence) that represents patterns of expectancy activation.

Brandon et al. (2004) claim that, if expectancy-based control systems are unconscious and automatised, then this could account for loss of control and craving, behavioural tolerance and difficulty in achieving abstinence. It is proposed that, as addiction develops, the activity is influenced less by conscious expectancies involving controlled processes (and assessable through self-report) and more by the unconscious expectancies involving automatic processes. On the other hand, the conscious accessibility of expectancies may relate to the effect that these have on behaviour.

It has been proposed that expectancies and actions may influence each other in a reciprocal fashion. For example, Smith et al. (1995) found that teenagers' expectancies for social facilitation from alcohol and their drinking showed a bidirectional relationship with each other.

Expectancies as part of a wider motivational system

Expectancy Theories have been combined with more general motivational accounts. For example, it has been proposed that alcohol abuse can be predicted from a causal chain that includes alcohol consumption and 'drinking to cope' as proximal determinants and coping skills and positive alcohol expectancies as more distal determinants (Cooper et al. 1988).

Cooper et al. (1988) reported a study in which drinking to cope emerged as the most powerful predictor of high alcohol consumption, apparently exerting an influence via direct and indirect pathways. Coping styles that involved showing avoidance of emotion emerged as stronger predictors of alcohol abuse than problem-focused coping. The predictive value of coping was moderated by alcohol expectancies: an avoidant style of coping with emotion predicted alcohol abuse only in drinkers expressing high levels of positive expectancies from alcohol.

Along the same lines, Fischer et al. (2003) found that positive expectancies of social facilitation from drinking moderated the effects of extraversion on drinking behaviour among a sample of undergraduate men and women.

Manipulating expectancies

Expectancies ought to be able to be manipulated, making them a suitable target for interventions. Tate et al. (1994) informed abstaining smokers that they should expect no complaints during abstinence, which led to fewer reported somatic complaints and less mood disturbance than controls not primed with any expectancies. Participants told to expect somatic but not psychological complaints reported more numerous and severe somatic withdrawal symptoms than those not told to expect this. Therefore, manipulation of expectancies on quit day may affect the withdrawal experience.

Issues and evaluation

Where Expectancy Theories deal with conscious beliefs about the costs and benefits of addictive behaviours, the fact that they show some level of association between expectancies and behaviours may not seem to represent a major advance on the common-sense model with which we started the chapter.

Where expectancies are construed as something more amorphous or difficult to pin down as such 'memory templates' or automatic processes, it is not clear what the concept refers to – what correspondence it has with the real world. It offers a level of abstraction that takes it out of the phenomenological or the physiological. On the other hand, it is interesting to see that this kind of theory is incorporating in some way the kinds of learning mechanisms that we will be considering in Chapter 5, without which we do not have a comprehensive theory of addiction.

A major limitation of the research involving these theories is that it rarely uses addiction per se as a target variable; most often it uses level of consumption and sometimes it uses problematic use. Thus, it is not clear how far expectancies play a specific role in the development of the damagingly powerful and repeated motivation that defines addiction.

The other problem faced by such theories is the one alluded to in the previous chapter about what constitutes support for a theory. The prediction of actual behaviour using even quite elaborate Expectancy Models is typically weak and this prediction is not compared with other formulations that make fewer assumptions. If we employ the method of looking for counter-examples to establish whether Expectancy Theories can provide a complete explanation of addiction, it seems that the theories are not sufficient.

Unstable preferences

It was pointed out earlier that it seems gratuitously limiting to postulate that underlying preferences do not change in addiction; after all they obviously change in many other areas of activity. People change their minds about what they like and dislike and what they want. One minute they choose to try to stop using a drug; at that time their thoughts are dominated by the negative aspects of the activity. Having then abstained for a while and facing the reality of the loss of reward and the discomfort associated with this, they change their mind and resume the behaviour. As Skog (2000) puts it: 'what we observe is not an inability to choose, but choices governed by strong appetites and conflicting motives' (p. 1309).

The concept of 'approach-avoidance conflict' is one that extends throughout motivational theory. At a distance something may look attractive but as one gets closer to it the unattractive features become more evident and dominate our thinking so we retreat from it at which point the unattractive features become less salient and we approach again.

The related concept of choice with unstable preferences has been elaborated by Skog (2000) (Box 3.6). His main tenet is that what looks like compulsive use is no more than unstable preferences resulting from conflicting motives.

Box 3.6 Skog's Choice Theory

This theory states that addiction can be regarded as a manifestation of conflicted choices that change as a function of the addict's current preferences.

Skog's Choice Theory of addiction seeks to explain addiction in terms of choices that people make rather than compulsion (Skog 2000, 2003). He points to the fact that in some sense addicts always have a choice. They are not physically forced to engage in the behaviour and do not require physical restraint. The appearance of lack of control arises because addicts change their minds. Their choices are conflicted and on some occasions the option to continue the behaviour dominates and on other occasions the option to exercise restraint dominates.

Stability and consistency of choices

Thus, the theory postulates that individuals differ in the stability and consistency of their preferences. This is certainly in accordance with common observation and with systematic research. It is also postulated that addicts may have a propensity to more unstable preferences. This may arise because of the addiction or be a factor that predisposes to development of addiction. Skog suggests that this might be a fruitful area for future research and indeed it may be. However, it is not clear whether a propensity towards unstable preferences is needed to understand addiction or why it should be greater in addicts.

The definition of choice

To be fair, Skog goes beyond metaphysics in his definition of choice. He states that if an action is made with regard to its possible consequences, if it is future-oriented, it must involve choice (Skog 2000). However, it is doubtful whether anyone working in the field of addiction would want to argue that it is only physiological or physical compulsion that is the appropriate model. Indeed, there are probably few addiction experts who believe that an addict would on a given occasion partake of their addiction in the certain knowledge that it would kill them immediately. So addiction in some sense must involve choice, even if that choice is highly constrained.

Issues and evaluation

In proposing his Choice Theory, Skog has argued that 'from the point of view of empirical research, convincing evidence for inability to choose is still missing' (Skog 2000, p. 1131). This is an example of a statement that appears to establish a theory (one involving 'compulsions') as conflicting with observation but only does so under a particular interpretation of the terms with which proponents of the theory could reasonably disagree. In focusing on the instability of preferences, Skog's theory captures a fundamental feature of human motivation, but in framing behaviour solely within the context of choice it arguably misses key aspects of the flow of behaviour in which alternative courses of action are not considered.

As long as we are willing to accept that people can change their minds about things rather quickly and then change them back again, and that a choice can be rational even if the preferences that determine it are ultimately self-destructive, there is no reason to abandon a Rational Choice Theory of addiction.

The denotative and connotative meaning of choice

However, this involves placing an interpretation on the term 'choice' that is very narrow and arguably misleading. If someone puts a gun to your head and threatens to pull the trigger if you do not drink a large glass of whiskey, it is true that you have a choice but the imperative to do as you are told is frankly so strong that most people would say that they were compelled to do the deed. On the other hand, if someone bursts a balloon in front of your face unexpectedly you would not be able to stop yourself blinking and would have no choice in the matter.

So acceptance of the Rational Choice Theory approach depends on what we mean by 'choice' and what we mean by 'rational'. This is something of a problem because the terms 'rational' and 'choice' have connotative as well as denotative meaning. 'Rational' carries connotations of calculating and purposeful, even adaptive; 'choice' carries connotations of free will and responsibility.

This is no doubt why this approach is so attractive to libertarian politicians who think that if people are too stupid, ill-informed or lacking in moral fibre to resist the ravages of drug addiction, it is their own fault and it is attractive to businessmen and shopkeepers who make a good living out of manufacturing and selling legal drugs because they are merely satisfying the desires of their customers.

Judgement and decision-making

There is a very large literature on decision-making, how it is done and in what ways it is rational or irrational, and many excellent books on the subject (e.g. Baron 2000). Much of this research has direct relevance for Choice Theories of addiction. Rather than attempt to summarise the field here, we will focus on the question of how risks are perceived and how people compare positive and negative features of alternatives when they are qualitatively different.

Looking first of all at the perception of risk, a number of useful observations have been made. Perhaps the most notable contribution to the field has been made by Paul Slovic (Box 3.7). Slovic's research has shown over the years how sensitive our judgements of risk are to the context in which those judgements are made and the manner used to elicit them. Of particular relevance here is the proposition, also made by others, that on most occasions when we have to judge risks we use feelings rather than analytical thought as the basis for our judgements.

Box 3.7 Slovic's Affect Heuristic

Slovic distinguishes between intuitive and analytical methods of making judgements and argues that the influence of the intuitive system which is based on feelings is an important factor in the development and maintenance of addictive behaviours.

The influence of 'feelings' on risk perception

Slovic and his colleagues have shown over a number of years that the choices we make between options involving numerically specified probabilities depend on how we are asked to express that choice and the context in which the choice is set. Of particular relevance here is a specific view on the role of feeling in the perception of risk (Slovic et al. 2002). Some general observations are as follows.

We have two very different methods of making judgements: an intuitive system and an analytic. The intuitive system is rapid and influences our feelings about what it is that we are dealing with that in turn is related to our imagination of it. The analytic system uses procedures, including formal logic and calculation, to arrive at judgements. Most judgements are made using the intuitive method.

How intuitive judgement can contribute to behaviours such as smoking

The intuitive method has many features that help to explain why people engage in addictive behaviours such as smoking.

1. When risks involve an accumulation over many instances of a behaviour, these tend to be discounted. Small individual risks do not engage our feelings of fear.
2. Risks that occur at some indefinable point in the future tend not to be prominent in our thoughts and so do not engage with motivational feelings.
3. Our ability to imagine a possible outcome as something fearful critically affects our feeling of motivation to avoid it. General abstract concepts such as 'harming health', and numerical probabilities, do not generally provide the kind of imagery that is engaging. In fact, in numerical terms people greatly overestimate the risk of lung cancer as a result of smoking. The lifetime risk is in the region of 15% for a smoker, whereas studies have found that people put the figure at more than 40% (Viscusi 2000). However, their emotive reaction to the prospect of getting lung cancer is much weaker than is warranted.
4. Related to this, currently experienced 'visceral factors' (drives such as hunger) have a much greater impact on our actions than mental representations of those factors in the future.
5. We tend to feel a greater sense of control over our fate than is warranted. In games of chance, for example, individuals often feel that there are ways in which they can influence events even when at some level they know this is impossible. The large majority of smokers believe, when they start, that

they will smoke for no more than 5 years and yet this is obviously not what happens. Even adult smokers overestimate their likelihood of success if they were to try to stop.

6. Possibly related to this, most of us experience an optimism bias. We may accept that there are risks attaching to particular activities but perceive our own personal risks as lower than these.

7. When judging risks and making choices, the size of potential losses or gains affects the way that we use judgements of probability. When losses or gains are very large, we are much less sensitive to differences in probability. For example, even the tiniest possibility of a cataclysmic event can lead people to expend huge resources to try to avoid it. And on the other side, the extremely low probability of, say, winning the national lottery is discounted when the potential prize is extremely large.

The Affect Heuristic

When considering the value that we place on particular options, Slovic notes that much of our thinking is dominated, not by an objective evaluation of the costs and benefits but by 'affect' – positive or negative feelings that are attached to those options. He takes this idea from Damasio (1994) although the observation has been made many times and indeed is a central plank of theories of conditioning.

Affective reactions derive from simple associations and non-analytical considerations such as mere repetition. The Affect Heuristic proposed by Slovic is an experiential system for ascribing risks and benefits to particular options. Slovic proposes that our positive or negative feelings about an option determine our judgements about its risks and benefits. Put simply, if we feel positively about something, we tend to judge the risks arising from it as low and the benefits as high.

Issues and evaluation

Some people might consider that the view that feelings affect our judgements of risks and benefits is fairly obvious. Slovic's contribution has arguably been in articulating this and the other sources of bias in a language that brings it within the domain of economic theory and cognitive psychology. His theory is extremely important, in that it represents the beginnings of a synthesis between theories of motivation based on learning mechanisms and drives and classical decision theory.

Cognitive biases

The influence that feelings have on beliefs and evaluations can be extended to non-conscious mental processes. Bias can occur not just because we believe things we want to believe but also in the very way in which our attention and memory operate.

That theme is the focus of what can be referred to as Cognitive Bias Theories of addiction (Box 3.8). These propose that addiction arises out of or is maintained by a tendency of the addict to pay greater attention to and selectively remember particular addiction-related information.

Box 3.8 Cognitive Bias Theories

Addiction is maintained by biases in the cognitive system, including beliefs, expectancies, self-efficacy, attributions and attention.

Cognitive bias and expectancies

The cognitive bias approach can be regarded as an extension of expectancy theory. The latter characterises addiction in terms of expectations, which may be accurate or inaccurate, for the individual concerned, about the future benefits and costs of engaging in the addictive activity. Cognitive Bias Theories propose that it is biases in beliefs and in attention and memory processes linked to these beliefs that are at the root of the problem of addiction.

Unconscious biases

Cognitive Bias Theories propose that expectancies that motivate behaviour reside in memory and that tasks that examine storage and recall of memory information can be used to detect biases that may be operating. A major advantage of this approach is that it does not rely on self-report and all the problems associated with this. It has been found, for example, that although smokers may endorse equal amounts of negative and positive outcome associations with smoking, they have a higher incidental recall of the positive outcomes.

Cognitive Bias Theories propose that the loss of control demonstrated by addicts can be explained by automatic and pre-conscious cue processing of stimuli related to the addiction. It is proposed that potential drug cues are evaluated 'pre-attentively'. They are then prioritised and subsequently trigger 'somatovisceral, behavioural and cognitive responses'. This information processing is subjected to automatic attentional and interpretative biases; these enhance the addict's awareness of his or her physiological arousal as well as action tendencies and cognitions (Ryan 2002).

Positive belief biases purportedly arise from the highly cue- and situation-dependent nature of memory structures. Experimental cognitive psychology techniques may be able to yield useful information about biases. Individuals may be aware of automatically triggered beliefs, but the ability to report these may be interfered with by a range of factors including cognitive dissonance and the demands of the situation.

Cognitive biases pertaining to addictive behaviours have been reported across a range of addictive behaviours, such as gambling (McCusker and Gettings 1997), cannabis use (Field et al. 2004), smoking (Waters et al. 2003) and heroin use (Franken et al. 2003).

Attentional biases

The Stroop colour naming task requires attention to the perceptual characteristics of words while suppressing processing of their meaning. In the original version of this task, people are presented with a list of colour words (e.g. 'red') written in colours different from the ones they are naming. They are asked to name as quickly as possible the colours in which the words are written. The task has been extended to non-colour words. Problem drinkers and smokers have shown a selective interference effect (increased colour naming times) for words semantically related to their addictive behaviour (e.g. 'cigarette' or 'beer') (Waters and Feyerabend 2000; Bruce and Jones 2004).

Visual probe tasks have also been found to add useful information about attentional responses to drug cues. Waters et al. (2003) found that a sample of heavy smokers were faster and more accurate in responding to a visual probe that replaced a smoking picture than to a neutral picture, indicating that they demonstrate an attentional bias to smoking cues. Attentional bias was also found to correlate with severity of cravings reported prior to undertaking the task, suggesting that the bias may be due to motivational processes.

In another visual probe study by Bradley et al. (2004), it was found that smokers showed an attentional bias for smoking pictures presented at exposures of 200 to 2000 ms compared with non-smokers but not at exposures at very short latencies (17 ms). Smokers also showed greater preferences for smoking-related than control cues. They interpreted these findings as showing that the biases were not due to pre-conscious processing.

Similar attentional biases have been found with problem gamblers. Boyer and Dickerson (2003) found that participants who reported difficulty in controlling their gambling behaviour took significantly longer time to name the colour of the words relating to poker machine gambling compared with those reporting that they could control their gambling behaviour.

Different results with different types of bias

It has been proposed that the three commonly used measures of cognitive bias (masked and unmasked Stroop test and visual probe tasks) may tap different underlying mechanisms. Mogg and Bradley (2002) found that scores on these tasks by a group of smokers were not correlated. The participants were asked to abstain from smoking 12 hours prior to a first session and to smoke as usual before a second session. An attentional bias for smoking-related pictures was found on the visual probe task and for smoking-related words in the unmasked condition of the modified Stroop task. Self-reported urges to smoke were most strongly predicted by the latter, rather than the deprivation manipulation. No evidence for a pre-conscious bias for smoking cues was found.

Frequent alcohol use and frequent drinking for enhancement but not for coping or social reasons have been found to be associated with a bias to attend to alcohol reward cues and to disinhibited behaviour (Colder and O'Connor 2002).

Issues and evaluation

It is clear from experimental studies that individuals who engage more frequently in addictive behaviours have attentional and memory processes that prioritise stimuli relating to these behaviours. However, it has not been demonstrated that this represents an abnormality that causes the behavioural problem of a repeated powerful motivation to engage in a rewarding but harmful activity or is a consequence of it.

In fact, as with Expectancy Theories, most of the research has focused on frequency of the behaviour as a target variable rather than the strength of the repeated motivation. As with other theories mentioned in this volume, this one draws attention to an interesting phenomenon that may contribute to addiction in some cases but cannot be considered a comprehensive theory. The experimental method adopted shows associations but these only account for a small amount of the variance and there are many individuals who are addicted who do not show evidence of the biases proposed.

This book has separated out Cognitive Bias Theories from Expectancy Theories for the purpose of exposition. In practice, as with so many of the theories in this book, there is considerable overlap in concepts and ideas.

Behavioural economics

An interesting approach to the understanding of addiction seeks to borrow concepts from the field of economics and apply them to the psychology of choice behaviour. Vuchinich and Heather (2003) have produced an excellent edited volume that explores this in detail, and in fact we have already considered two theories that fall within the ambit of this approach (the Rational Addiction Model and Skog's Choice Theory).

We should now consider behavioural economics more broadly. In its broader formulation, it is not entirely clear how far the mechanisms described in Behavioural Economic Theory are believed to operate within the realms of conscious decision-making but that is one interpretation so we will consider this theoretical approach here (Box 3.9).

Box 3.9 Behavioural Economic Theories

Economic conditions or principles influence the consumption of addictive substances, either determined by the availability of the drug or in terms of the decisions made by individuals regarding their drug use.

Addiction as a consumption behaviour

Behavioural economic theories of addiction seek to explain addiction in terms of the conditions that influence the consumption of addictive substances (Bickel et al. 1995). They view addiction as a process by which an increase in past consumption will determine an increase in current consumption and propose that proportional changes in consumption can be explained by proportional changes in cost, defined broadly (Bickel et al. 1997). Behavioural economic theories describe addictive behaviour at both an individual and population level.

Trade-offs and interactions

Behavioural economic theories focus particularly on the trade-off and interaction between different rewarding stimuli (reinforcers) and the resources that individuals will expend to experience those stimuli as a function of how far into the future those rewards will accrue.

Price elasticity

A central concept in economic theory is price elasticity. This is the ratio of the proportionate change in demand to the change in price. Inelastic consumption refers to a decrease in consumption that is proportionally *less* than price increases. Conversely, elastic consumption is a decrease in consumption that is proportionally greater than the increase in price. For example, a price elasticity of tobacco of −0.5 implies a 1% increase in price that, with all other factors remaining constant, would lead to a 0.5% reduction in demand. For the United Kingdom and the United States, the majority of studies have indicated that tobacco consumption is price inelastic, with a figure around −0.4 to −0.5 (Lewit 1989).

One major tenet of behavioural economic theories is that behaviours that seek out a reinforcer become more frequent as 'unit price' falls where unit price is defined as the *total resources*, including price, time and effort, needed to acquire a particular 'amount' of a reinforcing stimulus. This is the case whether the change in unit price arises from changes in the response requirement per episode of reinforcement or from a change in the amount of reinforcement delivered per response.

It has been suggested that pharmacological and conditioned effects may contribute to this finding. Macenski and Meisch (1998) found that unit price predicted consumption even at low doses of orally administered cocaine: the taste of the solution had acquired conditioned reinforcing properties that allowed it to function as a reinforcer despite a very low dose.

Addiction as a shift in the demand curve

The behavioural economic view sees addiction as a change in the relationship between unit price and drug consumption. Simplistically this can be thought of as a shift to the right of a 'demand curve' as a dependent drug user consumes more at a given unit price. However, this requires a more detailed explanation as the slope of the function is subject to change. Flat functions or those with a minimal slope are hypothesised to show 'inelastic demand'. It is predicted that as dependence progresses, the demand curve may shift to the right with drug demand becoming more inelastic with price changes having little effect on consumption. Higher intercepts and smaller slopes of demand curves associated with higher levels of dependence are expected to lead to stable patterns of intake and a greater difficulty in terms of controlling drug use.

Cross-price elasticity

The availability of one reinforcer may in principle have an effect on the demand for another reinforcer: 'cross-price elasticity' (Bickel et al. 1995). 'Substitution' refers to the situation in which the availability of one reinforcer reduces the consumption of another. A 'complement' is a reinforcer that increases the value of another.

There is little evidence to suggest that increasing the price of one substance results in consumers switching from one substance to another, as few significant cross-price effects have been found for alcohol or tobacco (Godfrey 1986). With regard to interactions between different substances, Jones (1989) found a subsystem of demand equations for tobacco, beer, wines and spirits using UK data for the period 1964–1983. Tobacco was found to be a complement to four types of alcoholic drink, with the results suggesting that, for example, a 1% increase in tobacco prices would lead to a decrease in beer and wine consumption of 0.2% and a decrease in spirits and cider consumption of 0.5%, with all other factors remaining constant.

Delay discounting

The concept of delay discounting is an important feature of behavioural economic theory. It is the phenomenon in which an individual selects a smaller but more immediately available reward over a later but larger one. Under one view, delayed rewards are discounted exponentially with a constant decay parameter. Under another view, discounting follows a hyperbolic function in which the decay is greater later on (Madden et al. 1999).

There are numerous examples of delay discounting and some evidence that individual differences in the function underpinning it may account for propensity to develop addictive patterns of behaviour. In one study, discounting of delayed rewards by pathological gamblers was compared with the delayed discounting by non-gambling participants (Dixon et al. 2003) in a hypothetical choice task in which participants made repeated choices between $1000 available after a delay (varied from 1 week to 10 years across conditions) and an equal or lesser amount of money available immediately. 'Indifference points' between immediate and delayed monetary rewards were calculated at each delay condition by varying the amount of immediate money across choice trials. The pathological gamblers discounted the delayed rewards more steeply than did the control participants, favouring the more immediately available rewards.

Discounting and impulsivity

Discounting has been proposed to account for the impulsivity evident in drug-dependent individuals and the loss of control associated with drug use. Impulsivity is related to behaviours other than addiction, which include delinquency, suicide, aggression, gambling and excessive spending.

Drug-dependent individuals have been shown to select brief but immediate drug intoxication or relief of transient withdrawal symptoms over a variety of prosocial but often deferred rewards (Madden et al. 1997). Also it seems that intravenous drug users often choose to share hypodermic needles instead of delaying their drug use until they have the opportunity to disinfect or obtain clean needles. Besides claims that drug users exhibit impulsive behaviour and that they score higher than controls on standardised measures of impulsivity, research has begun to compare the prevalence or degree of impulsivity across different types of drug dependence disorders to assess whether this is a general trait or whether impulsivity is specific to the type of reinforcer.

Loss of control

Loss of control is construed as somewhat different from impulsivity. In the case of loss of control, drug-dependent individuals report that they would prefer larger, more delayed rewards, but actually choose the smaller and immediate reward (Bickel and Marsch 2001). The key difference between loss of control and impulsivity is the inconsistency between behaviour and expressed preference in the case of loss of control compared with the consistent preference for an immediate smaller reward in the case of impulsivity. Bickel and Marsch (2001) provide the example of drug-dependent individuals expressing a strong preference for employment or family/friend relationships over drug use, but after a short period of time, they may use drugs instead of going to work or spending time with friends or family.

Factors affecting discounting

It is suggested that educational level may play a role in the operation of delay discounting. Jaroni et al. (2004) found that less educated smokers were more likely to discount future rewards than non-smokers.

State of tiredness may also play a role. There is evidence that the discounting effect is exacerbated in participants who have been sleep deprived (Reynolds and Schiffbauer 2004). This suggests that the operation of self-control requires mental effort which in turn requires mental resources that are depleted under sleep deprivation.

Polysubstance use, substitution and complementarity

Sumnall et al. (2004) examined the influence of price upon hypothetical purchases of alcohol, amphetamine, cocaine and ecstasy in a sample of polysubstance users. Self-reported demand for alcohol was inelastic. Amphetamine acted as a substitute for alcohol; cocaine was a complement drug and ecstasy was found to be independent of alcohol price increases. Demand for amphetamine, on the other hand, was found to be elastic as its price increased, and alcohol was identified as a substitute for amphetamine. Other substances were found to be independent. Demand for cocaine was elastic. Alcohol and ecstasy were substitutes for cocaine, yet amphetamine was independent. Finally, demand for ecstasy was elastic and cocaine was substituted as ecstasy price increased. These results suggest that consumption involves socioeconomic and psychopharmacological factors, although of course hypothetical situations and self-reports may not accurately represent actual behaviour.

In terms of 'substitution', it has been found that adolescents' choice to smoke appears to depend on substitute reinforcers or complementary activities to smoking and also individual differences in appraisal of the reinforcer value. For example, Audrain-McGovern et al. (2004) found that in a sample of adolescents the main 'substitutes' for smoking included school involvement, academic performance, physical activity and sports team participation. Complementary activities that influenced their decision to smoke included peer smoking or substance use.

Issues and evaluation

Behavioural economic theory offers a perspective on addiction that can be helpful. There is probably little in it that could not in principle be contained within other theoretical orientations but it does point to concepts that might otherwise be neglected. Of particular benefit are the concepts of the interaction between reinforcers with some acting as substitutes and some being complements.

One has to be very careful, however, in the application of economic ideas as general concepts. We cannot, for example, predict what will happen in terms of response substitution without knowing the precise purpose subserved by a particular reinforcer. We must also recognise that the worth of particular reinforcers is highly context dependent.

Finally, a detailed understanding is required of the behaviour one is dealing with; otherwise one can make some serious mistakes in interpretation of the evidence. A case in point is the price elasticity of cigarette consumption. We noted earlier that studies had found this to be in the region of -0.4 to -0.5. This means that a price rise in terms of purchasing power of 10% on average results in a reduction in consumption of about 4–5%. If one could address problems of black market sales, this puts tax increases at the top of the list of methods of reducing smoking in a population.

However, we have to recognise that a drop in consumption can arise either because smokers smoke fewer cigarettes, or because fewer people start smoking or because more smokers stop smoking altogether. There is less evidence on the effect of price rises on smoking cessation but what there is suggests that the price elasticity is more like −0.2.

One might still be satisfied that a reduction in consumption among those continuing to smoke is worthwhile but when smokers reduce their consumption in response to price rises, they do not end up inhaling less smoke – they smoke the remaining cigarettes more intensively. Therefore, unless a price rise is able to reduce the number of smokers, it appears not to have a useful effect on the true amount of smoking. This is perhaps not surprising if smoking does in fact represent nicotine-seeking behaviour with a preferred nicotine dose.

Some issues with mathematical and rule-based theories of choice

We noted earlier that there are many theories about behaviour that focus on beliefs and evaluations and how these combine to influence behaviour. The most general of these is probably one called Subjective Expected Utility Theory (see Baron 2000). This is a mathematical model of the decision-making process in which for each option being considered the decision maker examines how good or bad each of the possible consequences is, then gives this a weighting according to how likely he or she thinks it is to occur. The decision maker then adds up these 'weighted utilities' for each of the options being considered and chooses the one with the highest value.

Models as descriptions or as metaphors

Of course we know that people do not actually do this except on rare occasions, but theorists have argued that they *behave as though they do*, subject to some notable deviations. In the event, this model conflicts with how people actually think so it cannot be applied in most real-life situations.

For example, our decision-making is generally much more haphazard. We do not think numerically about the value of outcomes, and often we do not even think about outcomes but about 'characteristics' of the options (e.g. the aesthetic qualities of a car we are thinking of buying) and so on.

These limitations have, surprisingly, not been of great concern to psychologists and economists who are presumably willing to accept the patent inapplicability of the model to real behaviour for the sake of something that can be expressed in rather simple mathematical terms. A notable exception to this is found in the work of Janis and Mann (1977) who developed a more realistic model (Conflict Theory) in which the mode of decision-making varies according to person and situation.

The importance of the moment

But another limitation has been noted and it is that actions are influenced by what is going on at the time. This has been taken into account to a limited degree by the Theory of Planned Behaviour (TPB) (e.g. Hu and Lanese 1998) and to a greater extent by the Health Belief Model (HBM) (e.g. Garcia and Mann 2003). This addresses the issue by explicitly including the concept of 'intention'. Unfortunately, intention in the TPB has been construed in terms of a more or less enduring state that may span anything from minutes to months. The HBM introduces the idea of 'cues to action' or triggers. These are immediate situational determinants of behaviours such as exercising, attending for screening or attempting to stop smoking. The limitation is that the model treats triggers as independent of the motives that lead individuals to consider the action in question.

Transitions from one addictive behaviour to another

There are a number of theories that focus on ways in which preferences change over time and as a result of experience. One such account relates to the observation that many users of dangerous drugs, such as heroin, began their drug taking with so-called 'soft' drugs such as cannabis. Changes in preference as a result of continuing drug use have a manifestation in a particular theory of its development that has gained wide currency among the public and politicians: the Gateway Theory (Box 3.10).

Box 3.10   Gateway Theory

This theory argues that becoming a user of one drug, usually a drug with less powerful effects and a lower propensity to addiction, causes an individual to be more susceptible to using another, stronger and potentially more addictive or harmful drug. One example is the view that using cannabis makes it more likely that one will go on to use heroin (e.g. Kandel et al. 1992).

This theory proposes a number of mechanisms by which this might occur. First, the 'gateway' drug could simply provide a taste of the reward that a more powerful drug has to offer. Secondly, an individual may develop tolerance to the gateway drug so that its effects become weaker, and in order to achieve the original reward the user is motivated to seek a stronger drug. This would be the same principle that in some cases underpins the transition from a weaker form of the same drug to a stronger form or a mode of delivery that yields a more powerful effect. Thirdly, by becoming involved with a group of people who use or deal in the gateway drug, the user may encounter a greater opportunity or social pressure to take the stronger drug.

Soft to hard drugs
The major observation that underpins the theory is that many of those who use 'hard' drugs such as heroin started with use of 'soft' drugs such as cannabis.

However, transitions have also been examined between nicotine, alcohol and illicit drug use (Kandel et al. 1992; Lindsay and Rainey 1997; Kenkel et al. 2001; Beenstock and Rahav 2002; Chen et al. 2002; Tullis et al. 2003). The sequences appear to differ in different populations.

The problem of establishing causality

The problem is that mere observation of a transition from one drug to another does not necessarily imply a causal connection. It is equally plausible that the same characteristics that put people at risk of using 'hard' drugs also lead them to use 'soft' drugs, and use of soft drugs predates that of hard drugs as a result of availability or other environmental conditions.

One way to test a genuine causal relationship between use of one drug type and another is to assess how far factors that directly influence the first type (the gateway drug) at a population level later come to influence the second type. This has been done in one study in Israel in which it was found that price increases on tobacco reduced cannabis use, suggesting that tobacco may be a gateway to cannabis, but increase in the price of cannabis had no effect on later heroin use suggesting that in that country at that time cannabis was not a gateway drug for heroin (Beenstock and Rahav 2002). However, it is not difficult to come up with alternative explanations, and measurement error and choice of timescale may play a role in the findings.

Gateway Theory and behavioural economics

Gateway Theory has been formulated in terms of economic theory (Pacula 1997). It proposes that

'in the case of multi-commodity habit formation...the marginal utility of initiating a new drug is higher when there is prior consumption of the other drug. Further, it is found that the individual will initiate drug consumption with that drug that has the lowest marginal cost. The particular sequencing of drug use that is observed in empirical data is explained by differences in the marginal cost of consuming legal and illegal drugs' (from abstract).

Issues and evaluation

In terms of a general theory of addiction, the transition from use of one form of a drug to another needs to be able to be explained, but is likely to be highly dependent on the context. We are not yet in a position to say that using a 'soft' drug in itself makes it more likely that someone will start to use a 'hard' drug. In policy terms, we do not know whether relaxing restrictions on soft drugs makes the prevalence of hard drug use more likely. In terms of addiction, we cannot yet say anything useful about the influence of the use of one drug on development of *addiction* to another.

Recovery from addiction

A model that focuses more on attempts by individuals to change chronic behaviour patterns for the better is the Transtheoretical Model, sometimes called the Stages of Change (or Cycle of Change) Model. The model attempts to explain when, how and why individuals manage to do such things as stop smoking, restrain from or stop drinking alcohol, engage in more exercise and so on (Box 3.11). It seeks to do this by combining a number of ideas from other theories into a single framework which regards such changes as a process of transition between 'stages'.

Box 3.11   The Transtheoretical Model of behaviour change

The Transtheoretical Model (TTM) proposes that the process of recovery from an addictive behaviour involves transition through stages from 'precontemplation' in which no change is contemplated, through 'contemplation' in which it is contemplated in the foreseeable future, to 'preparation' in which plans are made for a definite attempt, to 'action' in which the attempt is made and then 'maintenance' in which the new pattern is established. Different processes are involved in the transition between different stages, and individuals can move backwards as well as forwards.

This model seeks to describe the processes that individuals go through in overcoming addictions and changing other chronic behaviour patterns. The Transtheoretical Model of behaviour change, also known as the Stages of Change (SOC) model, states that, with regard to chronic behaviour patterns such as smoking, individuals can be characterised as belonging to one of six 'stages' (Prochaska et al. 1985; Prochaska and Goldstein 1991; Prochaska and Velicer 1997): 'precontemplation' in which the individual is not thinking about changing in a defined period; 'contemplation' in which the individual is thinking about changing but not making any specific plans to change in a defined period; 'preparation' in which the individual intends to change; 'action' in which the individual is actively attempting to change; 'maintenance' in which the individual has engaged in the new behaviour pattern for a defined period; and 'termination' in which the individual has permanently adopted the new behaviour pattern. The 'termination' stage is a relatively recent addition to the model. The five main stages are described in more detail below.

Precontemplation stage
This stage represents individuals who are not interested in changing their behaviour and have no desire to do so in the immediately foreseeable future. Prochaska et al. (1985) define the foreseeable future as a 6-month time period, as this is the most far into the future that most people plan a specific health behaviour change. It is thought that the individuals who fall within this stage

have a lack of awareness or appreciation of the specific behaviour. However, these individuals are aware of the effects of this behaviour upon their health, but avoid involvement in health behaviour change programmes as this might involve rationalisation of their behaviour. Individuals may be at this stage as a result of failure at the desired behaviour change and resent their past efforts. Potential for progression from the precontemplation to the contemplation stage may be mediated through increasing awareness, which may be achieved through the mass media. Goals that are easily obtainable can increase self-efficacy or confidence that may also help progression to the contemplation stage.

Contemplation stage

Individuals at this stage are described as having the desire to change their behaviour within the next 6 months. Prochaska et al. (1985) claim that this intention arises despite the individual having knowledge of potential barriers or constraints. A plan for behaviour change is then drawn up with these barriers in mind. The benefits of the desired behaviour change may be obvious to the individual, although the types of barrier that they encounter may be specific to each individual. Having inadequate finances to fund the behaviour change may be relevant for one individual, whereas others may be concerned about the impact of the behaviour change in question on their social activities. Individuals in this stage require extra attention, intervention or strategies. The individual's progression towards the desired behaviour at a pace at which they feel most comfortable is emphasised and encouragement is required for motivation. Tailor-made messages are more preferable than general messages from the mass media at this stage.

Preparation stage

Individuals at this stage intend to make the behaviour change in the near future – that is to say, within the next month – and have usually made one previous attempt at the behaviour. The model has recently been changed so that a prior attempt to make the change is not necessary.

Action stage

The action stage may last from less than a month to as long as 6 months and is identifiable by some change of behaviour. This stage of change is usually the most identifiable as it involves a visible change in behaviour and usually receives the greatest external recognition. An individual in this stage will perceive the cons associated with the behaviour as greater than the plus points if they are to abstain from certain behaviours such as drug abuse or smoking. In the case of behaviours such as adherence to an exercise regimen, the pros of the behaviour should exceed the cons. If the individual continues the pattern of behaviour, he or she will proceed to the maintenance stage.

Maintenance stage

This stage starts after the action stage and can last for several years. The individual's level of self-efficacy is at its highest at this stage. In application of this model, it is important to bear in mind the need for relapse prevention in the form of a self-control programme designed to teach individuals who are trying to change their behaviour how to cope with the situation of relapse. Since this model is cyclical, it is possible for the individual to relapse back several stages rather than just the one stage.

Processes of change

The model proposes that individuals progress through stages sequentially but usually revert to prior stages before achieving maintenance and then termination (Prochaska and Velicer 1997). The model also states that different processes are involved in moving between different stages (Prochaska and Velicer 1997). It argues that interventions to promote change should be designed so that they are appropriate to an individual's current stage (Prochaska and Goldstein 1991). Moving an individual from one stage to another is purported to be a worthwhile goal because it will increase the likelihood that this person will subsequently achieve the termination stage (Prochaska and Goldstein 1991). Proponents of the model have argued that the model has revolutionised health promotion, claiming that interventions that are tailored to the particular stage of the individual improve their effectiveness (Prochaska and Velicer 1997).

Difficulties with the model

The following analysis draws primarily from research in smoking. It is in this area that the model was first developed and where much of the research relating to it has been carried out. To give some idea of the extent of the dominance of smoking, out of 1142 articles found in PubMed using the search phrase 'stages of change', 313 also had 'smoking' in the abstract or title, 110 had 'alcohol', 14 had cocaine, four had 'heroin' and six had 'gambling'.

Reservations have emerged about the model, many of which have been well articulated (Etter and Perneger 1999; Bunton et al. 2000; Whitelaw et al. 2000; Sutton 2001; Etter and Sutton 2002; Littell and Girvin 2002). One of these is a concern about the concept of the 'stage'. The model draws arbitrary dividing lines in order to differentiate between the stages. This has to mean that these are not genuine stages.

For example, an individual who is planning to stop smoking is in the preparation stage if this is within the next 30 days but only the contemplation stage if it is in 31 days' time (Sutton 2001). Boundaries between so-called 'stages' are therefore just arbitrary lines in the sand and statements of the kind '$x\%$ of smokers are in the "contemplation stage"' have little useful meaning. They should not be taken to mean, as they so often are, that 'x% of smokers are thinking about stopping smoking'

Secondly, this approach to classifying individuals assumes that individuals typically make coherent and stable plans. People responding to multiple-choice questionnaires are compliant and generally will try to choose an answer, but this does not mean that they think about things in the terms set by the response options. Apart from those individuals who set a specific occasion or date for change (e.g. in a New Year's resolution), intentions about change appear to be much less clearly formulated.

Larabie (2005) found that more than half of reported quit attempts in a general practice sample involved no planning or preparation at all – not even going so far as to finish the current packet of cigarettes. West and Sohal (2006) confirmed this in a large representative sample of smokers in England, and it has since been confirmed in other surveys. Another recent study found considerable instability in intentions to stop smoking over short periods (Hughes et al. 2005). A high level of instability in stages has also been found in other domains (De Nooijer et al. 2005).

Thirdly, it has been pointed out by others that the stage definitions represent a mixture of different types of construct that do not fit together coherently (e.g. time since quit, past quit attempts and intention) (Etter and Sutton 2002). It is not, as some of those using the model would like it to be, a statement of 'readiness' to change. Readiness or even preparedness is not actually assessed.

Fourthly, the model focuses on conscious decision-making and planning processes and draws attention away from what are known to be important underpinnings of human motivation. It neglects the roles of reward and punishment and of associative learning in developing habits that are hard to break (Baumeister et al. 1994; Mook 1996; Salamone et al. 2003).

Much of the problem of behaviour change arises from the fact that unhealthy habit patterns become entrenched and semi-automated through repeated reward and punishment (Robinson and Berridge 2003). These processes operate outside conscious awareness and do not follow decision-making rules such as weighing up costs and benefits. There is little or no consideration of the concept of addiction, which is clearly a crucial consideration when it comes to behaviours such as smoking.

Predictions made by the model have been found to be incorrect or less accurate than those of competing theories (Farkas et al. 1996; Herzog et al. 1999; Abrams et al. 2000). Strong claims have been made for the model (Prochaska and Velicer 1997) but the main body of evidence given in support of the theory is that individuals who are closer to maintenance at any one time are more likely to have changed their behaviour when followed up (e.g. Reed et al. 2005).

The relationship is often not strong, and by no means all studies find it (Hernandez-Avila et al. 1998; Littell and Girvin 2002) but the fact that it is present is given as evidence for the model. But this says no more than that individuals who are thinking of changing their behaviour are more likely to try to do so than those who are not, or that individuals who are in the process of trying to change are more likely to change than those who are just thinking about it. Put that way, it is just a statement of the obvious: people who want or plan to do something are obviously more likely to try to do it; and people who try to do something are more likely to succeed than those who do not.

Surprisingly, the proponents of the model appear not to report findings showing that the model is better at predicting behaviour than a simple question such as 'Do you have any plans to try to...?' or even 'Do you want to...?'. However, where others have made the comparison (e.g. SOC vs. a simple contemplation ladder that preceded it), little difference has been found (Abrams et al. 2000), or a simple rating of desire has been found to be better (Pisinger et al. 2005b). One might imagine that a scientific model would need to show an improvement at least on this kind of simple assessment. There have also been problems in the reliability of the assignment to categorical stages, as one might expect given that these are arbitrarily designated (Hodgins 2001).

Applications of the model

Proponents of the model may point to its having drawn attention to the fact that many people are not ready for interventions and progress can be made by moving them in the direction of changing their behaviour. However, in the years that the model has been in use, there appears to be no convincing evidence that moving an individual closer to action actually results in a sustained change in behaviour at a later date. In fact the history of behaviour change research is littered with studies that have succeeded in changing attitudes without accompanying changes in behaviour.

Where interventions have been developed that are based on the model, these have not proved more effective than interventions based on traditional concepts. A recent review comparing stop-smoking interventions designed using the SOC approach with non-tailored treatments found no benefit for those based on the model (Riemsma et al. 2003). Another review of the effects of applying the model to primary care behaviour change interventions has similarly found no evidence for a benefit (van Sluijs et al. 2004) and neither has there been found to be a benefit of applying the model in promotion of physical activity (Adams and White 2005). By contrast, there is good evidence that tailoring interventions in other ways, including triggers and motives, is more effective than untailored approaches (Lancaster and Stead 2002).

The popularity of the model

The popularity of the model can be put down to a number of factors. First, the seemingly scientific style of the assessment tool gives the impression that some form of diagnosis is being made from which a treatment plan can be devised. Secondly, the model also gives permission to go for soft outcomes such as moving an individual from 'precontemplation' to 'contemplation' which is of no proven value. Thirdly, it provides labels to categorise people rather than using everyday language: an individual is a 'precontemplator' not 'someone who is not planning on changing'. This appears to give the model scientific validation, which may or may not be founded on evidence.

Issues and evaluation

The above analysis suggests that the model tends to promote the wrong intervention strategy. For example, precontemplators tend to be provided with interventions aimed at 'moving them along' the stages, for example, by attempting to persuade them about the benefits of changing. However, if their apparent lack of interest in changing arises from their addiction, these individuals may respond favourably to the offer of a new and promising treatment as appears to have happened when the drug, Zyban, was launched as a smoking cessation aid (e.g. Zwar and Richmond 2002).

The model is also likely to lead to effective interventions not being offered to people who would have responded. There is now evidence in the case of smoking cessation that help should be offered to as wide a group as possible (Pisinger et al. 2005a, 2005b) but the SOC model can be taken as giving permission to those attempting to promote behaviour change to give weak interventions or no intervention to 'precontemplators'. This approach fails to take account of the strong situational determinants of behaviour. Behaviour change can arise from a response to a trigger even in apparently unmotivated individuals.

In the case of psychological theories for which there is accumulating evidence that they are not proving helpful, it is common to argue that better measurement is needed or that the theory has not been applied properly. This particular model is no exception (e.g. DiClemente et al. 2004). However, in the end, with some theories, one is often forced to accept that fundamental precepts of the theory are misplaced.

This analysis of the Transtheoretical Model is drawn mostly from West (2005), including large sections of text that are reprinted verbatim with permission.

So far in the development of a theory of addiction, we have arrived at what can be summarised as follows: addiction results from choices that people make in which they weigh up the benefits as they see it of engaging in the activity with the perceived costs; their evaluations of the costs and benefits may be subject to biases of many kinds, including feelings associated with the behaviour and its outcomes and a priority attaching to the present over the future. In some cases at least, preferences for the activities are altered by habituation, sensitisation and/or physiological changes which increase the costs of abstinence. Although it can be incorporated within this account, it is worth now drawing attention to something in our lives that quite obviously is very special: ourselves.

Identity

There is a large body of literature on the topic of 'identity' or 'self-labelling'. How we see ourselves is clearly of huge importance to our feeling of well-being and a major influence on our behaviour. This has been recognised in an interesting and insightful theory of behaviour change that encompasses addiction (Box 3.12).

Box 3.12 Identity shifts and behaviour change

Identity Shift Theory proposes that a value conflict develops as a result of increasing distress caused by behaviours. This prompts a small step towards behaviour change which if successful begins to lead to an identity shift. Increased self-awareness and self-confidence then fuel continued change (Kearney and O'Sullivan 2003).

The first step

Identity Shift Theory is used by its proponents to explain changes in a range of chronic behaviour patterns including overeating, smoking, excessive alcohol use and drug abuse. The version presented here developed out of a synthesis of the findings of a number of qualitative studies. The analyses revealed that key moments in achieving lasting behaviour change were a 'critical reappraisal of self and situation' which led to a small step towards change.

A new identity

If that step was successful it produced 'positive indicators' of a new identity. More behaviour change followed leading to a positive feedback cycle in which the new identity strengthened the behaviour change that reinforced the identity. Like many of the other theories considered, this theory notes the importance of social and environmental influences that act as prompts or constraints. It notes further that the constraints are powerful and numerous, which is why attempts at behaviour change so often fail. Figure 3.2 shows the elements and influences operating within the model.

Dissatisfaction plus trigger equals change

One of the major insights of this theory is the concept of a build-up of dissatisfaction with the current situation and a trigger, which might be quite trivial or might be major, that often results in an immediate and unplanned step on the journey to behaviour change. This fits well with the evidence from Larabie (2005) that many quit attempts involve no overt planning but result from triggers ranging from news of illness to weather conditions that prevent going out to buy a packet of cigarettes.

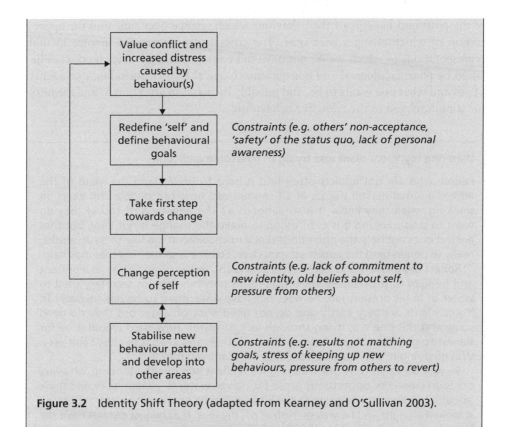

Figure 3.2 Identity Shift Theory (adapted from Kearney and O'Sullivan 2003).

Issues and evaluation

This theory highlights what seems to be a pivotal concept in addiction. However, it is not a comprehensive account but focuses on particular features of behaviour change. If one were to propose it as a comprehensive theory, it would fall foul of apparent counter-examples in which behaviour change takes place without, for example, reference to longstanding goals.

The importance of identity in the development and recovery from addiction has been included in other theories. For example, the Addicted Self Model (Fiorentine and Hillhouse 2000, 2004) proposes that the cessation of alcohol- and drug-dependent behaviour is more likely when the individual attributes failure to control the behaviour to a stable condition, disease, or some other permanent property of the self. The person has to accept that they must achieve complete abstinence.

Addiction as the exercise of choice based on desires

We have arrived at a theory of addiction in which the individual chooses in some sense to engage or not engage in the behaviour. The choice involves a weighing up of the costs and benefits of the behaviour which change over time and the appreciation of which changes over time. The costs and benefits may involve mental representations to which we do not have full conscious access. The choice is influenced by pharmacological and non-pharmacological factors, including one's sense of self and what one wants to be, and possibly by biases in attention to and memory for stimuli related to the addictive behaviour.

Watering my Yucca plant and trying to overcome addiction

People who are not addicts often find it hard to understand the mind of the addict. Journalists still ask us in all seriousness: how can people still keep on smoking when they know it is so dangerous? The answer is of course they do want to stop smoking but even trying to make the change is not easy. But that answer does not help the non-addict really to know what it is like to be an addict, really to understand the addict's perspective. So here is something that may help.

Robert has a lovely and expensive Yucca plant. It was given to him as a present and he likes it. It decorates his office. In his previous job, his secretary used to water it. In his present job, he does not have a secretary so he has to water it. Yucca plants are very hardy and do not need a lot of water but they do need some and this one was dying through lack of water. How hard would it be for Robert to give it some water every now and then and keep it healthy? Not very. Was he doing it? No. Does he care that the plant will die? Yes.

So why on earth is he not watering it? While it was healthy-looking, on every occasion when the opportunity arose for him to water it – when he would think about it because he was going to the kitchen, he did not need to water it because it looked all right and he was so 'rushed off my feet' that he just did not have the time. It could wait. The trouble is it can always wait. Eventually it got into really bad shape; most of its leaves are brown and it was close to death. Then perhaps it was too late. So he did not water it before because there was no single occasion when it really needed it at that moment and then he was not watering it because it was probably too late to do anything about it. He was in too deep.

There is nothing really pathological about this behaviour but for the sake of a very small effort Robert was killing something he liked. You almost certainly have your 'Yucca plant', most people do. What are we talking about? Procrastination of course. We will do it, we mean to do it, we intend to do it. . . then there is no point in doing it because it is probably too late, and then it is *actually* too late. What would it take for Robert to water his plant on a regular basis? Writing the first edition of Theory of Addiction to begin with – but then fortunately for all concerned a kind-hearted colleague took over watering duties. But if we can turn a blind eye to our Yucca plants, imagine how much harder it is for the addict to make that life-changing decision to give up their addiction. The smoker, the drinker, the cocaine sniffer, are all OK. . . until they are probably not and then definitely not.

For the addict, of course, once the life-changing decision has been made to give up the addiction, the trouble really starts. For them, continuing to water their Yucca plant requires them to walk on hot coals to the watering hole and trudge back again laden down with a heavy ewer, all the while missing out on a party that is taking place across the street, not knowing if they are going to make it or even whether it is really worth it because the plant may die anyway. It is not really surprising that many of them do not make it.

References

Abrams, D.B., Herzog, T.A., Emmons, K.M. and Linnan, L. (2000) Stages of change versus addiction: a replication and extension. *Nicotine Tob Res* **2**(3): 223–229.

Adams, J. and White, M. (2005) Why don't stage-based activity promotion interventions work? *Health Educ Res* **20**(2): 237–243.

Audrain-McGovern, J., Rodriguez, D., Tercyak, K.P., Epstein, L.H., Goldman, P. and Wileyto, E.P. (2004) Applying a behavioral economic framework to understanding adolescent smoking. *Psychol Addict Behav* **18**(1): 64–73.

Baron, J. (2000) *Thinking and Deciding*. Cambridge University Press, Cambridge, UK.

Baumeister, R.F., Heatherton, T.F. and Tice, D.M. (1994) *Losing Control: How and Why People Fail at Self-regulation*. Academic Press, San Diego, CA.

Becker, G.S. and Murphy, K.M. (1988) A theory of rational addiction. *J Polit Econ* **96**(4): 675–700.

Beenstock, M. and Rahav, G. (2002) Testing Gateway Theory: do cigarette prices affect illicit drug use? *J Health Econ* **21**(4): 679–698.

Bickel, W.K., DeGrandpre, R.J. and Higgins, S.T. (1995) The behavioral economics of concurrent drug reinforcers: a review and reanalysis of drug self-administration research. *Psychopharmacology (Berl)* **118**(3): 250–259.

Bickel, W.K., Madden, G.J. and DeGrandpre, R.J. (1997) Modeling the effects of combined behavioral and pharmacological treatment on cigarette smoking: behavioral-economic analyses. *Exp Clin Psychopharmacol* **5**(4): 334–343.

Bickel, W.K. and Marsch, L.A. (2001) Toward a behavioral economic understanding of drug dependence: delay discounting processes. *Addiction* **96**(1): 73–86.

Boyer, M. and Dickerson, M. (2003) Attentional bias and addictive behaviour: automaticity in a gambling-specific modified Stroop task. *Addiction* **98**(1): 61–70.

Bradley, B., Field, M., Mogg, K. and De Houwer, J. (2004) Attentional and evaluative biases for smoking cues in nicotine dependence: component processes of biases in visual orienting. *Behav Pharmacol* **15**(1): 29–36.

Brandon, T.H., Herzog, T.A., Irvin, J.E. and Gwaltney, C.J. (2004) Cognitive and social learning models of drug dependence: implications for the assessment of tobacco dependence in adolescents. *Addiction* **99** (Suppl. 1): 51–77.

Brown, S.A. (1985) Reinforcement expectancies and alcoholism treatment outcome after a one-year follow-up. *J Stud Alcohol* **46**(4): 304–308.

Brown, S.A., Christiansen, B.A. and Goldman, M.S. (1987) The Alcohol Expectancy Questionnaire: an instrument for the assessment of adolescent and adult alcohol expectancies. *J Stud Alcohol* **48**(5): 483–491.

Bruce, G. and Jones, B.T. (2004) A pictorial Stroop paradigm reveals an alcohol attentional bias in heavier compared to lighter social drinkers. *J Psychopharmacol* **18**(4): 527–533.

Buckley, P.F. (1998) Substance abuse in schizophrenia: a review. *J Clin Psychiatry* **59** (Suppl. 3): 26–30.

Bunton, R., Baldwin, S., Flynn, D. and Whitelaw, S. (2000) The 'stages of change' model in health promotion: science and ideology. *Crit Public Health* **10**: 55–70.

Chen, M.J., Grube, J.W. and Madden, P.A. (1994) Alcohol expectancies and adolescent drinking: differential prediction of frequency, quantity, and intoxication. *Addict Behav* **19**(5): 521–529.

Chen, X., Unger, J.B., Palmer, P., et al. (2002) Prior cigarette smoking initiation predicting current alcohol use: evidence for a gateway drug effect among California adolescents from eleven ethnic groups. *Addict Behav* **27**(5): 799–817.

Christiansen, B.A. and Goldman, M.S. (1983) Alcohol-related expectancies versus demographic/background variables in the prediction of adolescent drinking. *J Consult Clin Psychol* 51(2): 249–257.

Christiansen, B.A., Smith, G.T., Roehling, P.V. and Goldman, M.S. (1989) Using alcohol expectancies to predict adolescent drinking behavior after one year. *J Consult Clin Psychol* 57(1): 93–99.

Cohen, S. and Lichtenstein, E. (1990) Perceived stress, quitting smoking, and smoking relapse. *Health Psychol* 9(4): 466–478.

Colder, C.R. and O'Connor, R. (2002) Attention biases and disinhibited behavior as predictors of alcohol use and enhancement reasons for drinking. *Psychol Addict Behav* 16(4): 325–332.

Connors, G.J., O'Farrell, T.J., Cutter, H.S. and Thompson, D.L. (1986) Alcohol expectancies among male alcoholics, problem drinkers, and nonproblem drinkers. *Alcohol Clin Exp Res* 10(6): 667–671.

Cooper, M.L., Russell, M. and George, W.H. (1988) Coping, expectancies, and alcohol abuse: a test of social learning formulations. *J Abnorm Psychol* 97(2): 218–230.

Damasio, A.R. (1994) *Descartes' Error: Emotion, Reason, and the Human Brain*. Avon, New York.

Davies, J. B. (1997) *The Myth of Addiction: an Application of the Psychological Theory of Attribution to Illicit Drug Use*, 2nd edn. Harwood Academic Publishers, Chur, Switzerland.

De Nooijer, J., Van Assema, P., De Vet, E. and Brug, J. (2005) How stable are stages of change for nutrition behaviors in the Netherlands? *Health Promot Int* 20(1): 27–32.

DiClemente, C.C., Schlundt, D. and Gemmell, L. (2004) Readiness and stages of change in addiction treatment. *Am J Addict* 13(2): 103–119.

Dixon, M.R., Marley, J. and Jacobs, E.A. (2003) Delay discounting by pathological gamblers. *J Appl Behav Anal* 36(4): 449–458.

Etter, J.F. and Perneger, T.V. (1999) A comparison of two measures of stage of change for smoking cessation. *Addiction* 94(12): 1881–1889.

Etter, J.F. and Sutton, S. (2002) Assessing 'stage of change' in current and former smokers. *Addiction* 97(9): 1171–1182.

Farkas, A.J., Pierce, J.P., Zhu, S.H., et al. (1996) Addiction versus stages of change models in predicting smoking cessation. *Addiction* 91(9): 1271–1280; discussion, 1281–1292.

Farrell, M., Howes, S., Bebbington, P., et al. (2001) Nicotine, alcohol and drug dependence and psychiatric comorbidity. Results of a national household survey. *Br J Psychiatry* 179: 432–437.

Field, M., Mogg, K. and Bradley, B.P. (2004) Cognitive bias and drug craving in recreational cannabis users. *Drug Alcohol Depend* 74(1): 105–111.

Fingarette, H. (1988) Alcoholism: the mythical disease. *Public Interest* (91): 3–22.

Fiorentine, R. and Hillhouse, M.P. (2000) Self-efficacy, expectancies, and abstinence acceptance: further evidence for the addicted-self model of cessation of alcohol- and drug-dependent behavior. *Am J Drug Alcohol Abuse* 26(4): 497–521.

Fiorentine, R. and Hillhouse, M.P. (2004) The Addicted-Self Model of addictive behavior cessation: does it predict recovery for gender, ethnic, age and drug preference populations? *Am J Addict* 13(3): 268–280.

Fischer, S., Smith, G.T., Anderson, K.G. and Flory, K. (2003) Expectancy influences the operation of personality on behavior. *Psychol Addict Behav* 17(2): 108–114.

Fitzpatrick, M. (2003) Addiction myths. *Lancet* 362(9381): 412.

Franken, I.H., Stam, C.J., Hendriks, V.M. and van den Brink, W. (2003) Neurophysiological evidence for abnormal cognitive processing of drug cues in heroin dependence. *Psychopharmacology (Berl)* 170(2): 205–212.

Garcia, K. and Mann, T. (2003) From 'I Wish' to 'I Will': social–cognitive predictors of behavioral intentions. *J Health Psychol* 8(3): 347–360.

Gelkopf, M., Levitt, S. and Bleich, A. (2002) An integration of three approaches to addiction and methadone maintenance treatment: the self-medication hypothesis, the disease model and social criticism. *Isr J Psychiatry Relat Sci* 39(2): 140–151.

Godfrey, C. (1986) Government policy, advertising and tobacco consumption in the UK. A critical review of the literature. *Br J Addict* 81(3): 339–346.

Goldman, M.S. and Darkes, J. (2004) Alcohol expectancy multiaxial assessment: a memory network-based approach. *Psychol Assess* 16(1): 4–15.

Gossop, M., Griffiths, P., Powis, B. and Strang, J. (1994) Cocaine: patterns of use, route of administration, and severity of dependence. *Br J Psychiatry* 164(5): 660–664.

Gruber, J. and Koszegi, B. (2001) Is addiction "rational"? Theory and evidence. *Q J Econ* 116(4): 1261–1303.

Hernandez-Avila, C.A., Burleson, J.A. and Kranzler, H.R. (1998) Stage of change as a predictor of abstinence among alcohol-dependent subjects in pharmacotherapy trials. *Subst Abus* 19(2): 81–91.

Herzog, T.A., Abrams, D.B., Emmons, K.M., Linnan, L.A. and Shadel, W.G. (1999) Do processes of change predict smoking stage movements? A prospective analysis of the transtheoretical model. *Health Psychol* 18(4): 369–375.

Heyman, G.M. (2009) *Addiction: A disorder of choice*, Harvard University Press, Cambridge, Massachusetts.

Hodgins, D.C. (2001) Stages of change assessments in alcohol problems: agreement across self- and clinician-reports. *Subst Abus* 22(2): 87–96.

Hu, S.C. and Lanese, R.R. (1998) The applicability of the theory of planned behavior to the intention to quit smoking across workplaces in southern Taiwan. *Addict Behav* 23(2): 225–237.

Hughes, J., Keely, J., Fagerstrom, K.O. and Callas, P.W. (2005) Intentions to quit smoking change over short periods of time. *Addict Behav* 30(4): 653–662.

Janis, I.L. and Mann, L. (1977) *Decision Making, A Psychological Analysis of Conflict, Choice and Commitment*. The Free Press, New York.

Jaroni, J.L., Wright, S.M., Lerman, C. and Epstein, L.H. (2004) Relationship between education and delay discounting in smokers. *Addict Behav* 29(6): 1171–1175.

Jones, A.M. (1989) A systems approach to the demand for alcohol and tobacco. *Bull Econ Res* 41: 85–105.

Kandel, D.B., Yamaguchi, K. and Chen, K. (1992) Stages of progression in drug involvement from adolescence to adulthood: further evidence for the gateway theory. *J Stud Alcohol* 53(5): 447–457.

Kassel, J.D., Stroud, L.R. and Paronis, C.A. (2003) Smoking, stress, and negative affect: correlation, causation, and context across stages of smoking. *Psychol Bull* 129(2): 270–304.

Keane, H. (2004) Disorders of desire: addiction and problems of intimacy. *J Med Humanit* 25(3): 189–204.

Kearney, M.H. and O'Sullivan, J. (2003) Identity shifts as turning points in health behavior change. *West J Nurs Res* 25(2): 134–152.

Kenkel, D., Mathios, A.D. and Pacula, R.L. (2001) Economics of youth drug use, addiction and gateway effects. *Addiction* 96(1): 151–164.

Khantzian, E.J. (1997) The self-medication hypothesis of substance use disorders: a reconsideration and recent applications. *Harv Rev Psychiatry* 4(5): 231–244.

Koob, G.F., Caine, S.B., Parsons, L., Markou, A. and Weiss, F. (1997) Opponent process model and psychostimulant addiction. *Pharmacol Biochem Behav* 57(3): 513–521.

Koob, G.F. and Le Moal, M. (1997) Drug abuse: hedonic homeostatic dysregulation. *Science* 278(5335): 52–58.

Lancaster, T. and Stead, L.F. (2002) Self-help interventions for smoking cessation. *Cochrane Database Syst Rev* (3): CD001118.

Larabie, L. (2005) To what extent do smokers plan quit attempts? *Tob Control* 14(6): 425–428.

Lewit, E.M. (1989) U.S. tobacco taxes: behavioural effects and policy implications. *Br J Addict* 84(10): 1217–1234.

Lindsay, G.B. and Rainey, J. (1997) Psychosocial and pharmacologic explanations of nicotine's 'gateway drug' function. *J Sch Health* 67(4): 123–126.

Littell, J.H. and Girvin, H. (2002) Stages of change. A critique. *Behav Modif* 26(2): 223–273.

Macenski, M.J. and Meisch, R.A. (1998) Ratio size and cocaine concentration effects on oral cocaine-reinforced behavior. *J Exp Anal Behav* 70(2): 185–201.

Madden, G.J., Bickel, W.K. and Jacobs, E.A. (1999) Discounting of delayed rewards in opioid-dependent outpatients: exponential or hyperbolic discounting functions? *Exp Clin Psychopharmacol* 7(3): 284–293.

Madden, G.J., Petry, N.M., Badger, G.J. and Bickel, W.K. (1997) Impulsive and self-control choices in opioid-dependent patients and non-drug-using control participants: drug and monetary rewards. *Exp Clin Psychopharmacol* 5(3): 256–262.

Marcenko, M.O., Kemp, S.P. and Larson, N.C. (2000) Childhood experiences of abuse, later substance use, and parenting outcomes among low-income mothers. *Am J Orthopsychiatry* 70(3): 316–326.

McAuliffe, W.E. and Gordon, R.A. (1974) A test of Lindesmith's theory of addiction: the frequency of euphoria among long-term addicts. *Am J Sociol* 79(4): 795–840.

McCusker, C.G. and Gettings, B. (1997) Automaticity of cognitive biases in addictive behaviours: further evidence with gamblers. *Br J Clin Psychol* 36(Pt 4): 543–554.

Mogg, K. and Bradley, B.P. (2002) Selective processing of smoking-related cues in smokers: manipulation of deprivation level and comparison of three measures of processing bias. *J Psychopharmacol* 16(4): 385–392.

Mook, D.G. (1996) *Motivation: The Organization of Action*, W.W. Norton, New York.

Mooney, D.K., Fromme, K., Kivlahan, D.R. and Marlatt, G.A. (1987). Correlates of alcohol consumption: sex, age, and expectancies relate differentially to quantity and frequency. *Addict Behav* 12(3): 235–240.

Pacula, R.L. (1997) Economic modelling of the gateway effect. *Health Econ* 6(5): 521–524.

Parrott, A.C. (1998) Nesbitt's Paradox resolved? Stress and arousal modulation during cigarette smoking. *Addiction* 93(1): 27–39.

Peper, A. (2004a) A theory of drug tolerance and dependence I: a conceptual analysis. *J Theor Biol* 229(4): 477–490.

Peper, A. (2004b) A theory of drug tolerance and dependence II: the mathematical model. *J Theor Biol* 229(4): 491–500.

Pisinger, C., Vestbo, J., Borch-Johnsen, K. and Jørgensen, T. (2005a) It is possible to help smokers in early motivational stages to quit. The Inter99 study. *Prev Med* 40(3): 278–284.

Pisinger, C., Vestbo, J., Borch-Johnsen, K. and Jørgensen, T. (2005b) Smoking cessation intervention in a large randomised population-based study. The Inter99 study. *Prev Med* 40(3): 285–292.

Poirier, M.F., Canceil, O., Baylé, F., et al. (2002) Prevalence of smoking in psychiatric patients. *Prog Neuropsychopharmacol Biol Psychiatry* 26(3): 529–537.

Prochaska, J.O., DiClemente, C.C., Velicer, W.F., Ginpil, S. and Norcross, J.C. (1985) Predicting change in smoking status for self-changers. *Addict Behav* 10(4): 395–406.

Prochaska, J.O. and Goldstein, M.G. (1991). Process of smoking cessation. Implications for clinicians. *Clin Chest Med* **12**(4): 727–735.

Prochaska, J.O. and Velicer, W.F. (1997) The transtheoretical model of health behavior change. *Am J Health Promot* **12**(1): 38–48.

Rather, B.C., Goldman, M.S., Roehrich, L. and Brannick, M. (1992) Empirical modeling of an alcohol expectancy memory network using multidimensional scaling. *J Abnorm Psychol* **101**(1): 174–183.

Reed, D.N., Jr., Wolf, B., Barber, K.R., et al. (2005) The stages of change questionnaire as a predictor of trauma patients most likely to decrease alcohol use. *J Am Coll Surg* **200**(2): 179–185.

Reich, R.R., Goldman, M.S. and Noll, J.A. (2004) Using the false memory paradigm to test two key elements of alcohol expectancy theory. *Exp Clin Psychopharmacol* **12**(2): 102–110.

Reynolds, B. and Schiffbauer, R. (2004) Measuring state changes in human delay discounting: an experiential discounting task. *Behav Processes* **67**(3): 343–356.

Riemsma, R.P., Pattenden, J., Bridle, C., et al. (2003) Systematic review of the effectiveness of stage based interventions to promote smoking cessation. *BMJ* **326**(7400): 1175–1177.

Robinson, T.E. and Berridge, K.C. (2003) Addiction. *Ann Rev Psychol* **54**(1): 25–53.

Room, R. (1983) Sociological aspects of the disease concept of alcoholism. In *Research advances in alcohol and drug problems*, Vol. 7, (eds R.G. Smart, F.B. Glasser, Y. Israel, H. Kalant, R. Popham, and W. Schmidt), pp. 47-91. Plenum Press, New York.

Ryan, F. (2002) Detected, selected, and sometimes neglected: cognitive processing of cues in addiction. *Exp Clin Psychopharmacol* **10**(2): 67–76.

Salamone, J.D., Correa, M., Mingote, S. and Weber, S.M. (2003) Nucleus accumbens dopamine and the regulation of effort in food-seeking behavior: implications for studies of natural motivation, psychiatry, and drug abuse. *J Pharmacol Exp Ther* **305**(1): 1–8.

Schaler, P.D.J.A. (1999) *Addiction is a choice*. Open Court, Chicago, IL.

Shahab, L. and West, R. (2012) Differences in happiness between smokers, ex-smokers and never smokers: cross-sectional findings from a national household survey. *Drug Alcohol Depend* **121**(1–2), 38–44.

Shearer, J., Johnston, J., Fry, C.L., et al. (2007) Contemporary cocaine use patterns and associated harms in Melbourne and Sydney, Australia. *Drug Alcohol Rev* **26**(5): 537–543.

Sher, K.J., Wood, M.D., Wood, P.K. and Raskin, G. (1996) Alcohol outcome expectancies and alcohol use: a latent variable cross-lagged panel study. *J Abnorm Psychol* **105**(4): 561–574.

Siegel, S. (1988) Drug anticipation and the treatment of dependence. *NIDA Res Monogr* **84**: 1–24.

Skog, O.J. (2000) Addicts' choice. *Addiction* **95**(9): 1309–1314.

Skog, O.J. (2003) Addiction: definition and mechanisms. In *Choice, Behavioural Economics and Addiction*, (eds R.E. Vuchinich and N. Heather), pp. 157–175. Pergamon, Amsterdam.

Slovic, P., Finucane, M., Peters, E. and MacGregor, D.G. (2002) The affect heuristic. In *Intuitive Judgment: Heuristics and Biases*, (eds T. Gilovich, D. Griffin and D. Kahneman), pp. 397–420. Cambridge University Press, New York.

Smith, G.T., Goldman, M.S., Greenbaum, P.E. and Christiansen, B.A. (1995) Expectancy for social facilitation from drinking: the divergent paths of high-expectancy and low-expectancy adolescents. *J Abnorm Psychol* **104**(1): 32–40.

Solomon, R.L. (1980) The opponent-process theory of acquired motivation: the costs of pleasure and the benefits of pain. *Am Psychol* 35(8): 691–712.

Solomon, R.L. and Corbit, J.D. (1973) An opponent-process theory of motivation. II. Cigarette addiction. *J Abnorm Psychol* 81(2): 158–171.

Solomon, R.L. and Corbit, J.D. (1974) An opponent-process theory of motivation. I. Temporal dynamics of affect. *Psychol Rev* 81(2): 119–145.

Southwick, L., Steele, C., Marlatt, A. and Lindell, M. (1981) Alcohol-related expectancies: defined by phase of intoxication and drinking experience. *J Consult Clin Psychol* 49(5): 713–721.

Stewart, J. and Wise, R.A. (1992) Reinstatement of heroin self-administration habits: morphine prompts and naltrexone discourages renewed responding after extinction. *Psychopharmacology (Berl)* 108(1–2): 79–84.

Sumnall, H.R., Tyler, E., Wagstaff, G.F. and Cole, J.C. (2004) A behavioural economic analysis of alcohol, amphetamine, cocaine and ecstasy purchases by polysubstance misusers. *Drug Alcohol Depend* 76(1): 93–99.

Sutton, S. (2001) Back to the drawing board? A review of applications of the transtheoretical model to substance use. *Addiction* 96(1): 175–186.

Szasz, T.S. (1972) Bad habits are not diseases. A refutation of the claim that alcoholism is a disease. *Lancet* 2(7767): 83–84.

Tate, J.C., Stanton, A.L., Green, S.B., Schmitz, J.M., Le, T. and Marshall, B. (1994) Experimental analysis of the role of expectancy in nicotine withdrawal. *Psychol Addict Behav* 8: 169–178.

Tullis, L.M., Dupont, R., Frost-Pineda, K. and Gold, M.S. (2003) Marijuana and tobacco: a major connection? *J Addict Dis* 22(3): 51–62.

van Sluijs, E.M., van Poppel, M.N. and van Mechelen, W. (2004) Stage-based lifestyle interventions in primary care: are they effective? *Am J Prev Med* 26(4): 330–343.

Viscusi, W.K. (1998) Constructive cigarette regulation. *Duke Law J* 47(6): 1095–1131.

Viscusi, W.K. (2000) Comment: the perils of qualitative smoking risk measures. *J Behav Med* 13(2): 267–271.

Vuchinich, R.V. and Heather, N. (2003) *Choice, Behavioral Economics and Addiction*. Pergamon, Cambridge.

Warburton, D.M. (1985) Nicotine and the smoker. *Rev Environ Health* 5(4): 343–390.

Warburton, D.M. (1992) Nicotine as a cognitive enhancer. *Prog Neuropsychopharmacol Biol Psychiatry* 16(2): 181–191.

Waters, A.J. and Feyerabend, C. (2000) Determinants and effects of attentional bias in smokers. *Psychol Addict Behav* 14(2): 111–120.

Waters, A.J., Shiffman, S., Bradley, B.P. and Mogg, K. (2003) Attentional shifts to smoking cues in smokers. *Addiction* 98(10): 1409–1417.

Weiss, F., Ciccocioppo, R., Parsons, L.H., et al. (2001) Compulsive drug-seeking behavior and relapse. Neuroadaptation, stress, and conditioning factors. *Ann NY Acad Sci* 937: 1–26.

West, R. (1993) Beneficial effects of nicotine: fact or fiction? *Addiction* 88(5): 589–590.

West, R. (2005) Time for a change: putting the Transtheoretical (Stages of Change) Model to rest. *Addiction* 100: 1036–1039.

West, R. and Sohal, T. (2006) "Catastrophic" pathways to smoking cessation: findings from national survey, *BMJ* 332: 458–460.

Whitelaw, S., Baldwin, S., Bunton, R. and Flynn, D. (2000) The status of evidence and outcomes in Stages of Change research. *Health Educ Res* 15(6): 707–718.

Zwar, N. and Richmond, R. (2002) Bupropion sustained release. A therapeutic review of Zyban. *Aust Fam Physician* 31(5): 443–447.

Chapter 4

CHOICE IS NOT ENOUGH: THE CONCEPTS OF IMPULSE AND SELF-CONTROL

This chapter introduces the concept of impulses, urges, inhibition, self-control and voluntary restraint. These concepts are required to explain the experiences of addicts who make an effort to exercise restraint and whose failure is often not a simple 'change of mind'. It introduces evidence that, at least in some cases, addiction is accompanied by impaired performance of brain pathways involved in response inhibition. The concepts on pathological changes in motives and states that impel and restrain behaviour provide a way of explaining patterns of behaviour that do not fit a simple choice model, however, irrational that choice may be.

The last chapter took us from a Rational Choice Theory of addiction to an Irrational Choice Theory; but addiction was still conceived of as a choice process: a weighing up of the costs and benefits of an action and selection based on what is perceived to be the best outcome at the time. Under that view, the idea that addictive behaviour is driven by a damagingly powerful and repeated motivation is an illusion based on a failure to appreciate that the expressed desire to stop doing something at one time does not reflect the preferences operating at a later time after the attempt at restraint has begun.

Reports of feelings of compulsion

One problem with this view is that it does not accord with the experience of many addicts. At the point where they find themselves about to relapse back to their old ways, they frequently report a feeling of compulsion that is distinct from simple desire. It is not even that it is a 'strong desire': it is an urge that they are trying to resist. It also leads to neglect of the panoply of observational and research evidence for the importance of a failure of impulse control in the development and maintenance of addiction.

The concepts of compulsion, craving and self-control dominate what has been termed the Disease Model of addiction (see Jellinek 1960) (Box 4.1). This model proposes that the pathology underlying addiction involves changes in the brain that lead people to do things against their expressed will.

Theory of Addiction, Second Edition. Robert West and Jamie Brown.
© 2013 John Wiley & Sons, Ltd. Published 2013 by John Wiley & Sons, Ltd.

Powerful motives versus impaired control

Now would be a good point to bring in a distinction that has not figured highly in the theories considered thus far but is made in theories that we will consider later that are dominant in the discipline of behavioural pharmacology. The distinction is between compulsion that arises because the impetus to engage in a behaviour is so strong versus compulsion that arises because the ability to exercise restraint or control is so weak.

To put it simply, the question is how far an addict is someone who has such a strong desire for a drug, or indeed urge to use a drug, that it overwhelms powers of restraint that are unimpaired versus someone who has an admittedly strong desire or urge for a drug but an impaired ability to resist that desire. Definitions of addiction as 'impaired control' imply the latter but most of the theorising on the subject assumes the former. However, in the seminal formulation of Edwards and Gross (1976) of the Disease Model of alcohol dependence, the emphasis on failure to exercise control is evident, as, incidentally, is the philosophical difficulty in proposing a lack of choice. Edwards and Gross (1976, p. 1060) state: 'It is unclear, however, whether the experience is truly one of losing control rather than one of deciding not to exercise control.'

Box 4.1   The Disease Model of addiction

The Disease Model of addiction states that addiction involves pathological changes in the brain that result in overpowering urges.

The Disease Model of addiction seeks to explain the development of addiction and individual differences in susceptibility to and recovery from it. It proposes that addiction fits the definition of a medical disorder. It involves an abnormality of structure or function in the CNS that results in impairment (Jellinek 1960; Gelkopf et al. 2002). It can be diagnosed using standard criteria and in principle it can be treated.

Loss of control
Under this view, an addicted individual will express a sincere desire to stop engaging in the addictive behaviour and will show every evidence of making strenuous efforts to stop doing it *at the same time as* he or she carries on nevertheless. In fact the loss of control is manifest over short and long time spans. Over a period of a few hours, an alcoholic may begin a drinking session with the intention of having one or two drinks but finds that, according to his way of thinking, it is impossible to stop at that and more and more drinks are consumed: the power to resist has gone.

Over a longer time span, the alcoholic, or indeed the smoker, gambler or other drug addict formulates a plan not to engage in the activity but after a time (usually a short time) does in fact engage in the activity. The addict chooses to do one thing but does something else.

The importance of craving

At the heart of this theory is the concept of 'craving'. In the disease model, this has been defined as an 'urgent and overpowering desire' (Jellinek 1960). One way of thinking about this is as a feeling that impels the addict to take whatever steps are necessary and feasible to achieve the object of the addiction. However, it might even be proposed that it is a motivational state that goes beyond feelings: it overwhelms the individual in totality, dominating the thoughts, feelings and actions of the individual to the exclusion of all else.

This theory captures what seems to be the central phenomenology of addiction: a desire that is so strong and all-encompassing that it sweeps all other considerations before it in a myopic and single-minded search for the object of that desire. Even if in some sense there is a choice, it does not seem like it to the addict or to observers, and in the common understanding of the term there is no real choice, there is compulsion.

Self-cure

An observation that on the face of it poses difficulties for the disease model is that many 'addicts' stop engaging in the activity concerned without apparent difficulty. For years their behaviour has shown all the signs of compulsion but then one day they decide that enough is enough and cease.

It can only be presumed either that whatever abnormality there was in the individual's brain which led to the compulsion suddenly normalised or that the individual was never addicted in the first place. Both of these are just about possible at least for some individuals. It is also possible that this phenomenon is not quite what it seems: that heavily addicted individuals do not actually recover spontaneously in this way and that a distinction needs to be made between individuals who are heavy and regular users of a drug or who engage in an activity frequently but who are not addicted.

Issues and evaluation

Just as Rational Choice Theory can be regarded as misleading in implying that addicts are merely exercising preferences, the Disease Model has been criticised as misleading in implying that addicts are impotent onlookers and the only way of stopping them is physical restraint (Skog 2000).

As with the theories reviewed in the previous chapter, the main problem with this theory is observations that it does not account for. By focusing on compulsion, there are many aspects of addiction that it does not encompass. Specifically, it does not begin to address the issues of choice and identity that were the insights presented in the previous chapter.

The question of why some people become addicted to particular activities while others do not is a thread running through all the preceding discussion. We have postulated that it may relate to a host of different factors that make the addictive behaviour more rewarding or abstinence more distressing.

Personality and addiction typologies

One model that focuses specifically on personality as a predisposing factor in addiction is Cloninger's Tridimensional Theory (Cloninger 1987). It proposes three dimensions of personality: novelty seeking, harm avoidance and reward dependence (see Box 4.2). The potential link between these dimensions and susceptibility to addiction are striking, so it is surprising that research has not provided greater support for the theory (Howard et al. 1997).

Box 4.2   Tridimensional Personality Theory

Cloninger's Tridimensional Personality Theory argues that three fundamental dimensions of personality have direct implications for susceptibility to addiction and can also be used to divide addicts into subtypes (see Cloninger 1987).

Dimensional theories of personality

Cloninger's Tridimensional Personality Theory is an example of an approach to personality and its assessment that postulates that a small number of hypothetical dimensions of mental functioning explain a large amount of the variation that exists in the way in which people respond to their environment. It is from the same mould as Eysenck's Three-factor Personality Theory (see e.g. Roos 1977a, 1977b) and McCrae and Costa's Five-factor Theory (see, e.g. Conway et al. 2003; Miller and Lynam 2003), both of which have also been used to try to explain susceptibility to addiction.

Novelty seeking, harm avoidance and reward dependence

The Tridimensional Personality Theory proposes three fundamental dimensions: novelty seeking, harm avoidance and reward dependence (see Cloninger 1987). It is argued that the interaction between these dimensions leads to different patterns of responses to novelty, punishment and reward, and that this has implications for dependence on alcohol and drugs. It is further proposed that there are two fundamental subtypes of alcoholic (Type I and Type II). These two subtypes differ according to the age at which alcoholism develops; the relative contributions of predisposing genetic and environmental factors; the gender and personality traits of the alcoholic; and whether co-occurring psychiatric disorders, such as antisocial behaviour, are present. It is proposed that Type I alcoholics have later onset, less genetic involvement, are more likely to be female and have fewer problem behaviours.

Evidence

In a review of studies that have examined Cloninger's theory and its associated questionnaire assessment, novelty seeking was found to distinguish alcoholics from non-alcoholics and Type II from their Type I counterparts, and smokers from non-smokers. Tridimensional traits independently predicted early-onset alcohol abuse and serious delinquency and were significantly associated with concurrent substance abuse among adolescents. The review also found that most studies that compared non-alcoholic youth with positive and negative family histories of alcoholism reported non-significant differences between scores on a questionnaire designed to assess the three personality dimensions. Few alcoholics, cigarette smokers or sons of alcoholics displayed Type I (low novelty seeking, high harm avoidance, high reward dependence) or Type II (high novelty seeking, low harm avoidance, low reward dependence) personality profiles.

Thus, novelty seeking does predict early-onset alcohol abuse and criminality, and differentiates alcoholics exhibiting antisocial behaviour and persons with antisocial personality disorder (ASPD) from their non-antisocial counterparts. Findings for the harm avoidance and reward-seeking dimensions are less consistent though there is some support for the role of higher levels of harm avoidance in intensity of substance use (Howard et al. 1997).

However, more recently, Sannibale and Hall (1998) evaluated Cloninger's typology of alcoholism in a sample of 300 Australian men and women with a lifetime diagnosis of alcohol abuse/dependence. They found that the questionnaire measure used classified only 18% of the sample into either Type I or Type II. More women than men were classified as Type I (19% vs. 6%) but, contrary to expectations, similar numbers were classified as Type II problem drinkers (7% vs. 4%). As predicted, Type II problem drinkers had more symptoms of ASPD, more social consequences of drinking and higher sensation-seeking scores than Type I problem drinkers.

Issues and evaluation

Cloninger's typology of alcohol dependence is of importance primarily because it seeks to ground a theory of addiction in a more general theory of personality. It also recognises and attempts to systematise the heterogeneity that exists even within dependence on a particular substance. It clearly captures some important distinctions but evidence has often not supported its broader contentions.

Other typologies have also been proposed that are quite close to Cloninger's. Most notable is Babor's classification into Type A and B alcoholics (see Babor et al. 1992; Litt et al. 1992; Brown et al. 1994). This typology was based on a cluster analysis of alcoholics in treatment rather than derived from a personality theory. The two types of alcoholic differed across 17 characteristics. Type A alcoholics were characterised by later onset, fewer childhood risk factors, less severe dependence, fewer alcohol-related problems, and less psychopathological dysfunction. Type B alcoholics were characterised by childhood risk factors, familial alcoholism, early onset of alcohol-related problems, greater severity of dependence, polydrug use, a more chronic treatment history (despite their younger age), greater psychopathological dysfunction, and more life stress. The Type B alcoholics were less likely to be successful after treatment.

Self-efficacy

In the previous chapter, the concept of 'self-efficacy' was alluded to but not discussed in detail. Self-efficacy, like addiction, is a social construct, and has been defined in different ways. In general it reflects our confidence in being able to achieve certain outcomes and has been proposed as playing a major role in changing behaviour. Put simply, if we do not think we can do something, we do not try or if we do try we give up easily. This concept can be fitted into a simple choice framework as a factor entering into the cost–benefit analysis. However, it probably fits a little better in the present discussion about compulsion and control (Box 4.3).

Box 4.3   Self-efficacy Theory

Overcoming addiction is related to the extent of an individual's beliefs that he or she can organise and carry out activities in order to exercise restraint or achieve abstinence.

Self-efficacy is the level of an individual's confidence in his or her abilities to organise and complete actions that lead to particular goals (Bandura 1977; Bandura et al. 1977). Four main hypotheses form the core of the theory:

- Levels of self-efficacy affect the goals that people pursue.
- Self-efficacy affects the level of effort used to achieve those goals.
- Self-efficacy affects how long people will persevere in pursuit of their goals when encountering barriers.
- Self-efficacy affects the likelihood of the goal being achieved.

Self-efficacy may be influenced by the success or failure that an individual has previously experienced on the task in question though it is not the only source of influence. Thus it should, according to the theory, predict future behaviour over and above what is known about past experience.

Generalised versus specific self-efficacy
Self-efficacy can be related to specific tasks (such as stopping heroin use) or more general. Self-efficacy can extend beyond behaviour to a person's level of perceived control with regard to his or her thoughts, feelings and environment. The original Bandura Theory of Self-efficacy has been applied to addictive behaviours with some adaptation (see Marlatt 1996). It has been suggested that reduced self-efficacy may underpin loss of control in addiction (Brandon et al. 2004).

Marlatt (1996) has classified efficacy judgements in relation to the stages of drug and alcohol misuse. Resistance self-efficacy beliefs are the person's judgements of his or her ability to avoid substance abuse prior to its first use. Harm reduction self-efficacy beliefs involve judging one's ability to reduce the risks of the drugs once addicted.

Craving and self-efficacy
Craving and self-efficacy are postulated by Marlatt to be reciprocally related, with high levels of craving being the most disruptive to the addict's coping skills. Indeed, self-efficacy has been found to be inversely proportional to cigarette craving (Niaura 2000) and has also been found in some studies to be a predictor of success or failure of smoking cessation attempts even after controlling for concurrent smoking patterns (Gwaltney et al. 2001).

Changes in self-efficacy
It is thought that the act of giving up a drug has a positive impact on the individual's levels of self-efficacy. Carey et al. (1993) examined data from a sample of smokers over a 12-month period. Those who had successfully quit for 12 months had increased levels of self-efficacy, whereas those who continued smoking, or even attempted abstinence but relapsed, had decreased self-efficacy.

This has obvious parallels with the Identity Shift Theory described in the previous chapter. Self-efficacy ratings have also been reported to increase after an initial dose of methadone, to be unchanged when the individual is maintained on a stable dose of methadone and to decline during the weaning stage (Reilly et al. 1995).

Issues and evaluation
The ideas behind Self-efficacy Theory fit well with natural observations and with a simple Rational Choice Theory of behaviour. It also seems appropriate to focus special attention on self-efficacy because of the possibility that it may exert a large influence on addictive behaviour.

Unfortunately, the evidence to date has not established how important self-efficacy *per se* is in maintaining addiction. For example, consider someone who has all the signs of being heavily addicted to alcohol but is utterly confident that he could control his drinking whenever he so chooses. Would that confidence in itself be enough to enable him to overcome his addiction? This does not appear to have been tested but it seems unlikely.

Similarly, if we take a sample of smokers and assess their level of addiction carefully without reference to any beliefs about their ability to stop smoking, including observations of their past experiences of attempts to stop, would adding self-efficacy beliefs into the model substantially improve on the prediction of their ability to stop? Perhaps most importantly, we need evidence that an intervention that raises self-efficacy has a substantial impact on ability to exercise restraint.

The concept of self-efficacy forms a part of many theoretical accounts including social learning theory and the abstinence violation effect described later. As with other theories, it is drawn out here for the purpose of exposition.

The transition from lapse to relapse

We noted that the concept of self-efficacy permeated many of the choice-based models described in the previous chapter. It is also an important element of a theory that focuses on a particular phenomenon in addictive behaviour: the process by which a single lapse back to an old pattern of behaviour leads to full resumption of that behaviour. This process has been called the Abstinence Violation Effect (Box 4.4)

Box 4.4   The Abstinence Violation Effect

Precipitants of relapse are internal, stable and global attributions as to the causes of initial lapses – relapse is a learning experience that occurs due to inadequate coping resources.

The Abstinence Violation Effect (AVE) proposes that internal, stable and global attributions for the cause of a lapse of abstinence and concomitant feelings of guilt and loss of control increase the probability of a return to regular substance use. Cognitive factors play a crucial role in the likelihood of relapse. Marlatt argues that the AVE is a particularly destructive cognitive process (Marlatt 1979).

Genesis of the AVE
The AVE occurs when an individual views his or her drug use as a deviation from his or her commitment to absolute abstinence that elicits a state of 'cognitive dissonance'. The individual attempts to resolve this dissonance by assuming that some intrinsic personal quality makes abstinence impossible ('personal attribution'). Interpretations and attributions can then undermine future attempts at maintaining abstinence.

Effects of the AVE

The theory also has implications for how failure of an attempt at abstinence influences subsequent attempts. It argues that one of the most constructive ways of perceiving relapse, for the individual at least, is to identify circumstantial factors that made it difficult to resist, permitting contingency plans for the future to be developed. The AVE conceptualises relapse as a learning experience and that the individual's reaction and appraisal of the lapse will determine future commitments to abstinence.

Empirical evidence

It has been documented that alcoholics, smokers, opiate addicts, gamblers and overeaters are more likely to lapse when they experience negative emotional states (e.g. Cummings et al. 1985). Such findings support the proposition that addictive behaviour is often engaged in because of its effectiveness in controlling stress. Evidence for the importance of coping skills is provided by Miller et al. (1996) who found that the lack of these skills were the strongest predictors of relapse in a sample of alcoholics receiving outpatient care.

Walton et al. (1994) examined the role of attributions in the lapse and relapse process following substance abuse treatment. In a study of inpatients who had undergone 6 months of treatment they looked at the attributions made by recovering drug users who were tempted to lapse but remained abstinent in comparison with those who lapsed and those who relapsed. Predictions made by the Abstinence Violation Model were not supported in so far as lapsers and relapsers were similar in terms of internal/external attributions following a return to drug use. However, relapsers made more stable and global attributions compared with lapsers, and abstainers made more internal and stable attributions regarding their abstinence, compared with lapsers following their slip. Abstainers' attributions for success in remaining abstinent tended to be similar to the attributions made by relapsers for their failure to remain abstinent (i.e. for their relapse). These findings highlight the complexity in the attribution process in early recovery.

Shiffman and others (1996) found in a study of smokers that the indicators of the AVE, namely self-efficacy, attributions and affective reactions to the lapse, generally failed to predict progression to relapse, but participants who attempted restorative coping following a lapse were less likely to lapse for a second time. Those whose lapses were triggered by stress progressed more quickly on to a further lapse, whereas those triggered by eating or drinking or accompanied by alcohol consumption progressed more slowly. Those who were heavily nicotine dependent were more likely to have a second lapse, but neither the amount smoked in the first lapse nor its subjective reinforcement predicted progression.

Birke et al. (1990) used data from a sample of alcoholics and cigarette smokers to study the occurrence of the AVE predicting the likelihood of 'full blown relapse' following an initial lapse. No significant difference was found in the attribution style of abstainers and relapsers. Negative affect (such as anxiety or depression) and interpersonal conflict were found to be important precipitants of relapse while social pressure was not found to be linked to relapse.

Ross et al. (1988) examined the assumption that self-efficacy plays an important role in the resistance to relapse in the AVE. It was thought that combinations of unrealistically high standards and low self-efficacy for following those standards may relate to the risk of relapse. Newly admitted alcoholics and individuals who had remained abstinent for 1 year showed no difference in their self-imposed high standards, but successfully abstinent alcoholics were found to have higher self-efficacy expectations than alcoholics who were early in the recovery process.

Positive findings have been reported from a study testing the AVE hypothesis in a sample of marijuana users who reported a lapse back to marijuana use following completion of either relapse prevention treatment or a social support group promoting abstinence (Stephens et al. 1994). It was found that more internal, stable and global attributions for the cause of the lapse and perceived loss of control were related significantly to concurrently reported lapse. Furthermore, internal and global attributions for lapses predicted marijuana use during the subsequent 6 months.

Implications and interventions

The Relapse Prevention Model has been developed out of the AVE concept. In this model, no single treatment or package is endorsed owing to the diversity of attributions that may be attached to maintaining abstinence at an individual level. Instead, it is proposed that the therapist gain an overview of the wide range of different factors that can influence attitudes and expectations about a variety of drugs, and be willing to approach each individual's dependence with an open-minded view about the underlying factors.

The relapse prevention framework identifies four elements for developing an appropriate package based on the components of AVE:

1. An in-depth assessment of the individual's risk factors and discriminative stimuli (cues), as well as their existing coping skills and resources. The level of assessment required will be extensive, although further details will emerge and need to be added to the review over the course of the treatment.
2. Assisting the addicted individual in finding appropriate alternative strategies for avoidance or coping with risk situations. Strategies may consist of cognitive techniques (e.g. talking through difficult issues in order to identify the need and type of strategies required) and behavioural techniques (e.g. relaxation, distraction).

3. Enhancing the addict's self-efficacy and skill in using alternative strategies, for example, by assisting him or her to practise them and thereby identify and tackle potential difficulties.

4. Preparation for how to deal with a lapse may require discussion of the AVE, together with the development of a structured plan of what to do in such an eventuality (e.g. contact a particular person, go somewhere private for a period of reflection).

These four elements can take many different forms, depending on the characteristics of the therapist, the patient and the resources available.

Motivational interviewing

The relapse prevention approach has spawned a counselling technique known as 'motivational interviewing' (Miller and Johnson 2001). The idea of motivational interviewing is to engage the individual with the idea of sustaining and committing to their behaviour change in the longer term. This level of intervention relies on a dialogue between the therapist and the individual and a commitment to working together to identify risky situations and other problem areas and evaluate potential coping strategies in a supportive environment.

There is evidence that the motivational interviewing technique that is based on the relapse prevention model is of value (Rubak et al. 2005). For example, Allsop et al. (1997) randomised a sample of alcoholics to either a standard care package of basic drugs education, a relapse prevention package or extra discussion sessions. Those receiving the relapse prevention package showed significantly higher abstinence rates and spent a longer time drug free before relapse.

Issues and evaluation

Although not all of the postulates of the theory have been supported, the AVE theory captures some important features of the relapse process and accords well with observations in the real world. Its main tenets would need to be encompassed within any general theory of addiction. It is important to take note of Miller's admonition, however (Miller 1996), that the concept of relapse itself is problematic and an oversimplification of a complex and highly varied process of transition from abstinence to resumption of an addictive behaviour.

Impulse control

The concepts of self-efficacy and the AVE draw attention to beliefs and feelings that undermine attempts at change. It has been noted that impulse control problems as a personality type are associated with extent of addictive substance use (Conway et al. 2003). The failure of self-control has been explored in a more general way in a number of theories. One of these (Box 4.5) describes links between neuroanatomical structures and inhibitory mechanisms.

Box 4.5 Inhibition Dysregulation Theory

Addiction involves a progressive dysregulation of ability to inhibit behaviour that is rewarded (Lubman et al. 2004).

Lubman et al. (2004) present an argument that suggests that the inhibitory system involving brain regions related to aspects of response inhibition and selection underlies compulsive behaviours associated with drug addiction. They are not suggesting that addicted individuals are automatons under the direct control of substances or related stimuli acting on the brain, but rather that aspects of decision-making are compromised in perhaps either a direct way (i.e. a dysfunctional inhibitory system) or indirectly via a dysfunctional reward system.

Commonalities between addiction and disorders of control
It is noted that substance abuse is common in patients suffering from schizophrenia, depression and obsessive compulsive disorder (OCD) (Conway et al. 2002). It is also noted that inhibitory processes involving frontal cortical structures are deficient in patients with schizophrenia, bipolar mood disorder, attention deficit hyperactivity disorder and OCD (Murphy 1990; Bannon et al. 2002). Some aspects of addiction appear quite similar to OCD (Modell et al. 1992) as clinical descriptions of both disorders describe an inability to inhibit intrusive repetitive thoughts (i.e. obsessions or cravings) and ritualistic, regimented behaviour (compulsions or drug-taking behaviour) and both result in significantly impaired functioning.

Brain regions involved in inhibition
Significant under-activity has been found in the orbitofrontal cortex (OFC) and anterior cingulate cortex (ACC) of cocaine addicts and alcoholics who continue to use and in those abstinent for long periods (Volkow et al. 1997). These regions become highly active during cue exposure (Grant et al. 1996) and acute withdrawal (see Volkow et al. 1997).

Thus, the theory proposes that compulsive behaviour requires dysfunction within the two aforementioned highly interconnected cortical systems, the ACC and OFC, which are critically involved in self-regulation and together form the core of the inhibitory system. It is suggested that increased incentive states alone are not sufficient for compulsive behaviour to occur, but require dysfunctional inhibitory processes within the OFC and ACC.

Failure of inhibition and relapse

The Inhibition Dysregulation Theory appears to be supported by the findings of Miller and Gold (1994) that craving was only cited in 7% of cases as a primary factor for relapse, with 41% citing impulsive action (i.e. reduced inhibitory control). It has also been suggested that a failure consciously to consider future consequences of behaviours (Altman et al. 1996) may be associated with the underactivity of the inhibitory system.

It is hypothesised that the inhibitory system is overwhelmed by motives, resulting in the release, or disinhibition, of behaviour that is unduly dominated by 'pre-potent' and 'stimulus-driven' tendencies in the presence of addiction-related provocation. Lubman et al. (2004) explain further that this provocation leads to impulsivity (experienced as loss of control) with little consideration of adverse future consequences, resulting in recurrent compulsive drug taking. It is argued that clinical outcomes may be predicted more accurately by systematically probing the integrity of the inhibitory system under real-life motivational states, rather than measuring craving levels or inhibitory functions alone.

Interventions to enhance inhibitory control

Failure of inhibitory control is the target of many self-help clinical interventions such as Alcoholics Anonymous, and overcoming this is a feature of the technique known as 'motivational interviewing' mentioned earlier. Pharmacotherapeutic approaches that target aspects of dependence such as substitution treatments or withdrawal-oriented therapy are also argued to be consistent with a model of inhibitory dysregulation.

Inhibition dysfunction versus tolerance and withdrawal symptoms

This theory is a move away from the tolerance and dependence explanations of addiction towards a behavioural, compulsive drug-seeking explanation, reinforced by the effects of the drug and the struggle for abstinence. Lubman et al. (2004) attempt to bring together disparate findings involving neuroadaptation and sensitisation of the dopamine reward system (see Chapter 5), drug cue reactivity (see Chapter 5) and malfunction of the inhibitory system to create an integrated model.

Issues and evaluation

We have located this theory in a chapter that introduces the concept of compulsion and self-control, but like many of the theories reviewed thus far, it incorporates elements that include conscious choice, already discussed, and habit elements that will be considered further in Chapter 5. What is clear is that there is evidence of a failure of inhibitory mechanisms in the development of at least some cases of addiction, and we have the beginnings of an understanding of the neurological substrate of this.

Self-regulation as a broadly based concept

An account of self-regulation in all its aspects is set out by Baumeister et al. (1994) (Box 4.6). This wide-ranging review presents a persuasive case that self-regulation at many levels, from conscious restraint to response inhibition, plays a critical role in the balance of forces that operate on behaviour in all its manifestations. It notes that self-control is one aspect of wider self-regulation in which we self-consciously exercise our will in order to achieve particular goals.

Box 4.6   Self-regulation Theory

Actions arise from a hierarchy of multiple processes that may be in competition with each other. Higher processes involve more complex networks of meaningful associations and interpretations, and more distal or abstract goals. Self-regulation involves higher processes overriding lower processes. Self-regulation failure occurs when lower order processes win through.

Among the various theories that focus on impaired control or compulsion, Baumeister et al. (1994) have produced a highly developed account that emphasises the commonalities between addiction, poor self-management, obsessions, eating too much, aggression and many other behavioural problems. This theory allows for the possibility that there are stable individual differences in propensity to exercise self-control that may predate and contribute to development of addiction. Like the dysregulation of impulse control theory described earlier, it also allows for the possible effects of drugs of dependence on self-regulation and it also examines the effects of short-term influences such as tiredness, emotional state and environmental stimuli on self-regulation.

Issues and evaluation
The theory has enormous explanatory potential, for example, with regard to the link between antisocial personality and addiction, mental illness and addiction, associations between different forms of addiction and indeed the process of recovery from addiction.

It seems that we must include abnormalities of self-control in the theory of addiction. As noted earlier, the phenomenology of addiction also appears to involve a sense of urge or compulsion that may go beyond a weakening of impulse control mechanisms. It is now time to explore the concept of 'urge' in more detail.

Urges and craving

The term 'urge' has often been used synonymously with 'craving' but unfortunately this latter term has acquired many different meanings and this has tended to cloud the debate (Kozlowski and Wilkinson 1987). In common parlance 'urge' is a feeling of being impelled to do something. It is not necessarily the same as wanting to do it but often the two go together. A simple example of the difference between the two would be something like: 'Sammy had a strong urge to go to the bathroom but wanted to carry on playing on his computer'. Tiffany (1990) has developed a theory about how urges develop and what role they play in maintaining drug use (Box 4.7).

Box 4.7   A Cognitive Model of Drug Urges

The Cognitive Model of Drug Urges proposes that compulsive drug use involves more than subjective feelings of craving. It involves enactment of highly automated action sequences that are driven by cue–response associations. Craving should be viewed as two related dimensions. One arises from a conscious attempt to block automated action sequences. The other is anticipation of pleasure from the behaviour (Tiffany 1990, 1999; Tiffany and Conklin 2000).

The theory proposes that craving represents the addict's effortful cognitive processing devoted to interrupting drug use. It arises from attempts to block highly automated action sequences that are learned through repetition. Under this view, the addict's intention regarding whether or not to use drugs should influence features of reported craving. The model predicts that desire and intent to use drugs will be strongly 'coupled' in active smokers. However, desire and intention to smoke may become 'uncoupled' in individuals who are trying to quit smoking.

Two dimensions of urge
According to the theory, craving should be divided into two dimensions. One dimension is a feeling of urgent need linked with withdrawal symptoms and the other arises from expectation of pleasure from the activity concerned (Tiffany and Drobes 1991). Studies with smokers during *ad-lib* smoking and abstinence have been claimed to support this view (e.g. Cox et al. 2001). However, the type of evidence used is only weakly related to the hypothesis.

One line of evidence comes from 'factor analysis': a statistical method for assessing the extent to which scores on a number of measures (e.g. ratings given in response to questionnaire items) can be explained in terms of one or more underlying dimensions.

Factor analysis has been applied to responses to a questionnaire devised to test the theory, the Questionnaire of Smoking Urges (QSU). Unfortunately, when used with questionnaires, this statistical method is highly sensitive to the specific question wording to the extent of semantic overlap between questions, and to the sample and the circumstances in which the measurement is made. In addition, it does not give a clear decision as to how many underlying dimensions there are: more or less arbitrary rules have to be devised to make that determination.

In the case of the QSU, proponents of the theory claim that there are two underlying dimensions that are correlated with each other. However, one could argue that there is just one underlying dimension on which is superimposed some additional systematic variation attributable to similarities in wording and style of the items.

The second line of evidence is that the two scores derived from the QSU respond differently to interventions that affect craving in different ways. Unfortunately, the tests of this have not used the necessary statistical procedures that would tell us whether the pattern of responses are truly different or whether the difference could have occurred by chance. Thus, it is not enough to show that an intervention significantly affects one scale and not another. It is necessary directly to show a statistically significant difference in the effect of the intervention on the two scales (i.e. an interaction).

Automaticity and addiction
As regards the part of the theory related to automated action sequences, the theory is designed to explain the relationship between environmental cues and reports of craving and the fact that relapse to an addictive behaviour often occurs in the absence of cravings. Research has shown that although absent-minded lapses to smoking do occur, they are rare (Catley et al. 2000).

Issues and evaluation
It is clear that this theory, like others, stems from a need to integrate cognitive processing models with motivational systems that do not involve conscious awareness. The theory recognises that urges to engage in addictive behaviours do not simply derive from the anticipated pleasure that these will provide. The theory makes an important point about the urges potentially arising from an attempt to frustrate an automated action sequence. In this respect, it is the flipside of the 'restraint' coin.

Addiction as a failure of self-control over desires and urges

We have now arrived at a theory of addiction in which we have added the concepts of self-control and compulsion to an irrational choice theory with unstable preferences. This is still a theory in which conscious choice is the final common pathway, though many of the theories reviewed thus far (including the last one reviewed) have included non-conscious, automatic or semi-automatic processes.

There are still anomalies in a choice-type model. One is the observation, albeit not common, that addictive behaviours sometimes occur without conscious awareness being directed at them (e.g. lighting up a cigarette without thinking about it). More importantly, there seems to be a mismatch between the degree of urge to engage in some addictive behaviours and the apparent rewards that stem from them. The next chapter brings in the field of behavioural pharmacology as a possible means of addressing this weakness.

References

Allsop, S., Saunders, B., Phillips, M. and Carr, A. (1997) A trial of relapse prevention with severely dependent male problem drinkers. *Addiction* 92(1): 61–73.

Altman, J., Everitt, B.J., Glautier, S., et al. (1996) The biological, social and clinical bases of drug addiction: commentary and debate. *Psychopharmacology (Berl)* 125(4): 285–345.

Babor, T.F., Hofmann, M., DelBoca, F.K., et al. (1992) Types of alcoholics, I. Evidence for an empirically derived typology based on indicators of vulnerability and severity. *Arch Gen Psychiatry* 49(8): 599–608.

Bandura, A. (1977) Self-efficacy: toward a unifying theory of behavioral change. *Psychol Rev* 84(2): 191–215.

Bandura, A., Adams, N.E. and Beyer, J. (1977) Cognitive processes mediating behavioral change. *J Pers Soc Psychol* 35(3): 125–139.

Bannon, S., Gonsalvez, C.J., Croft, R.J. and Boyce, P.M. (2002) Response inhibition deficits in obsessive–compulsive disorder. *Psychiatry Res* 110(2): 165–174.

Baumeister, R.F., Heatherton, T.F. and Tice, D.M. (1994) *Losing Control: How and Why People Fail at Self-regulation*. Academic Press, San Diego, CA.

Birke, S.A., Edelmann, R.J. and Davis, P.E. (1990) An analysis of the abstinence violation effect in a sample of illicit drug users. *Br J Addict* 85(10): 1299–1307.

Brandon, T.H., Herzog, T.A., Irvin, J.E. and Gwaltney C.J. (2004) Cognitive and social learning models of drug dependence: implications for the assessment of tobacco dependence in adolescents. *Addiction* 99(Suppl. 1): 51–77.

Brown, J., Babor, T.F., Litt, M.D. and Kranzler, H.R. (1994) The type A/type B distinction. Subtyping alcoholics according to indicators of vulnerability and severity. *Ann NY Acad Sci* 708: 23–33.

Carey, M.P., Kalra, D.L., Carey K.B., Halperin S. and Richards C.S. (1993) Stress and unaided smoking cessation: a prospective investigation. *J Consult Clin Psychol* 61(5): 831–838.

Catley, D., O'Connell, K.A. and Shiffman, S. (2000) Absentminded lapses during smoking cessation. *Psychol Addict Behav* 14(1): 73–76.

Cloninger, C.R. (1987) A systematic method for clinical description and classification of personality variants. A proposal. *Arch Gen Psychiatry* 44(6): 573–588.

Conway, K.P., Kane, R.J., Ball, S.A., Poling, J.C. and Rounsaville, B.J. (2003) Personality, substance of choice, and polysubstance involvement among substance dependent patients. *Drug Alcohol Depend* 71(1): 65–75.

Conway, K.P., Swendsen, J.D., Rounsaville, B.J. and Merikangas, K.R. (2002) Personality, drug of choice, and comorbid psychopathology among substance abusers. *Drug Alcohol Depend* 65(3): 225–234.

Cox, L.S., Tiffany, S.T. and Christen, A.G. (2001) Evaluation of the brief questionnaire of smoking urges (QSU-brief) in laboratory and clinical settings. *Nicotine Tob Res* 3(1): 7–16.

Cummings, K.M., Jaen, C.R. and Giovino, G. (1985) Circumstances surrounding relapse in a group of recent exsmokers. *Prev Med* 14(2): 195–202.

Edwards, G. and Gross, M.M. (1976) Alcohol dependence: provisional description of a clinical syndrome. *Br Med J* 1(6017): 1058–1061.

Gelkopf, M., Levitt, S. and Bleich, A. (2002) An integration of three approaches to addiction and methadone maintenance treatment: the self-medication hypothesis, the disease model and social criticism. *Isr J Psychiatry Relat Sci* 39(2): 140–151.

Grant, S., London, E.D., Newlin, D.B., et al. (1996) Activation of memory circuits during cue-elicited cocaine craving. *Proc Natl Acad Sci USA* 93(21): 1204–1205.

Gwaltney, C.J., Shiffman, S., Norman, G.J., et al. (2001) Does smoking abstinence self-efficacy vary across situations? Identifying context-specificity within the Relapse Situation Efficacy Questionnaire. *J Consult Clin Psychol* 69(3): 516–527.

Howard, M.O., Kivlahan, D. and Walker, R.D. (1997) Cloninger's tridimensional theory of personality and psychopathology: applications to substance use disorders. *J Stud Alcohol* 58(1): 48–66.

Jellinek, E.M. (1960) *The Disease Concept of Alcoholism*. Hillhouse Press, New Brunswick, NJ.

Kozlowski, L.T. and Wilkinson, D.A. (1987) Use and misuse of the concept of craving by alcohol, tobacco, and drug researchers. *Br J Addict* 82(1): 31–45.

Litt, M.D., Babor, T.F., DelBoca, F.K., Kadden, R.M. and Cooney, N.L. (1992) Types of alcoholics, II. Application of an empirically derived typology to treatment matching. *Arch Gen Psychiatry* 49(8): 609–614.

Lubman, D.I., Yucel, M. and Pantelis, C. (2004) Addiction, a condition of compulsive behaviour? Neuroimaging and neuropsychological evidence of inhibitory dysregulation. *Addiction* 99(12): 1491–1502.

Marlatt, G.A. (1979) A cognitive-behavioral model of the relapse process. *NIDA Res Monogr* 25: 191–200.

Marlatt, G.A. (1996) Taxonomy of high-risk situations for alcohol relapse: evolution and development of a cognitive-behavioral model. *Addiction* 91(Suppl.): S37–S49.

Miller, C.E. and Johnson, J.L. (2001) Motivational interviewing. *Can Nurse* 97(7): 32–33.

Miller, J.D. and Lynam, D.R. (2003) Psychopathy and the five-factor model of personality: a replication and extension. *J Pers Assess* 81(2): 168–178.

Miller, N.S. and Gold, M.S. (1994) Dissociation of 'conscious desire' (craving) from and relapse in alcohol and cocaine dependence. *Ann Clin Psychiatry* 6(2): 99–106.

Miller, W.R. (1996) What is a relapse? Fifty ways to leave the wagon. *Addiction* 91(Suppl.): S15–27.

Miller, W.R., Westerberg, V.S., Harris, R.J. and Tonigan, J.S. (1996) What predicts relapse? Prospective testing of antecedent models. *Addiction* 91 (Suppl.): S155–172.

Modell, J.G., Glaser, F.B., Mountz, J.M., Schmaltz, S. and Cyr, L. (1992) Obsessive and compulsive characteristics of alcohol abuse and dependence: quantification by a newly developed questionnaire. *Alcohol Clin Exp Res* 16(2): 266–271.

Murphy, D.L. (1990) Neuropsychiatric disorders and the multiple human brain serotonin receptor subtypes and subsystems. *Neuropsychopharmacology* 3(5–6): 457–471.

Niaura, R. (2000) Cognitive social learning and related perspectives on drug craving. *Addiction* 95(Suppl. 2): S155–163.

Reilly, P.M., Sees, K.L., Shopshire, M.S., et al. (1995) Self-efficacy and illicit opioid use in a 180-day methadone detoxification treatment. *J Consult Clin Psychol* 63(1): 158–162.

Roos, S.S. (1977a) A psychophysiological re-evaluation of Eysenck's theory concerning cigarette smoking. Part I. The central nervous system. *S Afr Med J* 52(6): 237–240.

Roos, S.S. (1977b) A psychophysiological re-evaluation of Eysenck's theory concerning cigarette smoking. Part II. The autonomic nervous system. *S Afr Med J* 52(7): 281–283.

Ross, S.M., Miller, P.J., Emmerson, R.Y. and Todt, E.H. (1988) Self-efficacy, standards, and abstinence violation: a comparison between newly sober and long-term sober alcoholics. *J Subst Abuse* 1(2): 221–229.

Rubak, S., Sandbaek, A. , Lauritzen, T. and Christensen, B. (2005) Motivational interviewing: a systematic review and meta-analysis. *Br J Gen Pract* 55(513): 305–312.

Sannibale, C. and Hall, W. (1998) An evaluation of Cloninger's typology of alcohol abuse. *Addiction* 93(8): 1241–1249.

Shiffman, S., Hickcox, M., Paty, J.A., Gnys, M., Kassel, J.D. and Richards, T.J. (1996). Progression from a smoking lapse to relapse: prediction from abstinence violation effects, nicotine dependence, and lapse characteristics. *J Consult Clin Psychol* 64(5): 993–1002.

Skog, O.J. (2000) Addicts' choice. *Addiction* 95(9): 1309–1314.

Stephens, R.S., Curtin, L., Simpson, E.E. and Roffman, R.A. (1994) Testing the abstinence violation effect construct with marijuana cessation. *Addict Behav* 19(1): 23–32.

Tiffany, S.T. (1990). A cognitive model of drug urges and drug-use behavior: role of automatic and nonautomatic processes. *Psychol Rev* 97(2): 147–168.

Tiffany, S.T. (1999) Cognitive concepts of craving. *Alcohol Res Health* 23(3): 215–224.

Tiffany, S.T. and Conklin, C.A. (2000). A cognitive processing model of alcohol craving and compulsive alcohol use. *Addiction* 95(Suppl. 2): S145–153.

Tiffany, S.T. and Drobes, D.J. (1991) The development and initial validation of a questionnaire on smoking urges. *Br J Addict* 86(11): 1467–1476.

Volkow, N.D., Wang, G.J., Overall, J.E., et al. (1997) Regional brain metabolic response to lorazepam in alcoholics during early and late alcohol detoxification. *Alcohol Clin Exp Res* 21(7): 1278–1284.

Walton, M.A., Castro, F.G. and Barrington, E.H. (1994) The role of attributions in abstinence, lapse, and relapse following substance abuse treatment. *Addict Behav* 19(3): 319–331.

Chapter 5
ADDICTION, HABIT AND INSTRUMENTAL LEARNING

This chapter takes the development of the theory one step further by incorporating the idea of a mechanism linking stimuli to responses that does not involve conscious choice. Research with other animals has shown that they will learn to perform simple actions repeatedly if these are followed by rewards such as the availability of food. Animals will also make repeated responses for drugs that are addictive for humans. This raises the possibility that part of the motivation to take addictive drugs involves a learning mechanism that predates in evolutionary terms the development of conscious decision-making. Thus, addiction involves the development of a habitual behaviour pattern that is independent of any conscious evaluation that might be taking place about the costs and benefits of the behaviour. The impulses to engage in addictive behaviour that are generated by this mechanism can be so strong that they overwhelm the desire of the addicts to restrain themselves.

It was noted at the end of the previous chapter that some of the theories of addiction that work within a framework of choice theory have also found it necessary to postulate automatic, non-conscious processing to account for some of the phenomena of addiction. This chapter develops this idea using concepts of habit, instrumental (operant) learning and classical (Pavlovian) conditioning. These are ideas that are everyday currency in the world of behavioural pharmacology. There is in fact something of a gulf between this world and that of proponents of choice models of behaviour. Some kinds of conceptual link are made but only at a very superficial level.

Instrumental learning

In the world of the behavioural pharmacologist, addiction to drugs arises from the operation of reward and punishment. There are many different variants of this approach and this chapter will examine some of these in quite general terms. We begin with a simple account of instrumental learning in which no particular

---

Theory of Addiction, Second Edition. Robert West and Jamie Brown.
© 2013 John Wiley & Sons, Ltd. Published 2013 by John Wiley & Sons, Ltd.

pathology is involved; impaired conscious control arises simply because this reinforcement mechanism operates at a level that is outside conscious control and so sets up motivational forces that come into conflict with consciously held preferences (Box 5.1).

Box 5.1 Instrumental learning (operant conditioning) and addiction

Dependence on drugs and other activities arises from a normal instrumental learning mechanism that operates outside conscious awareness. Drugs such as heroin and nicotine reward behaviour that leads to them. Neuroadaptation in some cases also means that abstinence is aversive and so drug taking is strengthened by escape and avoidance learning mechanisms.

Addictive behaviours become entrenched and difficult to stop through a process that can occur without the individual being aware of what is happening, and it does not involve an active decision-making process. It does not even require the individual to feel positive pleasure from the behaviour. The process, reinforcement, involves a part of the brain that evolved many millions of years ago because it 'trained' animals to engage in behaviours that help with survival and reproduction. There are two facets to this process, positive reinforcement and negative reinforcement.

Positive reinforcement
This is the process by which a rat learns to press a lever to obtain food or a dog is trained to sit up and beg for treats. Drugs of dependence tap into the motivational system underlying this and in effect train the user to sit up and beg for the drug (O'Brien et al. 1992). The drug acts as a reward or positive reinforcer. With repetition, the cue–response–reward association becomes stronger and stronger.

Negative reinforcement
This is the second element of the instrumental learning process. Whereas positive reinforcement involves seeking out rewarding stimuli, negative reinforcement involves escaping from or avoiding unpleasant stimuli – punishment (e.g. Lewis 1990; Schulteis and Koob 1996). This kind of learning can be very powerful. Just as with positive reinforcement, many millions of years ago animals evolved a motivational system that enabled them to learn to escape from or avoid noxious or painful stimuli. It requires no conscious decision-making: it is automatic. A rat can readily learn to avoid treading on a part of the cage floor which delivers a small electric shock. A child quickly learns not to touch a hot surface. Equally, one can train a rat to press a lever to prevent an electric shock from occurring or to turn off an electric shock.

Addictive drugs tap into this system because after a relatively short period of use the body adapts physiologically to the presence of the drug. From that point onwards, periods of abstinence lead to the body compensating for the drug when it is not actually present: the physiological systems become unbalanced. Even a relatively brief interval without the drug can lead to a characteristic and unpleasant withdrawal syndrome (see the discussion in Chapter 3). Taking the drug turns these symptoms off. Like the rat pressing a lever to escape the shock, the drug user learns to take the drug to escape the withdrawal symptoms. Again, it is important to emphasise that according to the instrumental learning model, this is not a conscious process and no decision-making is involved.

Occasional reinforcement

The instrumental learning account of habit training extends further than noting that animals will respond to obtain rewards or avoid punishment. Many of the symptoms of withdrawal mirror feelings all of us feel from time to time anyway, such as depressed mood. The drug user is not very well placed to distinguish between those feelings caused by withdrawal and those that arise from other causes. This means that sometimes taking the drug will relieve them and sometimes it will not.

One might imagine that this would weaken the association between taking the drug and those symptoms but, paradoxically, it strengthens it. Odd as this may seem, a behaviour that is only reinforced on some occasions becomes more deeply entrenched, and more resistant to change, than one that is reinforced on every occasion. Lever-pressing is more firmly established in a rat if it produces food only once every 5 or 10 presses on average than if it produces food every time.

It has been noticed that when an animal has to press a lever, say, 20 times to get a morsel of food, as the end of the sequence of responses approaches, the response rate increases. That is, the responding speeds up and becomes more energised as the reward approaches. This has parallels in a tendency for people to place increasing priority on action sequences as they near their completion. It raises the possibility that the force of addiction arises in part from the same mechanism.

The evolutionary advantage of the strength of learning from occasional reinforcement is quite clear. The world is an unpredictable place, and animals need to be able to learn adaptive behaviours that on average work to their advantage, rather than just those that work every time. The animal cannot know each time whether the behaviour will have the required effect and so has to be driven to persist with it as long as it works often enough to make it worthwhile. With drug use, the end result is that taking the drug need only reduce depressed mood, say, every now and then for the pattern of behaviour to become established and maintained. The same is true for positive reinforcement: even if only a small proportion of cigarettes are rewarding, the reinforcing power of the cigarette may be very strong.

Avoidance

The instrumental learning model contains another potentially important feature. Animals, including humans, will learn to avoid as well as escape from discomfort. This means that the response can be maintained at a high rate even when no discomfort is experienced (because the avoidance is successful). Drug users do not need to experience withdrawal symptoms to keep them using the drug – the mere threat of these symptoms is enough to tap into the negative reinforcement mechanism. Again, according to the model, this does not involve a deliberate, conscious process, but one that typically operates outside of awareness. The behaviours driven by this process are performed urgently and compulsively.

Cues

The association between behaviour and reward becomes attached to particular cues (called 'discriminative stimuli'). This means that the behaviour tends to occur primarily in the presence of those cues or ones somewhat like them. Thus a habit that is very strong in one situation may not be strong in another. Cues can be anything from the environmental context (being at home or at a party vs. being at work) to a time of day (evening vs. morning). According to this view, craving is the subjective manifestation of the learned habit at a particular time and in a particular context. Thus, when a habit has been learned in the context of a particular set of cues, those cues may come to increase craving and unless that craving is opposed by a conflicting motivational pressure, it causes the behaviour to occur.

Secondary reinforcement

The mechanisms described above are supplemented by a very important phenomenon which strengthens the power of reinforcers to control behaviour. It was demonstrated early in the twentieth century that a neutral stimulus (such as a coloured light) could come to seem rewarding if it preceded a genuine reward (such as food). This process is known as 'classical conditioning' or 'Pavlovian conditioning' (after Pavlov, who demonstrated that salivation could be triggered in dogs as soon as a bell was sounded, even before food was presented, if the bell had previously been associated with food). It is one reason why certain smells, sounds and sights evoke certain reactions in some people but not in others.

These stimuli are called 'secondary reinforcers' because they derive their influence on behaviour only by association. However, there is evidence that they can increase the rate of responding for addictive drugs and may play an important role in dependence (Glautier and Drummond 1994).

Smoking provides a good example of this (Miyata and Yanagita 2001). For a smoker, one sensation that immediately precedes the nicotine hit is the 'scratch' of the smoke in the back of the throat. There is obviously nothing intrinsically rewarding about this, but smokers come to respond positively to it. Smokers do not know why this is the case, but it arises because this sensation has been so closely tied to the rewarding effect of nicotine. Besides this, the sight of the cigarette packet, the feel of the foil, the smell of the tobacco and so on all come to arouse an expectation of reward and form part of the addiction process (see also the section on 'evaluative conditioning' in Box 5.4). Similar effects are observed with drugs such as heroin and alcohol where stimuli associated with the pharmacological effects themselves become rewarding.

The power of the learning process

The strength of the learning process is influenced by a number of factors: the nature of the reinforcer itself, the schedule of reinforcement and also how long the schedule has been in operation. When one considers that a packet-a-day smoker repeats the processes of reinforcement 240 times a day (12 puffs for each of 20 cigarettes), 87 600 times a year and 2 190 000 times over a 25-year packet-a-day smoking career, it is not difficult to see how this might entrench the behaviour very deeply. It may be that it is this repetition that is driving the strong addiction in this case.

Overall

According to a simple instrumental learning model, drug use or another addictive activity not only becomes a deeply entrenched behavioural pattern ultimately under the control of the rewarding or punishing stimulus but also intricately tied into behavioural and social forces, and under impaired voluntary control.

Issues and evaluation

Instrumental learning offers a very powerful and attractive explanation for many aspects of drug addiction. Of particular importance is the fact that the process does not require conscious choice or awareness. This can help to explain how a conflict might occur between conscious desire to exercise restraint and motivational forces impelling the behaviour.

Much of this discussion is adapted from West and Shiffman (2004).

Mechanisms underpinning instrumental learning

We know something of the neural circuitry underpinning positive reinforcement (e.g. Nestler 2004). It is believed that whatever the drug or activity, ultimately the final common pathway through which reinforcement operates is the medial forebrain bundle and an important part of that is the mesolimbic pathway (Box 5.2).

Box 5.2   The Dopamine Theory of Drug Reward

There are many variations on the Dopamine Theory of Positive Reinforcement but they all propose that the action of dopamine on receptors in the nucleus accumbens plays a critical role.

The mesolimbic dopamine pathway

This is a theory about the mechanism by which addictive drugs exert their rewarding effects. There are numerous versions of the theory and our understanding of the circuitry is developing rapidly, but at its simplest it states that drugs with addictive potential increase the concentration of the neurotransmitter dopamine in a part of the brain known as the nucleus accumbens (NAcc). They further state that this increase in dopamine is necessary for addiction to occur. The nucleus accumbens lies towards the front of the brain and receives major input from a part of the midbrain called the ventral tegmental area (VTA) (Figure 5.1).

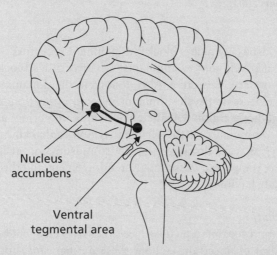

Nucleus
accumbens

Ventral
tegmental area

Figure 5.1   Location of the mesolimbic dopamine pathway (adapted from Tomkins and Sellers 2001).

Drugs of dependence influence dopamine concentrations in the NAcc in a number of different ways (Figure 5.2). Opioids, nicotine and alcohol block the inhibitory control of gamma-aminobutyric acid (GABA) on the VTA leading to an increase in firing of neurones leading to the NAcc. Cocaine and amphetamines act directly on the NAcc, blocking the natural process of re-uptake of dopamine that is released because of firing of the cells so that there is more dopamine in the extracellular space.

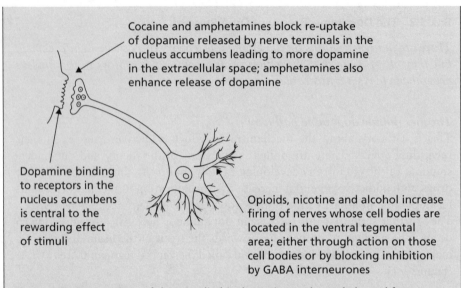

Cocaine and amphetamines block re-uptake of dopamine released by nerve terminals in the nucleus accumbens leading to more dopamine in the extracellular space; amphetamines also enhance release of dopamine

Dopamine binding to receptors in the nucleus accumbens is central to the rewarding effect of stimuli

Opioids, nicotine and alcohol increase firing of nerves whose cell bodies are located in the ventral tegmental area; either through action on those cell bodies or by blocking inhibition by GABA interneurones

Figure 5.2 Drug actions of the mesolimbic dopamine pathway (adapted from Tomkins and Sellers 2001).

Neuroleptic drugs which block dopamine receptors disrupt self-administration of psychomotor stimulants, whereas drugs blocking the noradrenergic receptors are ineffective. Also, lesions in the dopaminergic terminal field in the NAcc decrease psychostimulant self-administration. The actions of opiates in the cell body region (enhancing dopamine cell firing) and the actions of psychomotor stimulants in the terminal region (enhancing dopaminergic synaptic activity) increase dopaminergic neurotransmission. It is also thought that this pathway is involved in secondary reinforcement and the effects of cues on drug-seeking behaviour.

Issues and evaluation
The above description paints a picture that is relatively clear cut but in fact there is still a great deal of uncertainty about these mechanisms, not least because it is not clear how far humans share the same kinds of response as rats and mice, bearing in mind that rats and mice are different from each other in some important respects.

The neural basis for negative reinforcement is less well understood though some have argued that it may involve the same neural substrate as positive reinforcement (Koob and Nestler 1997). There is some evidence that drugs of dependence such as nicotine and cocaine cause changes in the functioning of the dopamine reward system that may underpin anhedonia during abstinence, but how this then goes on to motivate behaviour is not clear.

Weiss and Koob (2001) talk of 'functional neurotoxicity' as the basis for drug dependence (Box 5.3) but this does not assume pathological changes to the motivational process, only that drugs act abnormally on it and create additional motivation through neuroadaptation.

Box 5.3 Addiction arising from functional neurotoxicity of drugs

Chronic use of addictive drugs alters the functioning of brain reward circuitry and changes to other brain systems that lead to withdrawal symptoms and acquired drives.

Mechanisms underpinning withdrawal symptoms

This approach broadens simple dopamine theory referred to above, in proposing that the acute reinforcing effects of addictive drugs involve the part of the basal forebrain called the extended amygdala which includes the nucleus accumbens and amygdala and neurotransmitters such as dopamine, opioid peptides, serotonin, GABA and glutamate (Weiss and Koob 2001). Withdrawal from addictive drugs is proposed to cause unpleasant mood changes and dysregulation of brain reward systems involving some of the same neurochemical systems implicated in the acute reinforcing effects of drugs of abuse.

The 'functional toxicity' of the acute withdrawal state is accompanied by recruitment of the stress-related neurotransmitter system involving corticotrophin-releasing factor. During more prolonged abstinence, 'post-acute withdrawal', there may be continued dysregulation of the neural systems associated with drug reinforcement and stress. This may produce less pronounced but persistent functional neurotoxic effects and could be responsible for persistent vulnerability to relapse.

Addictive drugs differ from natural reinforcers

In a variant of this approach, it is proposed that drug rewards have larger and more prolonged rewarding or psychostimulant effects than naturally occurring stimuli (Wise and Bozarth 1987). A recent study found that presentation of an aversive conditioned stimulus suppressed drug seeking in rats with limited cocaine self-administration, but no longer did so after an extended cocaine-taking history. In contrast, after equivalent extended sucrose experience, sucrose seeking was still suppressed by an aversive conditioned stimulus. The effect of cocaine was not due to impaired fear conditioning, nor due to an increase in the incentive value of cocaine (Vanderschuren and Everitt 2004).

Acquired drives

It has been suggested that the development of a compulsive pattern of behaviour may stem from changes to drive mechanisms (Kostowski 2002). It may arise from a disturbed balance of the mechanism underlying drive-related behaviours, which controls appetitive reactions aimed at seeking out an addictive substance.

It is proposed that drug addiction may involve a change in the mechanism of satisfaction of drives and states of satiation. It argues further that, to understand how the motivational processes are changed with the development of addiction, it is necessary to consider the mechanism of drive satisfaction and satiation states that occur in relation to what it calls the 'consummatory reflex'.

When a given drive is satisfied, a state of 'fulfilment' results. This may stem from a so-called 'antidrive' mechanism. While a drive activity is characterised by general activation and tension, the drive satisfaction state is characterised by relaxation and relief. When a particular drive is satisfied, the other drives can then come into play. Hence the theory postulates that dysfunction of drive satisfaction leads to sustained activation related to the current drug-related drive, which blocks the operation of other drives. In effect, uncontrolled compulsive appetitive behaviour is released, and the operation of other drives is restrained, thus forcing the addict to focus on the drug-related drive.

Issues and evaluation

This emphasis on drive states offers a very attractive and plausible account of at least part of the addictive process. Addictive activities, and particularly drugs, create acquired drives which are unlike other drives in that they are resistant to satisfaction and therefore maintain a priority over other drive states. In this regard, it is noteworthy that individuals addicted to drugs as diverse as alcohol, heroin and nicotine show evidence of a reduction in drives relating to eating.

Classical conditioning

Several theorists have focused more closely on Pavlovian or classical conditioning and addiction (Box 5.4). These examine in more detail the role of cues in generation of impulses to engage in the behaviour. The overlap between the accounts makes it difficult to pick out any one of them as a theory.

Box 5.4   Classical conditioning and addiction

Stimulus–stimulus associations play an important role in the development of withdrawal symptoms and urges to take addictive drugs.

Classical conditioning and craving

Under a Classical Conditioning Model, drug craving arises because of a repeated pairing of environmental stimuli with drug effects (Drummond et al. 1990). For example, falling blood alcohol level (an unconditioned stimulus, UCS) induces a withdrawal syndrome including craving (unconditioned responses, UCRs). After a period of abstinence, it is possible for the stimuli associated with falling blood alcohol levels (conditioned stimuli) to elicit a conditioned withdrawal response which resembles alcohol withdrawal.

This account has been developed further. Drummond (2001) has proposed that 'cue-elicited craving' (as a response to the environmental stimuli) is different from 'withdrawal-related craving' (craving as part of the unconditioned withdrawal syndrome). He also proposes that cue-elicited craving may be more predictive of a relapse than withdrawal-related craving as relapse can only occur in situations of drug availability which is when cue-elicited craving occurs. Classical conditioning has also been proposed as the basis for urges and relapse long after the acute withdrawal phase has passed (Childress et al. 1988; Azorlosa 1994).

Classical conditioning and primary withdrawal symptoms

It has been argued that classical conditioning could underpin occurrence of the primary withdrawal syndrome itself and particularly craving (Melchior and Tabakoff 1984). The UCS is the drug effect, and in classical conditioning terms is thought of as a pharmacological challenge to internal regulation, which in some cases is compensated for by a response (UCR) which reflects the animal's defence against the drug-induced internal dysregulation.

A stimulus that precedes drug dose may then precipitate a defence reaction, termed a 'compensatory CR', when the drug effect is expected (see Siegel and Ramos 2002), which serves the purpose of maintaining this system of internal regulation as a response to the pharmacological challenge. The escalation of casual use to a level of use characteristic of addiction is explained by a strengthening of the learned associative link between the conditioned stimulus (CS) and UCS which increases the intensity of the CR. CRs that occur in the absence of a drug UCS will put the individual into a state of disequilibrium and induce withdrawal symptoms.

Classical conditioning and tachyphylaxis

The initial sensations associated with onset of drug actions could be interoceptive cues that predict the later full effect and so become conditioned stimuli themselves (McDonald and Siegel 2004). It is possible that these drug-onset cues (DOCs) are important in development of addiction as they come to elicit the response at least as reliably as any external drug-associated cues.

Cue exposure as a treatment

A psychological treatment approach has been proposed based on the idea that cues associated with drug taking precipitate cravings and relapse. The treatment, cue exposure, presents the cues without the opportunity to engage in the drug-taking behaviour. It is thought that this may lead to extinction of the classically conditioned association of the cues and drug effect thereby reducing the craving (Drummond et al. 1990; Childress et al. 1993; Sayette and Hufford 1994).

At present, evidence that this treatment approach is effective is weak. However, it needs to be recognised that even if the underlying theory were correct, there is no guarantee that there is a practicable procedure that would be powerful enough to have a major impact on cue-elicited craving and relapse. One needs to bear in mind that the conditioning process will have involved many years of pairing, and the opportunity to extinguish the association will involve a relatively few sessions at best.

Evaluative conditioning

It is well demonstrated that much of our behaviour is influenced by our likes and dislikes, and that for the most part these are acquired through experience (e.g. Martin and Levey 1978). Evaluative conditioning is one mechanism through which people learn to like things and can occur when a conditioned stimulus is paired with a UCS. The distinction from classical conditioning is that evaluative conditioning only concerns changes in evaluative responses to conditioned stimuli, whereas classical encompasses all other responses such as eye-blink, salivation etc. Researchers believe it is worth making the distinction because evaluative conditioning differs substantially from all other forms of classical conditioning. In particular, there is evidence that evaluative conditioning in comparison with classical requires less awareness of the CS–US contingencies, is more robust to extinction and is less dependent on the statistical contingency between CS and US (Hofmann et al. 2010). It is these latter two features which make an appreciation of evaluative conditioning important for explanations of the acquisition and maintenance of addiction.

Issues and evaluation

There can be no doubt that classical conditioning plays a critical role in the experience of drug addiction and the dependence syndromes surrounding it. It seems likely that it plays a significant role in the motivation to continue the addictive activity but it is not yet clear whether the same mechanism can be used to help addicts to recover.

More complex learning models

Variations on a straightforward instrumental learning model have been proposed that may better explain the details of drug-seeking behaviour, at least in animals. In their most general form, they propose that development of drug taking from hedonistic pleasure seeking to habitual and ultimately compulsive drug seeking involves interactions between Pavlovian and instrumental learning processes (see Everitt and Robbins 2005) and that susceptibility to addiction arises from vulnerabilities that predispose to this transition (see Everitt et al. 2008). A more specific version of this approach (Box 5.5) emphasises memory processes.

Box 5.5   Addiction as a learning/memory process

The development of more frequent drug-seeking behaviour involves multiple parallel learning and memory systems, not just a simple instrumental learning process (White 1996).

Three independent learning systems

According to this theory, all changes in behaviour, including the development of drug addiction, involve storage of new 'information' in the nervous system. This involves at least three more or less independent learning systems. Reinforcers operate on these systems in three ways: they activate the neural mechanisms involved in approach or avoidance responses; they produce states that are rewarding or aversive and they alter or strengthen the representation of the information stored in these systems. Each addictive drug maintains self-administration by tapping into these mechanisms in different ways. Each involves different brain structures.

Three actions of reinforcers

Figure 5.3 shows the theory in schematic form. The three actions of reinforcers are listed in the horizontal band at the top labelled 'Reinforcer actions' (in the

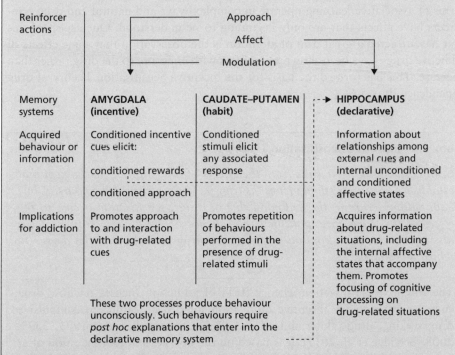

Figure 5.3   White's Multiple Memory System Theory of addiction (reproduced from White 1996).

column on the left). Each addictive drug is capable of mimicking some or all of these functions of natural reinforcers. These reinforcing actions influence behaviour by acting on learning and memory systems.

The systems are shown in the band labelled 'Memory systems'. Each system is named after a brain structure that is central to it. Each acquires a different type of behaviour or information: a one-word description of the kind of learning mediated in each system is below the name of its central structure. The kinds of behaviours these produce are described in the band labelled 'Acquired behaviour or information'. The role of each of these behaviours in the addictive process is described in the band labelled 'Implications for addiction'. White argues that most addictive drugs initiate more than one of these processes.

Issues and evaluation

This theory is an ambitious attempt to integrate classical and instrumental learning concepts and it also brings in conscious and non-conscious representational systems as would be necessary to understand human behaviour.

Research with other species is increasingly showing that instrumental and other forms of associative learning operate in complex ways and natural and drug reinforcers have effects that are only beginning to be understood. One aspect of this that has attracted a great deal of attention is the observation that some effects of addictive drugs have been shown to increase with exposure to the drug rather than decrease. This has formed the basis for the Incentive Sensitisation Theory of drug dependence (Box 5.6).

Box 5.6 Incentive Sensitisation Theory

Compulsive drug use results from the effects of drugs on the mechanism that establishes particular stimuli (cues) as triggers for appetitive behaviours. While habituation occurs to the hedonic value of drugs, sensitisation occurs to the effect of the drugs in establishing the salience of these cues. This creates a dissociation between how much pleasure a drug provides and the degree to which it is sought.

The Incentive Sensitisation Theory (IST) of addiction focuses on how drug cues trigger excessive incentive motivation for drugs, leading to compulsive drug seeking, drug taking and relapse (Robinson and Berridge 1993, 2003, 2008; Berridge et al. 2011). It is based on the observation that ingestion of at least some addictive drugs actually increases the effect of those drugs on certain behaviours in animals (such as locomotor activity and drug self-administration).

Sensitisation of incentive salience

This theory proposes that while drug pleasure becomes less important, during the transition to addiction the incentive motivation to use the drug increases. This arises from the long-lasting consequences of drug-induced alterations in NAcc-related circuitry that mediate 'incentive salience' (Figure 5.4).

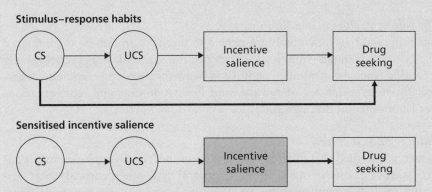

Figure 5.4 Changes occurring in development of addiction according the stimulus–response (S–R) Habit Learning Model (top) and the Incentive Sensitisation Theory (bottom). According to the Habit Learning Model, addiction is primarily due to the development of strong S–R habits (indicated by the thick arrow from a drug cue, the conditioned stimulus (CS), to a response). According to the incentive sensitisation view, the primary change is in the ability of drug cues to create a sensitised motivational response of incentive salience which then leads to compulsive drug pursuit (thick arrow) via an unconditioned stimulus (UCS) (Robinson and Berridge [2003]. Modified with permission from Annual Review of Psychology).

Incentive salience is a characteristic of the mental representation of a stimulus that can be characterised in terms of 'wanting' (a mental state that triggers behaviours that seek out a rewarding stimulus). The 'wanting' system can be activated implicitly and so can influence behaviour without a person necessarily having conscious emotion, desire or a goal.

For example, it has been reported that the brief subliminal presentation of faces expressing positive emotions (backward masked and so brief they do not cause any conscious feeling of emotion at the time they are presented) can activate implicit 'wanting' and so lead to an increase in subsequent consumption of a beverage (Winkielman et al. 2005). In addicts, doses of drugs that are too low to produce any conscious experience of pleasure can activate implicit 'wanting' as indicated by an increase in drug-seeking behaviour (e.g. Lamb et al. 1991).

Incentive salience and 'wanting'

Ingestion of addictive drugs causes the circuitry to become sensitised so that further ingestion produces a greater effect. Thus, drug-associated cues lead to pathological 'wanting' because excessive incentive salience is attributed chiefly to them. The sensitised neural systems responsible for excessive incentive salience can be dissociated from neural systems that mediate the hedonic effects of drugs, that is, how much they are 'liked'. In other words, 'wanting' is not 'liking'. Hedonic 'liking' is a different psychological process that has its own neural substrates (e.g. NAcc opioid neurotransmission).

The role of Pavlovian conditioning

It is proposed that individuals are guided to incentive stimuli by the influence of Pavlovian stimulus–stimulus (S–S) associations, and this is psychologically separable from the symbolic cognitive systems that mediate conscious desire, declarative expectancies of reward, and behaviour–outcome representations (see Robinson and Berridge 2003).

Brain regions involved

In fact, it is argued that different brain systems mediate cognitive versus incentive salience forms of motivation. Prefrontal and other cortical areas primarily mediate cognitive forms of desire and act–outcome representations, whereas NAcc-related circuitry (especially dopamine-related systems) play a more important role in Pavlovian-guided attributions of incentive salience (see Robinson and Berridge 2003).

Issues and evaluation

This theory allows for the possibility that excessive wanting may be compounded in at least some addicts by drug-induced dysfunction in prefrontal cortical systems normally involved in decision-making, judgement, emotional regulation and inhibitory control over behaviour. Cognitive deficits in the ability to inhibit or properly assess the future consequences of one's actions due to prefrontal dysfunction, combined with excessive incentive salience due to sensitisation of NAcc-related circuitry, lead to the compulsive pursuit of drugs out of proportion to the pleasure drugs provide and in the face of negative consequences.

The dissociation between wanting and liking is a powerful non-obvious statement that has a great deal of appeal. Moreover, the explanation in terms of sensitisation of one part of the motivational system versus habituation of another part is an important theoretical statement.

From the point of view of addiction in humans, the dissociation between 'wanting' and 'liking' in the Incentive Sensitisation Theory represents an important step towards the goal of understanding why the link between addictiveness of a particular drug and the degree to which it gives enjoyment is weak. The term 'wanting' under this view is not something that derives exclusively from anticipated pleasure. We will see later that there is merit in distinguishing feelings involving anticipated pleasure from those involving anticipated relief (which we may call 'need') and that this may allow us to retain the key important insights of incentive sensitisation theory while accounting for evidence which shows that indeed wanting and liking are strongly related. Under this view, incentive sensitisation is better thought of in terms of development of impulses to engage in a behaviour that may derive from direct stimulus–impulse associations or by development of increased wanting or increased needing. The idea of dissociation between pleasure seeking and impulse generation has been expanded on in more detail by Balfour (Box 5.7).

Box 5.7 Balfour's theory of differential drug effects within the nucleus accumbens

There are two major subdivisions of the nucleus accumbens which are presumed to be central to the rewarding effects of addictive drugs: the shell and the core. These mediate different parts of the instrumental learning process. Different effects of drugs on these different subdivisions may explain why different drugs show different patterns of addictive behaviour and in the case of nicotine why compulsive use can develop in the absence of powerful euphoriant effects.

A variant of the dopamine theory of reward has been proposed by Balfour (2004). It focuses on nicotine addiction but makes reference to addiction to other drugs. The theory attempts to relate the effects of nicotine on concentrations of dopamine in the extracellular space in the nucleus accumbens to its effects on the drug-seeking behaviour of animals. In doing so it offers an explanation for the fact that nicotine replacement therapies such as nicotine patches have only a small effect in improving the success rates of smokers wanting to quit.

Nucleus accumbens core and shell as separate systems
The theory notes that the nucleus accumbens consists of two major subdivisions: the shell and the core. It hypothesises that stimulation of the dopamine projections to the medial shell and the core of the nucleus accumbens play complementary roles in the development of addiction. Increased extra-synaptic dopamine in the medial shell confers hedonic properties on behaviours such as smoking which deliver nicotine, and this increases the probability that the response will be repeated as in the conventional model of operant learning.

However, nicotine also causes an increase in dopamine concentrations in the core and this confers 'incentive salience' to cues associated with delivery of the drug and leads to the development of stimulus–response ('Pavlovian') type behaviour in the presence of those cues. This effect of nicotine is enhanced by pre-treatment with nicotine. As Robinson and Berridge (2003) have proposed for psychostimulant drugs, there is sensitisation of this effect on dopamine levels in the accumbens core and this underpins the progression from normal to addictive use.

What is special about nicotine?
Balfour argues that nicotine is different from other addictive drugs in a number of respects that account for the different pattern of behaviour observed. One consequence of nicotine's actions is that the behaviour itself and the stimuli and cues associated with it are incentives in their own right. This would explain the observation that sensory characteristics of smoking such as the smell and feeling in the throat of the smoke being inhaled are sufficient to control behaviour in the short term (e.g. Pritchard et al. 1996).

Issues and evaluation
This is an elegant and insightful version of the Dopamine Theory of Drug Reward that, when applied to human behaviour, offers explanations of puzzling phenomena that go well beyond what simple common sense can provide. It suggests lines of preclinical and clinical research that could prove fruitful.

We have presented examples of the many formulations of the theories that attempt to explain addiction in terms of instrumental learning, supplemented by classical conditioning. These models have been developed to explain the behaviour of rats and other species in laboratory experiments but they have provided a wealth of ideas that may help in understanding human addiction.

Of particular value are the ideas that help explain why degree of addiction and degree of pleasure may be dissociated, why urges to engage in addictive activities are often affected by environmental triggers and the non-conscious processes that can lead to the behaviours in question.

The theories contain many speculative elements, especially when attempting to translate results from animal research to humans. From the point of view of developing a theory of human addiction, it is not clear how much further one needs to go than to acknowledge the existence of instrumental learning and classical conditioning mechanisms that operate outside of conscious awareness but influence behaviours and feeling states that can drive conscious behaviour. Moreover, these models cannot account for ways in which addictions respond to interventions that modify non-addictive behaviours (e.g. price rises) or spontaneous recovery.

Social learning

There is another aspect of learning that has been identified that needs to be included before any learning theory account can be considered complete. This is the propensity of humans to learn by both direct and vicarious experience. The details of this have been proposed in what has been called Social Learning Theory (Box 5.8).

Box 5.8   Social Learning Theory

Social Learning Theory extends the concept of instrumental learning as a basis for addiction to learning through observation and communication.

Social Learning Theory (SLT) (Bandura 1977) describes the effect of cognitive processes on goal-directed behaviour in humans. It considers the human capacity for learning within a social environment through observation or listening to others.

Starting with simple instrumental learning
It proposes that excessive human drug use is determined by consequences of the actual drug taking. The learning element of SLT is simple operant learning whereby an individual will repeat any behaviour that leads to a reward. Applied to drug use, a 'positive event' could be defined as the subjective euphoric effect that immediately follows a dose of a drug. However, some drug-taking experiences lead to adverse effects (e.g. nausea or disturbing flashbacks). The experience of a negative event following drug use is postulated to promote avoidance of drug taking in the future.

   According to SLT, the more frequent or intense the drug-taking experience, the more habitual it becomes. Similarly, the more frequent or intense the negative drug-associated experience becomes, the greater the likelihood it will be avoided. It is suggested that the individual becomes motivated to take the drug more often in order to achieve the drug effect. Such an effect may even increase to the point at which it interferes with other activities needed to sustain normal life.

Punishment and motivation to exercise restraint
Attempts to overcome the habit are conceptualised as reflecting the strength of the punishing outcomes. Most habits produce mixed effects, some pleasant, others aversive, and so the addicts may find themselves in an approach–avoidance conflict, where motivation fluctuates between wanting to use and wanting to stop.

Individual motives
Where social learning begins to take on a special character is in recognising that different classes of drug exert different types of effect and the effects that are most rewarding will differ between individuals and their desires, which also depend upon their past history, personality traits and current life circumstances.

   For example, an individual who takes a drug as a reaction to a social problem will face different issues when attempting to overcome addiction compared with an individual who uses drugs in a social environment where all his or her acquaintances also use the drug.

Application to relapse prevention

Marlatt and George (1984) have applied SLT to the understanding and treatment of addictions in the Relapse Prevention Model (see also the earlier discussion on the Abstinence Violation Effect). The Relapse Prevention Model focuses on the factors that will influence the success or failure of an attempt to maintain abstinence, but there is a great deal of overlap with processes that were involved in the initial development of an addiction.

Under the relapse prevention view, all addicts have a range of discriminative stimuli (cues) for drug use. After a period of abstinence, if the individual comes into contact with a cue he or she is at higher risk of relapse. If there are multiple cues present, then the risk escalates further. Marlatt and George (1984) propose a cognitive process whereby the cues arouse positive 'outcome expectancies' and thus trigger a motivation to use drugs.

The importance of personal resources

The ability of the addict to overcome such cognitive pressures depends upon factors such as their strength of will not to use the drug, their knowledge of alternative strategies for coping with the situation and their level of self-efficacy. The theory focuses attention on the personal 'resources' at the person's disposal to deal with motivational pressure to lapse or relapse. A high degree of self-efficacy combined with a strong motivation to remain abstinent may be insufficient if the addict does not have the knowledge or skill to resolve the situation in some way.

Effects of attempts at restraint on future attempts at abstinence

The outcome of the high-risk situation and the way in which the individual interprets it has important consequences for future progress. As noted in an earlier chapter, successfully resisting and continued abstinence contribute to increased self-efficacy and the individual will be more confident in his or her ability to handle future threats successfully. This increase in self-efficacy may increase the likelihood of attempting alternative strategies in high-risk situations and thus improve his long-term chances of abstinence. In contrast, a lapse, either because of unprepared coping strategies or a lack of self-efficacy, then leaves the individual at risk of relapse.

Issues and evaluation

This theory has a great deal in common with simple instrumental learning theories and indeed simple rational choice theories but focuses attention on the concept of 'personal resources' that are needed to resist motivational pressures to lapse or relapse. In that regard, it has the potential to add value to these approaches.

Associative learning

The theories in this chapter have focused on associative learning mechanisms that operate outside of conscious awareness. It is noteworthy, however, that in most cases they have found it necessary to introduce mentalist concepts such as choice, psychological resources and self-control to provide an explanation of the phenomenon of addiction in humans.

One must exercise extreme caution when extrapolating from rat and mouse motivation to human motivation, but the fact that addictive drugs can come to control the behaviour of these other species suggests a non-self-conscious mechanism by which they do so in humans. It gets more speculative when one gets into the territory of specific effects on specific neural pathways, and even in rats and mice there is still a great deal of uncertainty about what is going on. However, the experiments suggest some very plausible hypotheses about instrumental and classical conditioning effects in humans that look as though they are relevant.

References

Azorlosa, J.L. (1994) The effect of chronic naltrexone pretreatment on associative vs. non-associative morphine tolerance. *Drug Alcohol Depend* 36(1): 65–67.

Balfour, D.J. (2004) The neurobiology of tobacco dependence: a preclinical perspective on the role of the dopamine projections to the nucleus accumbens [corrected]. *Nicotine Tob Res* 6(6): 899–912.

Bandura, A. (1977) Self-efficacy: toward a unifying theory of behavioral change. *Psychol Rev* 84(2): 191–215.

Berridge, K.C., Robinson, T.E., Poland, J. and Graham, G. (2011) Drug addiction as incentive sensitization. In *Addiction and Responsibility* (eds. J. Poland and G. Graham). pp. 21–53. MIT Press, Cambridge, MA.

Childress, A.R., Ehrman, R., McLellan, A.T. and O'Brien, C. (1988) Conditioned craving and arousal in cocaine addiction: a preliminary report. *NIDA Res Monogr* 81: 74–80.

Childress, A.R., Hole, A.V., Ehrman, R.N., Robbins, S.J., McLellan, A.T. and O'Brien, C.P. (1993) Cue reactivity and cue reactivity interventions in drug dependence. *NIDA Res Monogr* 137: 73–95.

Drummond, D.C. (2001) Theories of drug craving, ancient and modern. *Addiction* 96(1): 33–46.

Drummond, D.C., Cooper, T. and Glautier, S.P. (1990) Conditioned learning in alcohol dependence: implications for cue exposure treatment. *Br J Addict* 85(6): 725–743.

Everitt, B.J., Belin, D., Economidou, D., Pelloux, Y., Dalley, J.W. and Robbins, T.W. (2008) Neural mechanisms underlying the vulnerability to develop compulsive drug-seeking habits and addiction. *Philos Trans R Soc B Biol Sci* 363(1507): 3125–3135.

Everitt, B.J. and Robbins, T.W. (2005) Neural systems of reinforcement for drug addiction: from actions to habits to compulsion. *Nat Neurosci* 8(11): 1481–1489.

Glautier, S. and Drummond, D.C. (1994) A conditioning approach to the analysis and treatment of drinking problems. *Br Med Bull* 50(1): 186–199.

Hofmann, W., De Houwer, J., Perugini, M., Baeyens, F. and Crombez, G. (2010) Evaluative conditioning in humans: a meta-analysis. *Psychol Bull* **136**(3): 390–421.

Koob, G.F. and Nestler, E.J. (1997) The neurobiology of drug addiction. *J Neuropsychiatry Clin Neurosci* **9**(3): 482–497.

Kostowski, W. (2002) Drug addiction as drive satisfaction ('antidrive') dysfunction. *Acta Neurobiol Exp (Wars)* **62**(2): 111–117.

Lamb, R.J., Preston, K.L., Schindler, C.W., et al. (1991) The reinforcing and subjective effects of morphine in post-addicts: a dose–response study. *J Pharmacol Exp Ther* **259**(3): 1165–1173.

Lewis, M.J. (1990) Alcohol: mechanisms of addiction and reinforcement. *Adv Alcohol Subst Abuse* **9**(1–2): 47–66.

Marlatt, G.A. and George, W.H. (1984) Relapse prevention: introduction and overview of the model. *Brit J Addict* **79**(3): 261–273.

Martin, I. and Levey, A.B. (1978) Evaluative conditioning. *Adv Behav Res Ther* **1**(2): 57–101.

McDonald, R.V. and Siegel, S. (2004) Intra-administration associations and withdrawal symptoms: morphine-elicited morphine withdrawal. *Exp Clin Psychopharmacol* **12**(1): 3–11.

Melchior, C.L. and Tabakoff, B. (1984) A conditioning model of alcohol tolerance. *Recent Dev Alcohol* **2**: 5–16.

Miyata, H. and Yanagita, T. (2001) Neurobiological mechanisms of nicotine craving. *Alcohol* **24**(2): 87–93.

Nestler, E.J. (2004) Molecular mechanisms of drug addiction. *Neuropharmacology* **47**(Suppl 1): 24–32.

O'Brien, C.P., Childress, A.R., McLellan, A.T. and Ehrman, R. (1992) A learning model of addiction. *Res Publ Assoc Res Nerv Ment Dis* **70**: 157–177.

Pritchard, W.S., Robinson, J.H., Guy, T.D., Davis, R.A. and Stiles, M.F. (1996) Assessing the sensory role of nicotine in cigarette smoking. *Psychopharmacology (Berl)* **127**(1): 55–62.

Robinson, T.E. and Berridge, K.C. (1993) The neural basis of drug craving: an incentive-sensitization theory of addiction. *Brain Res Brain Res Rev* **18**(3): 247–291.

Robinson, T.E. and Berridge, K.C. (2003) Addiction. *Ann Rev Psychol* **54**(1): 25–53.

Robinson, T.E. and Berridge, K.C. (2008) The incentive sensitization theory of addiction: some current issues. *Philos Trans R Soc B Biol Sci* **363**(1507) 3137–3146.

Sayette, M.A. and Hufford, M.R. (1994) Effects of cue exposure and deprivation on cognitive resources in smokers. *J Abnorm Psychol* **103**(4): 812–818.

Schulteis, G. and Koob, G.F. (1996) Reinforcement processes in opiate addiction: a homeostatic model. *Neurochem Res* **21**(11): 1437–1454.

Siegel, S. and Ramos, B.M. (2002) Applying laboratory research: drug anticipation and the treatment of drug addiction. *Exp Clin Psychopharmacol* **10**(3): 162–183.

Tomkins, D.M. and Sellers, E.M. (2001). Addiction and the brain: the role of neurotransmitters in the cause and treatment of drug dependence. *Can Med Assoc J* **164**(6): 817–21.

Vanderschuren, L.J. and Everitt, B.J. (2004) Drug seeking becomes compulsive after prolonged cocaine self-administration. *Science* **305**(5686): 1017–1019.

Weiss, F. and Koob, G.F. (2001) Drug addiction: functional neurotoxicity of the brain reward systems. *Neurotox Res* **3**(1): 145–156.

West, R. and Shiffman, S. (2004) *Smoking Cessation*. Health Press, Oxford.

White, N.M. (1996) Addictive drugs as reinforcers: multiple partial actions on memory systems. *Addiction* **91**(7): 921–949; discussion, 951–965.

Winkielman, P., Berridge, K.C. and Wilbarger, J.L. (2005) Unconscious affective reactions to masked happy versus angry faces influence consumption behavior and judgments of value. *Pers Soc Psychol Bull* **31**(1): 121–135.

Wise, R.A. and Bozarth, M.A. (1987) A psychomotor stimulant theory of addiction. *Psychol Rev* **94**(4): 469–492.

Chapter 6

ADDICTION IN POPULATIONS, AND COMPREHENSIVE THEORIES

This chapter is in two parts. The first part notes that the phenomenon of addiction can be studied at the level of populations and social groups. The rules governing the extent and nature of addiction in populations may not be the same as those that apply to individuals. The second part describes two theories of addiction that explicitly span the levels of analysis described in previous chapters and attempt a comprehensive description of the phenomenon. It concludes by establishing what is required for a new synthetic theory.

Addiction in populations

All the preceding chapters have focused on addiction as a phenomenon affecting individuals. Cultural, social and economic factors were examined in terms of their effects on individual motivation. However, social groups and populations are also a legitimate focus of study. The rules governing group and population behaviour may not be the same as those governing the behaviour of individuals. There should, however, be linkage between the two. Thus, it should be possible to use knowledge of individual behaviours to derive rules governing populations, and observation of the behaviour of populations should provide clues as to the principles governing individual behaviour.

The spread of addictive behaviours in populations

We have already seen an example of the theory that is focused on the behaviour of populations: the Rational Addiction Theory. It was decided to include that in Chapter 3 on rational choice because that is where the main assumptions of the theory lay. However, it did make predictions about the effects of population-level interventions such as price rises on consumption of addictive goods. The discussion of Behavioural Economic Theory could also be considered to apply at both the individual and population level. One theory that specifically applies at the population level is Diffusion Theory (Box 6.1).

Theory of Addiction, Second Edition. Robert West and Jamie Brown.
© 2013 John Wiley & Sons, Ltd. Published 2013 by John Wiley & Sons, Ltd.

Box 6.1 Diffusion Theory

Prevalence of particular addictive behaviours in populations can be understood in terms of diffusion of uptake or cessation of these behaviours from subgroups in the population to other groups. The diffusion takes place in an abstract medium of social networks as well as geographical proximity (Ferrence 2001).

Ferrence (2001) provides an excellent review of the concept of diffusion in populations as it applies to addiction. She notes that the earliest description resembling the idea of this model was the Law of Imitation, which stated that proximity would lead to imitation via a trickle-down process in which 'inferiors' would imitate their 'superiors', described in terms of a societal epidemic.

General diffusion theories

Rogers et al. (1983) proposed a description of the diffusion process of behaviours or products that involve a number of considerations. The spread of a behaviour will be affected by (1) perceived advantage over alternatives, (2) compatibility with values, (3) perceived risks of experimentation, (4) observability of the behaviour, (5) impact on social relationships, (6) extent to which the behaviour can be stopped again, (7) communicability, (8) time and commitment required and (9) mobility of the population.

Although this seems like a rather haphazard selection of factors and one might consider others that were not included in the list, it provides some means of predicting whether new behaviours will diffuse into a population.

In another account, diffusion has been described as involving five stages: innovation development, dissemination, adoption, implementation and maintenance (Oldenburg et al. 1999). There are proposed to be two routes of innovation under Diffusion Theory: natural (spontaneous) diffusion and planned diffusion.

Epidemics and contagion

Studies of natural diffusion typically use an 'epidemic model', originally used to detail infectious spread through populations. Terminology such as 'susceptibility' to a drug and 'contagiousness' are used. The 'contagiousness' analogy is particularly useful for describing the mechanisms by which drug use is spread through populations: friendship networks, neighbourhoods and communities or institutional settings such as workplaces, schools or prisons. This model has been used in several studies to document the social diffusion process in groups of opiate users (e.g. Bejerot 1972; Richman and Dunham 1976). Such findings provide some evidence for the compatibility and observability features that promote diffusion.

Des Jarlais (1997) examined the diffusion of unprotected sex and the sharing of drug-use equipment in developing and developed countries. He found rapid diffusion rates of 10–50% of HIV from unprotected sex. With regard to smoking initiation, Einstein and Epstein (1980) described a contagion phenomenon in which 40% of a sample of adult smokers claimed that they began smoking as a result of another individual introducing them to the idea, most commonly in a group setting. The idea of 'inoculation' was introduced by Pfau et al. (1992), who used the term in order to suggest ways in which adolescents could become more resistant to smoking.

Patterns of diffusion

Diffusion may begin at a single point and spread outwards, as would an epidemic (see Ferrence 2001). An urban hierarchy model pinpoints the starting point of diffusion frequently to be in large cities, with spread reaching to smaller communities and eventually to remote areas. This would be expected from particular characteristics of cities, such as well-served transport links. Historically, imports would arrive at cities first and reports suggest that sailors would be among the first to experiment with drug use.

The spread of tobacco is used as an example of cultural diffusion. In North and South America, pipe tobacco smoking was commonly used throughout the day by indigenous males. The first tobacco use by Europeans was in the late fifteenth to early sixteenth century, indicating that there was a lapse of just 12 years between reported smoking by an English explorer and accounts of widespread smoking in England. It may also be noted that the provision of free cigarettes to army soldiers during World Wars I and II resulted in positive normative and economic reinforcement for cigarette smoking (Ferrence 2001).

Issues and evaluation

One of the problems with research in Diffusion Theory is that the likelihood of discovering non-obvious 'emergent' features at a population level that go beyond a simple rational choice level of explanation of individual behaviour is not clear. Population trends are observed and interpreted in Diffusion Theory terms but they could be explained in other terms. Moreover, interventions that claim to be informed by Diffusion Theory appear no different from ones that are developed based on simple common-sense principles. Nevertheless, the promise of Diffusion Theory as a model for the spread of behaviours through populations is great and it just remains for researchers to develop the concepts to a point at which important insights can be derived that can drive policy.

Other approaches have also been taken to explain why illicit drug use of particular kinds develops at a particular location at a particular time in particular sub-populations (Agar and Reisinger 2002). One of these is Trend Theory. It has commonalities with Diffusion Theory and argues that important factors are the distribution/supply system and susceptibility of the population as a result of the prevailing political climate. Like Diffusion Theory, it focuses on some features and does not appear to attempt a comprehensive model. Also like Diffusion Theory it is hoped that with further conceptual work it can drive observations and hypotheses that go beyond application of the simple common-sense model.

Comprehensive theories of addiction

By adding in instrumental learning and automatic (non-conscious) processes to a theory in which desires and urges were tempered by self-control, it was possible greatly to expand the scope of the theory of addiction. The focus on choice, urge and habit still, however, fails to capture the experience of addiction which ranges from one of abject misery, conflict, shame, anger and feelings of worthlessness to complacency, defiance and a strong sense of identity in which the activity in question forms an integral part.

What we have is not much more than the shell of a theory. The theory needs to describe the feelings, beliefs, urges and habits that form our motivational system and how these influence each other and are influenced by our inheritance and experiences before we ever have our first taste of the addictive behaviour. It needs to be scientific in the sense that the concepts are sufficiently well specified that they can be used to make predictions but they need to be understandable in terms that capture the human experience of addiction. The theory should be specified at the level of the individual but provide a basis for models and theories that work at the level of groups, cultures and societies.

Two comprehensive theories

Modern accounts typically involve at least some integration between many of the important constructs described thus far. The variation is in the particular components that are included and the explanation of how they interact in both typical and addictive behaviour. A common theme is the division of reflective processing and automatic processing (e.g. Strack and Deutsch 2004). Many theories centred on this distinction are not particularly comprehensive. However, these types of models and their application to health behaviour need to be understood within the appropriate historical context. Namely, the preoccupation of health psychology with designing interventions to target primarily reflective processes based on the assumption that changing conscious cognitions would engender substantial changes in behaviour (Marteau et al. 2012; Sheeran et al. 2012). The 'radical' suggestion that behaviour can be changed by targeting automatic processes should not lead to the conclusion that everyone can be empowered to make healthy choices by subtly altering choice architecture (as in Thaler and Sunstein 2008). Instead, the idea should encourage a fuller understanding of behaviour and an appreciation of the range of policies and techniques that might help change the behaviour (Marteau et al. 2011; Michie et al. 2011).

A metaphor that has been commonly used to describe the interaction between these systems is of a rider on an animal (often horses or elephants) (Haidt 2007; Friese et al. 2011). The rider does not have direct control over where the animal takes him or her but has to communicate as best he or she can, and exert whatever influence he or she can, with whatever means are at his or her disposal to achieve his or her goals. The risk run by models that rely too heavily on this idea is invoking the age-old notion of the 'homunculus' – the little person inside our heads controlling things (Ryle 1949). It is important, but often difficult, to avoid this because it simply transfers the burden of explanation of behaviour to another agent which then itself has to be understood. The key is in understanding that the rider refers to a part of the brain that represents the world in terms of propositions and is capable of representing itself in that way while the animal experiences feelings and drive states and is subject to conditioning of these to stimuli.

There are also neurobiological theories that attempt integration by incorporating high-level psychological notions such as personal growth (Esch and Stefano 2004). However, there are very few truly synthetic theories. An excellent example of a theory that provides the closest thing yet to being comprehensive is Orford's (2001) Excessive Appetites Theory. This captures the notions of choice and instrumental learning in a common conceptual framework and adds further insights concerning attachment and processes of self-change (Box 6.2).

Box 6.2   Excessive Appetites Theory

Addiction involves appetitive behaviours that have the potential to become so excessive as to spoil lives, appearing at the skewed end of the norm of consumption for the population. It arises from ecological, socio-economic or cultural factors interacting with features of the behaviour and the individual.

The Excessive Appetites Theory (Orford 2001) provides a comprehensive account of how people take up, establish and give up an addiction. The model notes that a range of objects and activities exist to which humans are at risk of developing a strong attachment, finding their ability to moderate their behaviour considerably reduced.

Addiction and appetitive consumption
Orford suggests that addiction can be explained in terms of an appetite for certain experiences and that the initial pleasure experienced towards the addictive stimulus can transform into a lack of control if one experiences a certain degree of need for it and conflict about the extent to which one is seeking it. Consequently, 'addiction' is referred to as 'appetitive consumption' in the theory of excessive appetites.

Addiction to drug and non-drug rewards
The excessive appetites theory proposes that non-drug forms of addiction are possible, such as gambling, sex or exercise as the initial delight, feelings of

necessity and erosion of social control elements are applicable to these kinds of stimuli. The way in which the mechanism of addiction operates is different from behaviour to behaviour and drug to drug.

With regard to cocaine, for example, the drug-induced euphoria becomes so pleasant that it becomes more important to individuals than their own health or diet. Alcohol, it is argued, provides a means of coping with stress by increasing feelings of self-efficacy, deadening sensation, preventing coherent thought or releasing inhibition. Psychomotor stimulants such as amphetamine affect arousal and so it has been proposed that they improve performance on tasks requiring sustained attention in addition to producing euphoriant effects.

The social response to 'addiction'

The range of appetitive activities all have in common the potential to become so excessive that they spoil the quality of people's lives and give rise to concern among family and friends. The excessive activities are costly to communities as well as to individuals and families, attract terms such as 'addiction', 'dependence' and 'disease' and provoke the setting up of mutual help and expert treatment systems. The development of a strong appetite gives rise to a new, acquired motivation for activity in the form of secondary emotional cycles which add an important drive reduction element with the examples of chasing losses (gambling), neuroadaptation (some drugs) and maintaining secrecy (most activities).

Core addictions

Orford names certain excesses that constitute the 'core addictions'. These are drinking, gambling, drug taking, eating, exercise and sex. They are all activities which ordinarily are unexceptional and unproblematic, but which may cause many people great conflict because of the strong attachment that they are feeling towards them.

Multiple interacting determinants of addiction

The degree of a person's involvement in each of these appetitive activities has multiple interacting determinants. These include features of character or personality, but some of the strongest determinants are ecological, socio-economic or cultural, including the availability of opportunities for activity and the normative influence of friends. The wide range of determinants includes those that operate to restrain activity or which offer disincentives, as well as those that operate to promote activity, or offer incentives. Each of these activities can serve numerous personal functions for different individuals, and even within the same person. They include forms of mood modification as well as enabling many different forms of self-expression and enhancing many different kinds of self-identity.

Two methods of escalation

Under the Excessive Appetites Theory, Orford (2001) postulates that there are two ways in which casual consumption escalates into uncontrollable levels of consumption.

First, there is the 'law of proportionate effect', which suggests that appetitive consumption will escalate when the individual perceives the incentives of the appetitive activity to be relatively great and the restraints to be relatively weak. This is intended to capture the elements of choice and self-control.

Second, it is argued that Learning Theory explains the development of strong attachment. The development of increasing attachment is manifest in the form of increasingly generalised activity and the erosion of the discriminations that would ordinarily maintain moderate activity. Strong appetite development gives rise to a new acquired motivation for activity in the form of a secondary emotional cycle, which adds an important drive reduction component to the excessive appetites model. A strong attachment to an appetitive behaviour runs an increased risk of incurring costs, which may be physical or social, immediate or long term, affecting the self or others.

Addiction and conflict

The consequences of conflict are an important part of addiction. They may be thought of as a set of tertiary processes and their effect can be to further amplify the addiction process. They include demoralisation, poor information processing, and alterations of social role and social group.

The importance of norms

In order to understand the development of appetitive consumption more fully, Orford argues that it is important to examine how appetitive behaviours are distributed within populations. Surveys of the consumption of alcohol within mainly Western populations have been found to produce a frequency distribution curve skewed towards the highest levels of consumption. Therefore, the amount of alcohol consumption for the majority of the population is 'moderate' and mostly unproblematic. The minority consume in excess of this 'norm': the greater the deviation, the smaller the proportion who show that pattern of behaviour. Norms are not just statistical descriptions of population distributions. They are potentially one of the most important sources of influence on behaviour.

The social norm is extremely important in this account. Orford refers back to the work of Allport who argued that all behaviour that is subject to social control follows a skewed frequency curve (e.g. time of arrival for work or speed for crossing a junction). Furthermore, the majority of people conform to norms, rules or laws governing behaviour and only a minority would deviate excessively. Allport claims that social control over behaviour is usually highly effective and most people will more or less conform to a norm or rule of law governing behaviour.

The implication is that individuals with essentially the same opportunity to engage in behaviours that have the potential to be addictive and with the same underlying propensities will become addicted or not depending critically on the norms operating in the social group to which he or she belongs.

Deterrence and restraint

Orford also refers to Hyman's idea of deterrence. Orford uses the analogy of barriers to the formation of a river – competition from other tributaries, insufficient rain or extreme heat. The evolution of appetitive behaviour to higher levels of consumption can be impeded by a range of deterrents including (with the example of alcohol) gastric distress, headaches, dizziness or a psychological make-up that regards intoxication as unpleasant. The idea is that our appetitive consumption would naturally escalate given the opportunity. It is environmental and physiological constraints and deterrents that prevent our consumption from escalating further than it does. This emphasis upon appetitive activity as a dynamic, changing process through time is an important departure from simple dispositional theories of excessive behaviour.

Multiple levels of motivation

The theory incorporates Classical Learning Theory mechanisms to explain the development of the strongest of attachments to appetitive behaviour. The combination of operant learning based on mood modification together with other positive rewards associated with the activity, negative reinforcement, 'coping' functions of the activity, and the establishment of associations between multiple cues and the appetitive activity, plus the abundant opportunities that exist for the development of behaviour-enhancing expectations, attributions, images and fantasies, provide a powerful set of processes for the development of a strong attachment. Circumstances are favourable for the development of a strong appetite when the availability of the activity is high, inclination strong and restraints weak.

Orford argues that other theories are overly specific and fail to account for the diversity of emotional rewards associated with even one form of appetitive consumption, let alone the whole range. Neuropharmacological explanations based on a single reward system in the brain are viewed as simplistic. The social context in which these behaviours take place has also been largely overlooked. A single substance or activity may serve very different functions depending on an individual's social circumstances and needs. Theories that attempt to specify the exact nature of emotional changes are unlikely to be able to provide anything like a comprehensive account of appetitive emotional reward.

Cognitive schemata are believed to operate within learning and memory processes. Following the Multiple Regulation Model (Leventhal and Cleary 1980), it is proposed that excessive appetites result from a strong emotional memory and that it is the memory schema that is responsible for provoking desire or craving.

Secondary processes and amplification

The Excessive Appetites Model talks of secondary processes that play an important role in amplifying an individual's level of consumption. The first of these is termed 'acquired emotion regulation cycles', which operate when the individual's appetite for the stimuli strengthens, providing further incentive for consumption by serving new emotional regulating functions.

Orford conducted semi-structured interviews with problem gamblers and concluded that, in addition to the arousal and excitement generated by the gambling (primary processes), there is a powerful set of attachment-promoting secondary processes that add a strong drive reduction component. The main component of this secondary motivational cycle is a strong negative feeling state associated with an increased desire to recoup losses by further gambling. Orford suggests that this chasing could be an equivalent to neuroadaptation. The Abstinence Violation Effect (see Chapter 4) is another secondary process and is characterised by feelings of guilt and self-blame, self-attributions for lapses that are internal, global and uncontrollable and feelings of helplessness and hopelessness.

Recovery from addiction

Orford argues that cases of spontaneous remission from addictive patterns of behaviour represent a major challenge to any theory of addiction. To account for this, he places the conflict that addicts experience at the heart of the theory (Figure 6.1) and at the heart of the process for motivating attempts to exercise restraint.

There are proposed to be at least two stages in the process of change. The first is cognitive – in the form of the decision or resolution to change. The second is a behavioural or action-oriented response stage. Social and spiritual moral processes can also be important. Social reactions to excess, including the responses of concerned and affected others, are influential in the process of giving up an excessive appetite. Orford claims that motivation for 'self-liberation' plays a central role in the process. Psychological and pharmacological treatments also clearly play a part in recovery. There exist a very wide range of treatment rationales and procedures but they produce a rather similar and modest result in the short term.

Issues and evaluation

This model is extraordinary in its scope and captures features of addiction that others do not. It is truly comprehensive in combining ideas from Learning Theory with those from Choice Theory as well as social psychology and sociology. It even encompasses the population-level analysis. Its recognition of the power of norms in terms of motivating and restraining addictive behaviours is perceptive and has powerful implications for interventions. A particularly striking conclusion from the model is worth quoting verbatim:

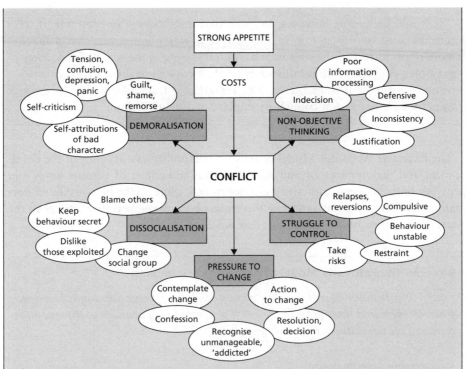

Figure 6.1 Consequences of conflict from the Excessive Appetites Model (adapted from Orford 2001).

'at the very core of addiction, according to this view, is not so much attachment per se but rather conflict about attachment. The restraints, controls and disincentives that create conflict out of attachment are personally, socially and culturally relative. No definition of addiction or dependence, however arbitrary, will serve all people, in all places, at all times. From this perspective, systems such as DSM and ICD which claim universality may in fact be standing in the way of scientific progress by leading us to believe that such absolutes might exist' (Orford 2001, p. 29).

This implies a radical rethink of the concept, definition and assessment of addiction that is worth serious consideration. Perhaps, the model has been too radical because, compared with more constrained accounts such as the Incentive Sensitisation Theory, it has not yet generated a large body of research.

It may also be that its strength in terms of its ability to account for the huge diversity that exists in the phenomenon of addiction has made it difficult for researchers working within the conventional tradition of behavioural science to connect with it. It does not readily generate experiments in which particular correlations between variables would be predicted.

It would be wrong, however, to claim that the theory is not testable. If we refer back to the discussion in Chapter 2, it was pointed out that a much more rigorous test of theories in behavioural science is the search for counter-examples. A single genuine counter-example is enough to show that the theory or an element of it is incorrect. The remarkable thing about the Excessive Appetites Theory is that counter-examples are difficult to find.

The Excessive Appetites Model provides a comprehensive account of the development and maintenance of and recovery from addictions of various kinds and provides links between addictive behaviours and what might be considered normal motivation. A similar synthetic theory has been developed that applies to the development of gambling addiction (Box 6.3).

Box 6.3   The Pathways Model of pathological gambling

Pathological gambling arises out of a complex interaction of ecological, social, psychological and biological factors that generate three primary pathways into different manifestations of the problem.

Recognising heterogeneity

The Pathways Model of pathological gambling (Blaszczynski and Nower 2002) provides a conceptual model of gambling that addresses the multiple biological, psychological and ecological variables contributing to the development of pathological gambling. It argues that there is no single conceptual theoretical model of gambling that adequately accounts for the multiple biological, psychological and ecological variables contributing to the development of pathological gambling. It claims further that advances in this area are hampered by imprecise definitions of pathological gambling, failure to distinguish between gambling problems and problem gamblers and a tendency to assume that pathological gamblers form one, homogeneous population with similar psychological principles applying equally to all members of the class.

Multiple levels of the motivation system

The proposed model attempts to integrate the 'complex array of biological, personality, developmental, cognitive, learning theory and ecological determinants of problem and pathological gambling' (Blaszczynski and Nower 2002, p. 487). It is proposed that three distinct subgroups of gamblers manifesting impaired control over their behaviour can be identified. These groups are (1) behaviourally conditioned problem gamblers, (2) emotionally vulnerable problem gamblers, and (3) antisocial, impulsivist problem gamblers.

Figure 6.2 shows the three pathways. These pathways reflect the dominance of different processes that arise out of interactions between individual and environmental factors.

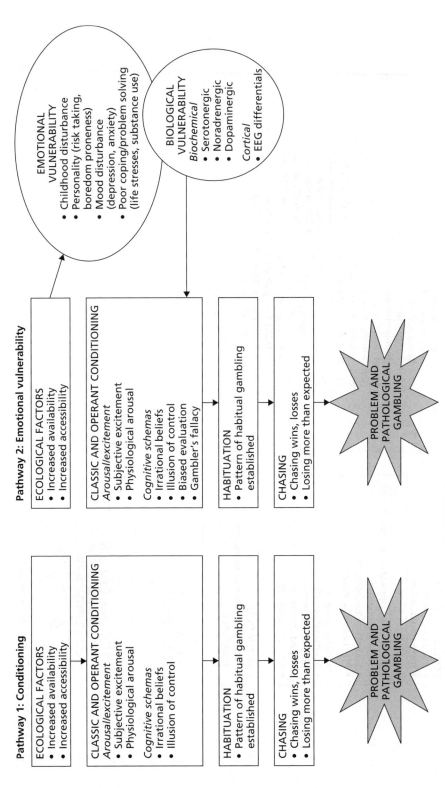

Figure 6.2 The three pathways to pathological gambling (adapted from Blaszczynski and Nower 2002).

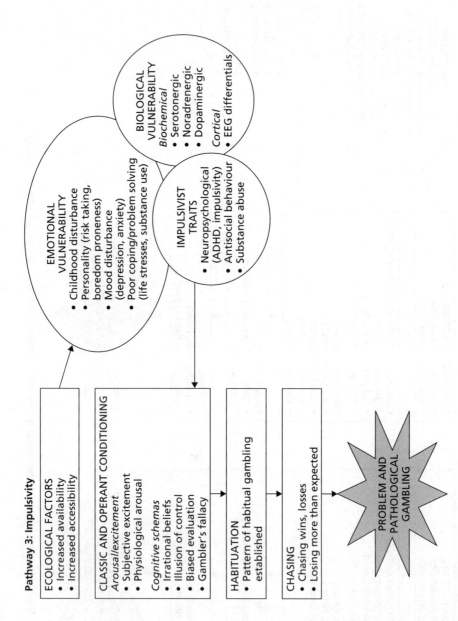

Figure 6.2 (*Continued*)

Issues and evaluation
Although this model addresses only the issue of gambling, it has potential relevance to other addictions and particularly in its attempt to integrate decision-making, environmental factors, personality and instrumental learning mechanisms.

The two theories mentioned in this chapter and some of those in previous chapters seem to be able to capture the experience of addiction and they do so by recognising the diversity of patterns, feelings and routes to addiction. This diversity presents a major challenge to theory development. A synthetic theory needs to be more than a listing of influences and factors: it must synthesise.

What is addiction and how can we explain it?

More than choice

It is apparent that addiction can be explained in terms of actions people make in response to desires, urges and impulses to engage in particular behaviours in the face of attempts to exercise restraint. It is also apparent that it would be wrong always to characterise these merely as choices.

Choices only occur when individuals consciously consider alternatives. Much of the time, addicted individuals do not consider alternatives; they may consciously and deliberately engage in the behaviour but it forms part of the flow of activity in which they are engaged and they do not step back from it and weigh up the options. Other times they do. It varies. Moreover, the nature and extent of conscious direction of the behaviour clearly varies. Sometimes, as in the case of smoking on occasions, the activity attracts very little of the actor's attention.

A balance of forces

Activities are addictive for individuals to the extent that the desires, urges or impulses are abnormally powerful and/or the restraints are abnormally weak. A wide range of factors can influence the development and maintenance of addiction including factors relating to the individual (physiological susceptibility, personality traits, beliefs and values), factors relating to the activity (degree to which it provides pleasure, satisfaction or relief from distress, taps into incentive learning mechanisms and causes neuroadaptation that amplifies the rewarding effects of the activity and the punishing effects of abstinence), and factors relating to the environment (opportunities, reminders, cues, situations that create needs that the activity can satisfy, and social norms).

There is something special about the addict or his or her situation

For most people in most circumstances, most activities are not addictive. In fact arguably no activities are addictive to most people in present-day Western societies in which there are strong constraints on our lives that militate against excesses. Heroin provides a very strong euphoriant effect and yet is used by a tiny proportion of society. In fact, only a minority of people who try it recreationally become addicted. Cigarettes provide only a modest amount of pleasure but are used by many more people in society and about the same proportion of those who try it become addicted as with heroin. It is all a matter of the balance between forces promoting the behaviour and the forces opposing it.

From the general to the specific

The further development of our understanding of addiction must, of course, deal with the specifics of why particular drugs or activities are addictive. We need to be specific about the causes of withdrawal symptoms, how incentive learning is affected by different drugs and how genetic and developmental factors affect susceptibility to becoming addicted. We need to know more about the diffusion of addictive behaviours throughout social groups and populations. However, we also need to develop a better conceptual framework in which all these advances can be placed.

What is needed is a truly synthetic theory that accounts for the big observations and can incorporate those more specific theories that offer unique insights, but is more than just a placeholder for this information. It must add value with a unifying construct that itself generates new ideas.

References

Agar, M. and Reisinger, H.S. (2002) A heroin epidemic at the intersection of histories: the 1960s epidemic among African Americans in Baltimore. *Med Anthropol* **21**(2): 115–156.

Bejerot, N. (1972) Registering addicts and dangerous drugs in Scandinavia. *Int Pharmacopsychiatry* **7**(1–4): 126–130.

Blaszczynski, A. and Nower, L. (2002) A pathways model of problem and pathological gambling. *Addiction* **97**(5): 487–499.

Des Jarlais, D.C. (1997) HIV/STDs and drug use. *AIDS STD Health Promot Exch* (2): 1–3.

Einstein, S. and Epstein, A. (1980) Cigarette smoking contagion. *Int J Addict* **15**(1): 107–114.

Esch, T. and Stefano, G.B. (2004) The neurobiology of pleasure, reward processes, addiction and their health implications. *Neuro Endocrinol Lett* **25**(4): 235–251.

Ferrence, R. (2001). Diffusion theory and drug use. *Addiction* **96**(1): 165–173.

Friese, M., Hofmann, W. and Wiers, R.W. (2011) On taming horses and strengthening riders: recent developments in research on interventions to improve self-control in health behaviors. *Self Identity* **10**(3): 336–351.

Haidt, J. (2007) *The Happiness Hypothesis: Putting Ancient Wisdom and Philosophy to the Test of Modern Science*, Arrow, New York.

Leventhal, H. and Cleary, P.D. (1980). The smoking problem: a review of the research and theory in behavioral risk modification. *Psychol Bull* **88**(2): 370–405.

Marteau, T.M., Hollands, G.J. and Fletcher, P.C. (2012) Changing human behavior to prevent disease: the importance of targeting automatic processes. *Science* **337**(6101): 1492–1495.

Marteau, T.M., Ogilvie, D., Roland, M., Suhrcke, M. and Kelly, M.P. (2011) Judging nudging: can nudging improve population health? *BMJ* 342(7791): 263–265.

Michie, S., Hyder, N., Walia, A. and West, R. (2011) Development of a taxonomy of behaviour change techniques used in individual behavioural support for smoking cessation. *Addict Behav* 36(4): 315–319.

Oldenburg, B.F., Sallis, J.F., Ffrench, M.L. and Owen, N. (1999) Health promotion research and the diffusion and institutionalization of interventions. *Health Educ Res* 14(1): 121–130.

Orford, J. (2001) Addiction as excessive appetite. *Addiction* 96(1): 15–31.

Pfau, M., Van Bockern, S. and Kang, J.G. (1992) Use of inoculation to promote resistance to smoking initiation among adolescents. *Commun Monogr* 59: 213–230.

Richman, A. and Dunham, H.W. (1976) A sociological theory of the diffusion and social setting of opiate addiction. *Drug Alcohol Depend* 1(6): 383–389.

Rogers, A., Willekens, F. and Ledent, J. (1983) Migration and settlement: a multiregional comparative study. *Environ Plan A* 15(12): 1585–1612.

Ryle, G. (1949) *The concept of mind*. Hutchinson, London.

Sheeran, P., Gollwitzer, P.M. and Bargh, J.A. (2012) Nonconscious processes and health. *Health Psychol* epub.

Strack, F. and Deutsch, R. (2004) Reflective and impulsive determinants of social behavior. *Pers Soc Psychol Rev* 8(3): 220–247.

Thaler, R.H. and Sunstein, C.R. (2008) *Nudge: Improving Decisions about Health, Wealth, and Happiness*, Yale University Press, New Haven, CT.

Chapter 7

DEVELOPMENT OF A COMPREHENSIVE THEORY

This chapter takes the reader through the development of a comprehensive theory of addiction starting with the simplest common-sense rational choice model, extending it to a model that involves concepts of self-control and impulse, then habit. This sets the scene for the final two chapters, which describe a theory of motivation that forms the basis for a synthetic theory of addiction.

The preceding chapters worked systematically through the various approaches that have been adopted to understanding addiction at a broad level. This chapter presents a functional classification of those approaches before recapitulating the journey from rational choice to integrative theories with additional commentary and with a greater focus on the issue of how far each element that is added to a comprehensive theory of addiction is necessary.

A reminder of what we are talking about

The following vignettes are adaptations of real stories provided by addicts. The internet contains many more like these that help to give a flavour of the complexity and variety of the experience of addiction. It may be useful to keep these in mind when considering the intellectual and academic considerations in the development of a theory of addiction.

'I am 18 years old and I used to be a drug addict. I started taking drugs when I was 13 and it just got worse. I suppose I thought it was cool at first and when I did it again I never thought I would get addicted. I started out with smoking weed and I also drank and smoked cigarettes. Then I went on to cocaine. When I was doing cocaine I would do it for 4 or 5 days at a time and not eat or sleep properly. I got depressed when I came down and wanted more cocaine. When I got sick I decided then that I had to stop. I had lost my boyfriend, my job and I dropped out of school. I stopped for about a month but then started up again. I am doing better now. I have not used for a few weeks but I don't know if I will start using again. I wake up every morning not knowing if I am going to be able to stay off today. If I last out the day I feel very good about myself but the next day it starts all over'.

'I wake up in the night because the drink has worn off and my nerves are screaming out. I have a splitting headache, my mouth is dry, and my guts are

---

Theory of Addiction, Second Edition. Robert West and Jamie Brown.
© 2013 John Wiley & Sons, Ltd. Published 2013 by John Wiley & Sons, Ltd.

churning. I crawl to the medicine cabinet to try and find something to make it go away. Then I find my way to the kitchen for water. I am dizzy and want to throw up – my head is about to explode. I swear that I'm never going to put myself through this again. I feel like death – in fact I pray for it. But somewhere inside myself I know that by evening I will be drunk again'.

A functional classification of theories of addiction

The previous chapters in this book set out the main theories of addiction beginning with rational choice theories and ending with more integrative theories. This was useful as a didactic tool but is not necessarily the best classification system for these theories. Before going on to describe how to integrate the main features of theories of addiction it will be helpful to introduce a more comprehensive classification system. Figure 7.1 shows a system that has recently been developed (West 2013) and Table 7.1 briefly describes the theoretical approaches and gives examples.

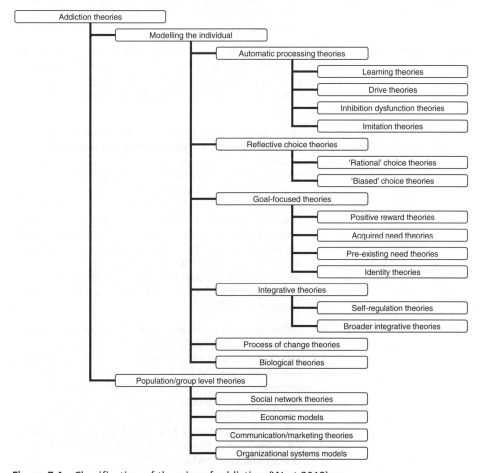

Figure 7.1 Classification of theories of addiction (West 2013).

Table 7.1 Categories of theories of addiction together with examples

Learning theories	*Addiction involves learning associations between cues, responses and powerful positive or negative reinforcers (pleasant or noxious stimuli).* Examples are operant learning, classical conditioning, incentive-sensitisation theory (Berridge et al. 2011), behavioural momentum and inertia theory (Nevin and Grace 2000).
Drive theories	*Addiction involves development of powerful drives underpinned by homeostatic mechanisms.* Examples are the disease model of addiction (Jellinek 1960; Gelkopf et al. 2002) and control systems dynamical model of smoking urges (Riley et al. 2011).
Inhibition dysfunction theories	*Addiction involves impairment of the mechanisms needed to control impulses.* Examples are dysfunction of inhibitory brain circuitry (Lubman et al. 2004; Dalley et al. 2011) and dysfunction of the prefrontal cortex in addiction (Goldstein and Volkow 2011).
Imitation theories	*Addiction involves, or at least begins with, imitation of behaviour patterns and assimilation of ideas and identities.* Examples are social learning theory (Bandura 1977) and automatic imitation (Heyes 2011).
'Rational' choice theories	*Addiction involves making a rational (in the sense that preferences are decided using reason and analysis and then acted upon) choice that favours the benefits of the addictive behaviour over the costs.* Examples are subjective expected utility theory (Edwards 1961), multi-attribute utility theory (Keeney and Raiffa 1993), prospect theory (Tversky and Kahneman 1992), theory of planned behaviour (Ajzen 1991), protection motivation theory (Rogers and Prentice-Dunn 1997), theory of rational addiction (Becker and Murphy 1988) and positive and negative expectancy theories (for a review, see Jones et al. 2001).
'Biased' choice theories	*Addiction arises at least in part from the influence of emotional and other biases on the process by which options to engage or not engage in addictive behaviours are compared.* Examples are unstable preference theory (Skog 2000; 2003), temporal discounting models (Bickel et al. 2007), cognitive bias models (McCusker 2001; Field and Cox 2008), affect heuristic (Slovic et al. 2002; Slovic et al. 2007), gateway theory (Kandel 1992; 2002) and conflict theory (Janis and Mann 1977).

Table 7.1 (*Continued*)

Positive reward theories	*Addiction arises out of the pleasure and satisfaction caused by the activity. The greater the pleasure and satisfaction, the greater the risk of addiction.* This is a very large body of theory and underpins many of the learning theory approaches. Specific examples that focus on specific nuances of positive reward are failure of habituation to positive reward (Di Chiara 1999; McAuliffe and Gordon 1974; for a review, see de Wit and Phan 2010), body image theory of steroid addiction (Kanayama 2009) and weight control theory of tobacco smoking (Cawley et al. 2004).
Acquired need theories	*Addiction involves development of physiological or psychological needs as a result of engaging in the addictive behaviour which are then met by the addictive behaviour.* Examples are drug withdrawal theory (Eddy et al. 1965; Koob et al. 1992) and opponent-process theory (Solomon 1980; Solomon and Corbit 1973 1974; Koob 2008; George et al. 2012).
Pre-existing need theories	*Addiction involves engaging in behaviours that meet important pre-existing needs.* Examples are self-medication theory (Khantzian 1997), attachment theory (Flores 2004) and affect-regulation theory (Cooper et al. 1995).
Identity theories	*Addiction arises from, and is at least partly maintained, by aspects of one's self-identity (how one views oneself).* Examples are identity theory (Walters 1996; Kearney and O'Sullivan 2003), prototype–willingness model (Gerrard et al. 2008) and self-affirmation theory (Harris and Epton 2009).
Self-regulation theories	*Addiction involves a failure of an individual's strategies, skills and capacity for self-control to counter the immediate impulses and desires underlying the addictive behaviour; this failure can in part be caused by 'ego depletion'.* Examples are cognitive control theory (Miller and Cohen 2001), executive dysfunction theory (Fernandez-Serrano et al. 2010; Hester and Garavan 2004; Madoz-Gurpide et al. 2011), self-regulation theory (Baumeister and Vohs 2007; Vohs and Baumeister 2011), self-determination theory (Deci et al. 1994; Ryan and Deci 2000; Deci and Ryan 2012) and implementation intentions (Gollwitzer 1999; Sheeran et al. 2005).

(*continued*)

Table 7.1 (*Continued*)

Broader integrative theories	*Addiction involves a wide range of processes that may involve different processes for different behaviours, populations, contexts and individuals. Social and environmental factors interact with different pre-existing dispositions to trigger initiation of the behaviour and this leads, through an interactive process, to changes in the personal environment and personal dispositions to increase the strength of motivation to engage in the behaviour.* Examples are the pathways model of pathological gambling (Blaszczynski and Nower 2002; Nower and Blaszczynski 2004), externalising and internalising pathways to addiction (e.g. Sher et al. 1991; Hussong et al. 2011) and excessive appetites theory (Orford 2001).
Process of change theories	*Initial enactment of the addictive behaviour, development of addiction, attempts at recovery and success or failure of those attempts involve different processes that can be delineated and influenced by different interventions.* Examples are cognitive dissonance theory (Festinger 1957; Blume and Schmaling 1996) elaboration likelihood theory (Cacioppo and Petty 1984; Petty et al. 1991; Petty and Briñol 2012), transtheoretical model (Prochaska et al. 1992; Norcross et al. 2011), acceptance and commitment theory (Hayes et al. 1999) and relapse prevention (RP) model (Hendershot et al. 2011; Larimer et al. 1999; Marlatt and George 1984).
Biological theories	*Addiction is primarily a 'brain disease' in which neural pathways of executive function become disordered and particular motivational processes become amplified as a result of an interaction between behaviours and their effects in the brain, particularly, ingestion of particular drugs.* It may seem strange to make such a large class of theories, and many of the other categories are of course 'biological'. This category is intended to capture theories that propose specific neural mechanisms. Examples are neural circuitry in addiction (Brewer and Potenza 2008; Everitt and Robbins 2005; Schultz 2011), individual differences in neural circuitry (Everitt et al. 2008; Hariri 2009; Muller et al. 2010) and expectancy-reward theory (Baker et al. 2011).

Table 7.1 *(Continued)*

Social network theories	*The rates of transition into and out of addiction on the part of individuals within a group or population is a function of the social connections between individuals who are and are not promoters of addiction or non-addiction, and the nature of those connections.* Examples are diffusion theory (Ferrence 1996; 2001), social contagion theory (Einstein and Epstein 1980; Rende et al. 2005; Smith and Christakis 2008) and actor–network theory (Latour 2005; Young et al. 2010).
Economic models	*The prevalence, incidence and/or rate of addictive behaviours in populations can be predicted by functions from economic theory including current and future financial and other costs relating to the behaviour and/or competing/alternative behaviours.* Examples are price elasticity (French et al. 2006; Gallet and List 2003; John 2008; O'Riordan 1969; Liu et al. 1999; Van Ours 1995) and cross-elasticity models (Mytton et al. 2007; Mytton et al. 2012).
Communication/marketing theories	*The development of and recovery from addiction is influenced by the persuasive communications and marketing activities of those promoting or seeking to combat the behaviours concerned.* This is more of a theoretical orientation than a body of theory. Example is social marketing (Evans 2006; Hastings and McDermott 2006; Hastings 2007).
Organisational system models	*Addictive behaviours can be understood in terms of systems of mutually interacting components at a societal level (e.g. government, tobacco industry, public). The effects of innovation introduced into the system can be nullified by compensatory changes in another or can propagate through the system or even be amplified.* Examples are tobacco use management system (Borland et al. 2010; Young et al. 2012) and systems approach to healthcare delivery (de Savigny and Adam 2009).

In an ideal world, such a classification would form a neat hierarchy. Unfortunately, it is not possible to fit all the approaches into such a hierarchy. That is because of significant overlap between approaches and the fact that they have to be distinguished using multiple features. Thus, some of the theories could be located in more than one category. In those cases, the choice of category has been determined by what appears to be a dominant feature of the theory. For more details of this classification system, see West (2013).

Addiction as reflective choice

The functional classification given in Figure 7.1 and Table 7.1 shows the huge breadth of approaches. It should be easy to see that each one offers a form of understanding and an approach to combating the problem. It is of course foolish to take just one or a few of these approaches and pretend that this is all there is. Thus, the pre-existing need approach suggests that if we can improve the mental health of those who might be susceptible to addiction this could lead to prevention and/or cure. Acquired need theories lead us to focus on interventions such as drugs that reduce craving and withdrawal symptoms. Rational choice theories suggest that we should incentivise, punish, persuade or educate in order to prevent or manage addiction. Inhibition dysfunction theories lead us to look for ways of building inhibitory capacity, either through drugs or training, and so on.

What none of the theories do is to tell us how we can integrate these approaches to arrive at a rational strategy for combating addiction that is appropriate for the particular individual, group or population, the behaviour concerned and the social and environmental context. That is the ambitious goal of the rest of this book.

The simplest common-sense model

The journey towards a synthetic model of addiction started with the simplest common-sense theory of addiction that there is addiction that involves a choice to engage in an activity that is based on a weighing of the costs and benefits. The activity appears driven by a repeated powerful motivation when the activity is unusually frequent or intense or costs are very high; however, under this view, there is no true compulsion and the behaviour is rational. To understand why a particular activity is addictive for someone, one just needs to look at how strong the benefits are to him or her or how little that person cares about the costs. Figure 7.2 illustrates the main elements and influences in this kind of model.

At its most extreme, this theory asserts not only that addiction involves a rational choice, but also that the addict is well informed about the consequences of his actions and is fully consistent in trying to maximise the benefits and minimise the costs. It is even possible to understand how this can happen: addictions are either very pleasurable for the addict or they provide for a very strong need, such as the need to escape from anxiety, or both of these.

The basis of addicts' preferences

Note that something can be rewarding for many reasons: it can give pleasure, serve a useful function or relieve discomfort. At the same time, addicts are often people who have little to lose as a result of their addiction (at least in their eyes). In many

Conscious evaluation of...

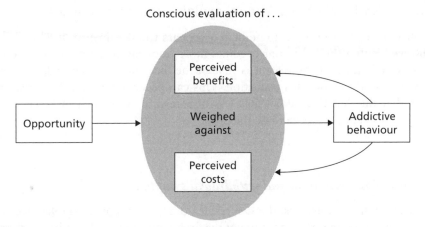

Figure 7.2 Addiction as rational choice. Given the opportunity, the individual makes decisions to seek out or enact the behaviour depending on analysis of the costs and benefits. A high frequency or intensity of activity simply reflects the preferences of the individual given current circumstances. Increases in frequency or intensity derive from feedback from the behaviour to the costs and benefits of engaging in it.

cases, they have low self-esteem while in others they may exhibit a general lack of care over anything, including themselves. Either way they do not place great value on their welfare. In some cases, they do not care much about the welfare of others either; for example, they are willing to steal, if necessary, in order to fund their addiction.

According to this approach, if one wants to know whether an activity has widespread addictive potential, one simply looks at how much pleasure it can give or how much it can serve other important needs. If one wants to know what kind of a person will become addicted to an activity, look at his or her physiological or psychological response to the activity to see how rewarding it is and look also at how little the person cares about the harm that the behaviour is likely to cause. If one wants to know what kinds of situations are conducive to addiction, look at those that make it easy and cheap to engage in the activity.

Costs and benefits of different modes of drug delivery

Remember, when considering addiction to drugs, that the way that a drug is used dramatically affects the cost–benefit equation: injecting heroin is potentially more harmful but also, for some, there are greater benefits than smoking it (Pates et al. 2005).

Remember also the social dimension to addiction; for example, the pharmacological actions of a drug have a different value depending on the social circumstances in which a drug is taken. What is more, social costs and benefits of an addictive behaviour play an important part in its development, maintenance and termination.

What the Rational Choice Theory explains and encompasses

This theory can explain why an addiction appears to take time to develop. What is observed is that the behaviour becomes more frequent or its intensity (or dose) increases or both; and the reason is that in the individuals concerned, the cost–benefit equation favours this transition. This can occur for a number of reasons. One is that the fledgling addict gets less of a reward from each instance of the activity and so chooses to increase the dose.

Tolerance, dose escalation and withdrawal symptoms

In the case of drug addictions, this can result from 'pharmacological tolerance': the body adapts to the repeated ingestion of the drug with changes that work to restore normal functioning. However, tolerance can occur to non-drug stimuli as well. In fact, it is normal for us to become accustomed to pleasures; things that once used to delight and excite us gradually lose their appeal and we need more intense stimuli to gain the same experience.

It may be noted that a wide range of rewards are amenable to 'dose' escalation in response to habituation. Stimuli that involve risk and excitement fall into this category. Money is no doubt another example. It may also be noted, however, that habituation to some of these seems to have limits. Once tolerance has developed within a few weeks to the effects of nicotine, there is little further change. Thus the timing, extent and duration of dose escalation will be variable.

This rational choice approach allows for the possibility that one difference between an activity that goes on to become addictive and one that does not is that the 'habituation' process (as it is commonly called) for some reason leads the individual to seek more intense forms of the stimulus to compensate for it rather than just giving it up. Another reason why an activity may become more frequent is that the development of tolerance results in abnormal functioning in the absence of the drug or activity.

In the case of addiction to substances, there is a good deal of evidence of such abnormal functioning and the unpleasant symptoms that result from abstinence. Once this starts to happen, a drug user has a new reason to keep taking the drug on a regular basis. In the case of heroin and alcohol, for example, the 'withdrawal symptoms' begin within a few hours, as the drug concentrations in the body drop, and so the users need to dose themselves several times a day to keep these at bay.

The situation regarding tolerance is actually more complex than this. In some cases, particularly stimulant drugs such as nicotine and cocaine, there may be what is called 'acute tolerance' or 'tachyphylaxis' to the hedonic effects (e.g. Foltin and Fischman 1991; Perkins et al. 2003). Repeated doses taken over a short space of time have a reduced effect. This can result from an active physiological process in which the system attempts to restore balance or a passive process in which the system is unable to respond with the same intensity as before. With acute tolerance, the effect lasts only a short space of time and further doses of the drug have a smaller effect. This is one possible explanation, within the rational addiction theory, for 'bingeing'.

Explaining attempts at restraint

The theory can also explain why addicts sometimes stop engaging in the activity, a phenomenon sometimes called (misleadingly) 'spontaneous recovery' or 'self cure'. It postulates that for some people there comes a point when the benefits of *stopping* the activity are judged to be greater than the costs.

The alcohol addict reaches a point where life is so unpleasant and the prospect of a better life without alcohol is so great that he or she decides to stop, and does so. The addict has not changed his or her evaluation of anything, and in this extreme version of the rational choice theory, he or she would not regret having been a heavy drinker. This addict always considered the possibility that the damage caused by his or her drinking would eventually lead him or her to stop, but he or she was prepared to take the risk.

Similarly, the addicted smoker may reach a point where the harmful health effects or the price of cigarettes outweigh the pleasure of smoking and so the decision is made to stop. Alternatively, the smoker decides to reduce the risk by switching to a lower tar cigarette believing it to be safer, or by trying to reduce the number of cigarettes smoked. Under this view, the addict is in control and if he or she does not choose to stop the activity it is because the costs of doing so outweigh the benefits.

It is not clear whether any researchers are seriously proposing this extreme version of the Rational Choice Theory but Becker and Murphy's (1988) Theory of Rational Addiction (Chapter 3) comes close. This is an economic theory that has spawned a large body of research and arguably been very influential even though in psychological terms the assumptions underlying it are simplistic (see Chapter 3).

It is also possible to view accounts that come under the heading 'Expectancy Theory' as falling into this category. Such theories seek to identify what addicts expect to get from their behaviour and how they view the costs (Chapter 3).

Implications of the Rational Choice Theory

The policy implications of the extreme version of the Rational Theory of Addiction are clear. To reduce the prevalence of an addiction, make it more costly, in the broadest sense. Treat it like any consumer behaviour. Make it harder to get and more expensive. One can also increase the personal cost of the behaviour by making it illegal or stigmatising it. For drug addictions in which rapid onset of withdrawal symptoms plays a role in maintaining the frequency of the activity (such as heroin addiction), the frequency can be reduced by making a drug available that alleviates these symptoms (such as methadone). Essentially, the addiction is countered by increasing the costs relative to the benefits.

It is worth noting that it will not always be easy to predict what the precise effect of any single intervention or combination of interventions will be. This is because the costs and benefits have to be seen in the context of those operating on other choices that we make. For example, increasing the price of a drug will have a smaller effect or even no effect in individuals who can easily absorb the cost without sacrificing other goods or activities that they value.

Rational Choice Theory as a psychological theory

The Rational Choice Theory is a psychological theory that provides a framework for including pharmacological theories concerning how habituation to drugs occurs and how drugs achieve their rewarding effects. It also provides a framework for psychological, social, psychobiological or even biopsychosocial theories explaining the rewarding effects of drugs or other addictive activities. In addition, it provides a basis for economic theories of consumption of addictive 'goods' expressed in terms of equations relating costs and adoption at the level of populations.

Addiction as irrational choice

Unstable preferences

The extreme version of Rational Addiction Theory goes a surprisingly long way towards explaining addictive behaviour but it is contradicted by some 'big observations'. (The term 'big observation' has been used in this book to describe evidence from observation of people in their natural habitat or scientific studies that are uncontested and which address major issues in addiction.) The assumptions that preferences are stable and addicts are well informed must be wrong.

Failure of genuine attempts to exercise restraint

To be fair, these assumptions were never going to be realistic. If preferences are stable and addicts are good at predicting what will happen in the future, it is impossible (without resorting to a great deal of special pleading) to explain what is one of the core features of addiction: that genuine attempts to restrain use fail.

Clinics for alcohol addicts, heroin addicts, gambling addicts and cigarette addicts are largely populated by people who are in the process of making a serious attempt to stop their behaviour, but who will resume their addictive behaviour within days, weeks or months. For example, 75% of serious attempts to stop smoking do not even last a week (West 2009). If these addicts had stable preferences and could foresee the consequences of their actions, this would only happen if the individuals concerned never intended to stop the activity for good.

Admittedly this could happen in some cases. For example, a heroin addict who was attending a treatment service because of a court order might have no intention of staying off heroin for long; he or she is just responding rationally to a situation where for the time being it is better to be abstinent. Similarly, a heroin addict might seek treatment while he or she is unable to secure his or her street supply of heroin for whatever reason. It could also happen that an alcohol addict decides to 'dry out' for a while but with no intention of staying off alcohol indefinitely.

On the other hand, there are certainly large numbers of cases where addicts show every sign of wanting to stop for good and yet still resume the activity. Either their preferences must have changed or they must have misjudged the effects of abstaining, or both. This should not be surprising. Even a casual observer of human behaviour knows that what we like and dislike, and what we regard as good and bad, vary over time and circumstance and that we are often ill-informed about the consequences of our actions. It is unrealistic to assume that the situation would be any different for addiction.

Misjudging the effects of restraint and changing preferences

To explain relapse that was unplanned before the attempt at restraint, we can keep a rational addiction theory alive by postulating that the addict misjudges how much he or she will miss the activity. The smoker who decides to make a quit attempt has not reckoned with the strength of the desire to smoke or the unpleasantness of life without cigarettes. Since both are typically greatest in the first days of abstinence and then diminish, this is when the most relapse would occur.

Thus, nicotine withdrawal symptoms mostly peak in the first week, and urges to smoke peak in the first 48 hours (the two not being quite separable); that is, when the rational, but not well-informed, smoker is most likely to decide to go back to smoking (West and Shiffman 2004). However, even after weeks or months an individual may choose to resume the addictive activity because life without it is not what he or she hoped it would be. This would be a good reason for resuming the behaviour that was over and above any particular life circumstances that could reasonably have been foreseen.

Deliberate relapse

Surprisingly, there has been little research into what might be called deliberate relapse. That is, how often someone who has decided to abstain from an addictive behaviour then deliberately decides to go back to it as a self-conscious choice stemming from a cost–benefit analysis. Just by way of illustration, a Google Scholar search on the phrase 'deliberate relapse' resulted in only six hits, none of which had anything to do with addiction, and the suggestion that one might have meant 'deliberate prolapse'! A search on the phrase 'choosing to relapse' yielded one discussion at a conference in which 'choosing to' was in parentheses.

It seems like an obvious test of a theory that proposes that addiction involves self-conscious choice to take people who have relapsed and ask whether they recall having made a deliberate choice to resume their addictive behaviour. There are a lot of studies that have examined 'reasons for relapse' but this is not the same thing, as is evidenced by the fact that one of the most common ones given is craving. In that case, the addict may be reporting that they have responded to an urge rather than making a decision.

In a rare example of this kind of study, Vangeli et al. (2010) surveyed 199 smokers who had relapsed a month or more after starting a quit attempt with a stop-smoking group. She found that only 27% considered that they had made a deliberate decision to return to smoking – most commonly they thought they would smoke just a few cigarettes and then resume being a non-smoker.

Returning to the journey, under a realistic rational decision theory, addiction is still a rational choice: the addict chooses to start, increase, stop or decrease the frequency and intensity of the activity in response to prevailing costs and benefits that are accurately perceived at the time. Relapse occurs because the cost–benefit balance that prompts an attempt to restrain use alters once that attempt is under way. A theory that is close to this approach is Skog's Choice Theory (Chapter 3).

Irrationality

This theory goes quite a bit further towards explaining addiction but there is a problem with the concept of rationality, at least as we are using it. A rational decision-maker is not biased in his or her beliefs. This is different from being uninformed. When you roll a die you do not know what number will come up but if it is a normal die you know that there is an equal chance of a 1 or a 6. If you think that a 1 is more likely because it has not come up in the last 100 rolls so it is 'due', that is irrational. Similarly, if you think that a 1 is more likely because you really 'need it' to come up to get you out of a gambling debt, that is irrational too. There is a vast literature on irrationality in human decision-making (Baron 2000), and it is obvious that we all exhibit it to a greater or lesser degree, some more than others and more on some occasions than on others.

Biased beliefs and addiction

There is evidence that many addicts are biased in their beliefs about their activity: not surprisingly they often underestimate the costs and overestimate the benefits. How far this contributes to their addiction is another matter; there are no obser-vations that absolutely require us to postulate biased beliefs to account for an addictive pattern of behaviour. So all we can say is that addicts are biased in their beliefs and perhaps this contributes to their problem but perhaps it does not. So we do not necessarily have to abandon the 'rational' part of the Choice Theory of addiction in order to explain the phenomenon, but since we know that human judgement is frequently biased, there seems no reason to preclude such bias from our theory.

Beliefs and feelings

The preceding discussion has not discriminated explicitly between beliefs and feel-ings. Yet it is obvious that believing that something is 'a good thing' and anticipating it with pleasure are very different. It is also obvious that sometimes we work out what to do by trying to calculate what the best outcome will be and sometimes we go with our emotions. Sometimes the two conflicts with each other and one or other (usually the emotion) wins out. Thus, we need to include in the Irrational Choice Theory the influence of feelings on judgement. One of the most important applications of this to addiction theory has come from Slovic et al. (2002) (Chapter 3).

Biased attention and memory

There is another level at which irrationality might help to promote addiction: not so much in conscious beliefs and values, but in our memory for, and the attention we pay to, information relating to it (Cognitive Bias Theories, Chapter 3). There is an extensive literature showing that addicts pay closer attention to information relating to smoking, alcohol, drug taking or whatever, than non-addicts. As with the notion of irrational beliefs, this could help to explain the development and maintenance of addiction, but it could also be a consequence of it and not play an important causal role. Establishing which of these is the case will not be easy.

The theory is now a Choice Theory (with degree of rationality unspecified) with unstable preferences. Such a theory still, of course, provides a comprehensive framework that can accommodate pharmacological, social and economic theories.

Addiction, compulsion and self-control

Not all important activities involve choice

The flow of behaviour

One problem for a Choice Theory is that most of our behaviour, including addictive behaviours, does not involve choice at all. Choice involves conscious consideration of alternatives, by definition. Yet in the flow of behaviour we usually do not consider alternatives, we react to stimuli or execute plans that we have made. It is unrealistic to assume that each time an alcohol addict takes a drink he or she is weighing up the costs and benefits. We need to recognise that there is a flow to behaviour in which one thing leads to another and that the extent to which we deliberate over it is highly variable.

Salvaging Choice Theory

Proponents of Choice Theory may attempt to salvage the approach in two ways. One method is to propose (as many have done) that the term 'choice' is being used in a more abstract way and is not intended to refer to actual mental events. Choice Theory in this view is a statistical model of behaviour and not a description of any particular process.

Expectancy theories typically fall into this category. It is absurd to propose, for example, that all intentional behaviour involves individuals making a quantitative judgement about the likelihood of each possible outcome and multiplying this by a quantitative judgement about how good or bad the outcome is and then summing the results. It does not happen that way.

It is possible to argue that the theories are not intended to describe actual processes, but rather model the outcomes: it is 'as if' behaviour is controlled in this way. This works up to a point when it comes to analyzing population level data but clearly it is preferable to postulate mechanisms that exist where the opportunity arises. Moreover, as will be seen in the next chapter, the approach that is then used to test these ideas (using regression analyses) is very limited when it comes to the task of building better theories and does not allow falsification.

The other way around the point that most behaviour does not involve choices is to argue that choices are being made but these are not 'conscious' choices. The problem with this approach is that the concept of choice then loses much of its meaning and the theory becomes too poorly specified to be of value.

The need for 'self-control'

Even more of a problem for the Choice Theory of addiction is that it has no place for the concept of self-control. In this account, choices are made on a cost–benefit analysis as the addict sees things, and the presumption is that the addict makes (as he or she sees it) the best choice at the time, even though he or she may regret it later. If the addict does regret it later, the choice is changed.

The experience of addiction as effortful exercising of restraint

Yet the experience of addicts is that they try consciously to exercise restraint and that this feels difficult and it usually fails. Note that this is very different from them just saying that they are in two minds, or are conflicted about whether or not to engage in the activity. They have actively to stop themselves doing something and this requires mental effort. This idea is by no means esoteric or metaphysical. Figure 7.3 shows this model in simple terms.

Self-control is a well-documented phenomenon that applies in many areas of behaviour (Baumeister et al. 1994). There is an interesting question about whether self-control, in the form of forcing yourself to do something you do not want to, involves a different process from self-control in restraining yourself from something you feel impelled to do. There are grounds for believing that it does. In one case, inhibitory processes must hold sway while in the other, behavioural activation is required.

Impulsiveness

The personality trait 'impulsiveness' has a long history of research behind it. Its level is partly determined genetically and it is associated with antisocial behaviour, and with addiction to drugs and gambling. Impulsivity as a trait provides another possible explanation for why some people become addicted to certain activities while others do not.

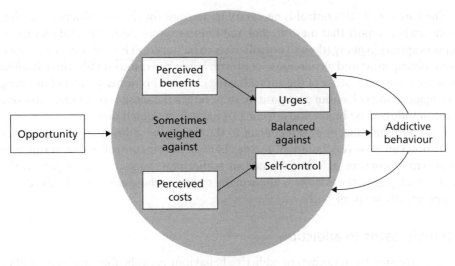

Figure 7.3 A Choice Theory of addiction with self-control added.

The self

In the phenomenology of self-control, there are some further concepts that we cannot do without. We must postulate the existence of a part of us that is exercising 'control' (or not) and we must further postulate a difference between desires on the one hand and judgements about what is good or bad, right or wrong, beneficial or harmful on the other. Self-control involves consciously prioritising what we should do (or not do) over what we want to do or feel an urge to do.

Response inhibition

The concept of restraint has an analogue in biological theories of behaviour: 'response inhibition'. Pathways in the brain that are involved have to some extent been mapped out and it is possible to measure the degree to which inhibition is operating using experimental procedures. One of these is what is known as 'differential reinforcement of low rate responding'. In this set-up, a hungry rat, pigeon or monkey (typically) can be trained to press a lever to receive food. If a morsel of food appears every ten or so responses, the animal will press the lever at a high rate. If we now change things so that a high rate of responding is not rewarded, but instead the animal has to respond at a low rate, it must inhibit the behaviour in order to get food. In the right conditions, animals can learn to do this and we can then look at the effects of various manipulations on their ability to do so. A particular drug, for example, might interfere with the ability of an animal to learn to slow down the rate of responding (e.g. Pattij et al. 2004). Response inhibition in non-human animals is not the same as self-control in humans. For a start, self-control involves a self-conscious act of will; but there may be enough commonalities to use it as a model; we shall see.

The concept of self-control is necessary to account for the 'big observation' that many addicts report that they attempt and fail to exercise restraint, and that those reports appear in many (though not all) cases to be sincere. The restraint is described as involving effort and a conscious act of will. When the restraint fails, there is often (but not always) no sense of the addict having changed his or her mind and deciding to engage in the behaviour as a positive step; rather the sense is of a failure to exert control followed by regret and a feeling of having let oneself down.

If we add the concept of self-control to the theory, we allow the possibility that addiction can involve a failure of the mechanism of self-control. So, with this new explanatory concept at our disposal, an addict may be someone for whom the desire to engage in the activity is abnormally strong or the ability to resist the desire is abnormally weak or both.

Multiple paths to addiction

The progression from normal to addictive behaviour is explicable now in a number of ways: changes to the individual's circumstances, development of habituation or sensitisation to the rewarding effects of the activity, onset of unpleasant symptoms during abstinence and now a progressive reduction in the addict's ability to exercise restraint. With regard to all of these, we have the beginnings of an understanding of the brain mechanisms that underpin them. Chapter 4 examined theories relating to self-control (see also Lubman et al. 2004).

Addiction, instrumental learning and habit

Addiction is not always linked to enjoyment or relief of distress

We are now close to a complete explanation of addiction at a broad-brush level. However, it is still contradicted by some big observations. If this theory is correct, then, with other things being equal, the more rewarding an activity for an individual the more addictive it should be for that individual. For example, there should at least be some positive relationship between how much a smoker enjoys smoking and his or her difficulty in stopping.

Enjoyment and addiction are not necessarily linked

Yet this is not what is typically observed. In the case of smoking, for example, research has failed to find a relationship between how much smokers say they enjoy smoking and the likelihood of being able to remain abstinent when they make a serious attempt to stop (West 1995; Fidler and West 2011). Neither is there a relationship between ability to stop and any of the commonly reported rewards of smoking such as relief from stress or boredom and control of weight (West 1995). What is consistently observed instead is that success at stopping is related to the dose of nicotine that smokers take in each day: the higher the nicotine dose, the greater the difficulty in stopping (Norregaard et al. 1993; Rigotti et al. 1994; Gariti et al. 1999).

It has also been found that more dependent smokers have generally lower hedonic tone than less dependent smokers, who have lower tone than non-smokers, and that while individual cigarettes tend to reverse the adverse mood, the effect is short-lived (Adan et al. 2004).

Level of addiction is more closely related to dose

Where it has been tested, it seems that it is the nicotine dose rather than the frequency of the behaviour that is most important. Thus, the number of cigarettes per day has been found to predict failure of quit attempts (Vangeli et al. 2011), but saliva cotinine concentration (which provides a much better indication of the actual nicotine dose obtained because it takes account of puffing and inhalation patterns) does a better job.

This dissociation between personal level of enjoyment and level of addiction has been observed with other drugs than nicotine. However, it would be wrong to presume that the two were completely unconnected. We also need to bear in mind that all addictions, by definition, involve a reward-seeking behaviour, with reward being used to refer to pleasure, satisfaction, utility or relief from discomfort. The point is only that the association between the level of reward provided by an activity and level of addiction to it is complex and not universal. This means that addiction involves something else.

Returning to the concept of withdrawal symptoms

There remains a possible explanation that does not involve any new concepts. It goes back to something we have already discussed. Perhaps, the likelihood of relapse is instead related to the severity of withdrawal symptoms experienced. The worse the withdrawal symptoms, the greater the motivation to resume the activity. Unfortunately, this does not help because, where it has been looked at, severity of withdrawal symptoms (measured prior to relapse) and likelihood of relapse are only very weakly associated with each other.

In the case of smoking, some studies have found that severity of one withdrawal symptom, depressed mood, predicted relapse (West et al. 1989; Swan et al. 1996) but the result is not consistent and it is always weak (Norregaard et al. 1993). Much more consistent relationships have been found between severity of withdrawal symptoms and relapse when smokers who have relapsed are asked about their symptoms. The problem here is that this could just be a self-justification of their failure. In the case of other drugs, the association has not been studied so well unfortunately, but the observation in the case of smoking is enough to establish the principle.

Enjoyment and craving are not necessarily linked

For smokers, not only is enjoyment not related to relapse when trying to stop, it is only weakly related to the strength of urge to smoke during a quit attempt. This seems strange on the face of it. A common-sense understanding of urge to smoke would lead us to believe that it stems from wanting something enjoyable. Yet this is not the case. Urge to smoke is modestly associated with the severity of other withdrawal symptoms but, again, we could not claim that it represents a desire to escape from those symptoms. Reports of the strength of urges to smoke have been found to predict relapse, as one would expect, though again the relationship is only modest and not always detected.

So we have a situation, at least in the case of smoking, where, in the course of a quit attempt, urge to smoke and relapse cannot be fully explained by the perceived rewards or the discomfort that would be alleviated. We could perhaps explain relapse without extending the theory by using our existing notion of impaired self-control. However, this would not help to explain the strength of urge.

Automatic responses, habit and instrumental learning

Habit

There is perhaps a feature of motivation that we can call on that can help us out. It is the notion of habit. Habits are widely observed and to postulate their existence is uncontroversial. These are behaviour patterns that through repetition become so routine that they become at least partly or fully 'automatic'. They occur without conscious intent.

Habit as unthinking behaviour

It would be reasonable to propose that at least some cases of relapse in addictive behaviours occur because of an automated process in which conditions that have so often in the past led to the behaviour occurring do so again without a conscious decision-making process on the part of the addict (see Baxter and Hinson 2001). There are certainly reports of smokers lighting up cigarettes without thinking about it. It is therefore necessary to postulate habit, arising through repetition, as a contributory factor. On the other hand, it is not common enough to account completely for relapse that is not motivated by expectation of enjoyment or relief of withdrawal symptoms because there are enough reports of conscious urges to smoke precipitating relapse that it would be unrealistic to ignore all of them.

Habit as learned behaviour

If habit, in the sense used above, cannot do the whole job, perhaps habit in the sense used by learning theorists can. Everyone knows that it is possible to teach dogs, horses and other animals to perform certain actions by rewarding them with tasty food, affection or other stimuli that they seem to like. We also know that we can train animals to do things that enable them to escape from or avoid punishment. We can also, up to a point, stop them doing things by punishing them.

The same is obviously true for humans. The difference is that in the case of humans we think of the effects of reward and punishment as influences on the choices that people make whereas in the case of animals we think of the effects in terms of shaping their behaviour patterns. Most of us assume that people make a conscious choice to seek out rewards and minimise punishment while other animals do things through a more automated process – since they presumably do not have the facility for conscious decision-making.

What if it were the case that human animals have retained something of the same automated process whereby rewards and punishments shape behaviour through a mechanism that does not involve conscious choice? It turns out that we have (see Mook 1996).

It is relatively easy to show that you can influence someone else's behaviour by rewarding it in subtle ways so that they do not consciously notice the connection, but nevertheless they find themselves engaging in the activity more often. A group of students in a lecture theatre can, if they feel so inclined, gang up to ensure that the right side of the class looks attentive and nods and smiles while the other, not too blatantly, is less obviously attentive. Quite quickly the lecturer will be focusing attention on the side of the class that is rewarding him and if the class does it right, he will not even be aware that he is doing it.

That is a rather trivial example, but with careful observation of human behaviour it is clear that much of our behaviour is shaped by rewards and punishments without our making any conscious choices or weighing up preferences. The process is automatic, just as we presume it is with other animals. This process is known as instrumental (also 'operant') learning and has been very widely studied. We know what kinds of things are rewarding, under what conditions they are rewarding and we know something about the brain pathways involved.

Using instrumental learning to train a behaviour

The basics of using operant learning to train a behaviour are as follows: you choose a relatively simple action that the person or animal can readily perform (such as pressing a lever); you then either wait for it to be performed spontaneously, or you induce it in some way. Once it has been performed you reward it. It is usually more effective if you provide the reward as soon as possible after the action has been completed.

Obvious rewards are any kind of food if the animal is hungry, or tasty food if it is less hungry, affection if the animal is a dog or person, liquid if the animal is thirsty and so on. Once the behaviour has been rewarded, it is more likely to occur when the conditions that preceded it are repeated. These conditions can involve a specific stimulus such as a green light or a combination of environmental conditions such as a particular room or internal conditions such as feeling hungry, or indeed a combination of these.

Stimulus–response–reward associations

Connections are made between the conditions that preceded the behaviour (cues), the behaviour itself (the response) and the reward (also known as the 'positive reinforcer'). Remember that the process is automatic and does not involve conscious

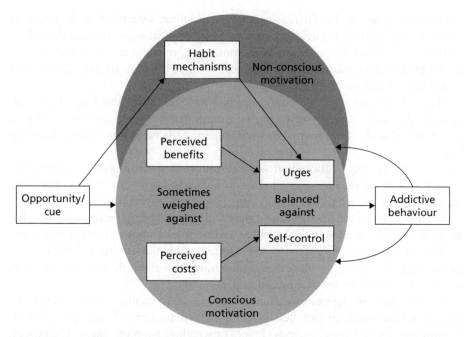

Figure 7.4 A simplified diagram of a Choice Theory of addiction with self-control, and instrumental learning added.

choice. Rewarding a response to a cue makes that response more likely when the cue is next presented (Figure 7.4).

There is an important and difficult question about what constitutes a response here. There are lots of muscles moving at any one time and not all of them are always coordinated into what we would recognise as a response. Even those that are contracting may contract in different ways to achieve their goal. Does the way someone holds his or her little finger at the time, or a turn of the head, get included in the response, and if not why not?

Intermittent reinforcement

A striking aspect of the process of instrumental learning is that the association between the cue and the response is often stronger when the response is only rewarded some of the time than when it is rewarded every time it occurs. If you set up a situation where on average you reward, say, every ten responses but the animal or person does not know exactly which one it will be, you can generate high rates of responding and strong persistence.

It is easy to see how this might have evolved. The real world is fairly unpredictable. Animals need to be able to engage in behaviours that are useful for survival even if they do not get the desired result every time. If you artificially set up a situation where a response is rewarded every time, an animal (a) does not need to make the response very often to meet its needs and (b) notices (in some sense) immediately when the reward is not forthcoming and starts to slow down or stop its responding accordingly. A situation in which a response is rewarded on the basis of a variable number of responses is called a 'variable ratio schedule of reinforcement'.

Setting up the optimal conditions for learning

Bearing in mind all this, if one wanted to train the average human to pull a lever as often as possible one would find a reward that was always effective no matter whether the human was hungry or thirsty (such as money), one would attract the attention of the human to the lever with bright flashing lights, and one would use a variable ratio schedule of reinforcement with a low probability of a high payout. If one wanted to get the human to pay money for the privilege of pulling the lever, one would have to arrange it so that the payouts were sufficiently frequent or large that the behaviour would continue even if the human was losing money on the deal in the long run.

Of course, this is what slot/gaming machine owners do and it seems to work well for them. Over the years, they have discovered that motivation to use the machines can be enhanced in various ways, for example, by creating the illusion of some degree of control through the pressing of 'Hold' buttons, but the principle is essentially a variable ratio schedule of a monetary reinforcer with the size and frequency of the payouts carefully controlled to maximise lever pulling behaviour.

Habit strength

So operant behaviour is regarded as a kind of habit because the mechanism underlying it does not require conscious choice – the cue elicits the action which is repeated at a rate that reflects the 'habit strength'. Behavioural pharmacologists use variants of this kind of responding as a 'model' of drug dependence (Chapter 5). They can show that many species of animal will respond repeatedly for drugs that are addictive for humans: morphine, nicotine, cocaine and amphetamines.

The mechanisms underlying instrumental learning

This is a demonstration that drugs of dependence can influence behaviour through a habit mechanism. The neurobiology underlying this process is beginning to be understood. Drugs of dependence all seem to increase the concentration of dopamine in the extracellular space in the nucleus accumbens (NAcc). They do it in different ways but it is apparent that if you can stop this happening, animals will stop finding ingestion of these drugs rewarding.

The fact that drugs are rewarding to animals does not necessarily mean that human drug taking involves the same learning mechanism. But we know that humans have similar brain structures and that where we can measure and influence the activity it seems to follow similar patterns; we also know that human behaviour often looks as though it is under operant control. All this together makes operant learning a good choice for an explanation of the dissociation between the conscious choice process and drug-taking behaviour.

Adding habit to choice and compulsion

We can incorporate operant learning into the theory as follows. Addictive behaviours in humans are at least partly under the control of an operant learning mechanism which is automatic in the sense that it does not involve conscious choice. At various times (not necessarily every time) when someone takes an addictive drug or engages in an addictive activity, the concentration of dopamine in the extracellular spaces in the NAcc increases and this causes the activity to be more likely to be repeated in the presence of the stimuli that preceded it.

The mechanism is not influenced by beliefs about what is good or bad or right or wrong and so can come into conflict with conscious choices that the individual makes. The individual may consciously 'choose' not to smoke or have a drink but feels a strong impulse to do so. Note that operant learning does not require the rewarding stimulus to give pleasure, although it usually does. It looks as though there are different parts of the NAcc, though usually linked together, that are involved in the hedonic experience arising from a behaviour versus the power of a cue to elicit that behaviour (Balfour 2004; Wonnacott et al. 2005).

Explaining the dissociation of conscious likes and evaluations and addiction

We can now explain quite easily why degree of addiction can be dissociated from enjoyment and other conscious feelings about what is good and bad, liked and disliked: there is a mechanism at work that drives behaviour automatically without regard to these experiences. The subjective manifestation of that mechanism is the feeling of urge or compulsion on occasions when attention is drawn to it (e.g. because it conflicts with conscious wishes that motivate attempts at restraint), but when attention is not drawn to it (e.g. when there is no conflict), there is no subjective manifestation and the behaviour is simply automatic, as when a smoker lights up without realising that he has a cigarette already lit.

Explaining the time course of relapse risk

This addition to the model provides a further explanation for why relapse rates are higher early on in an attempt to stop doing something but there is always a risk of relapse at any time afterwards. In fact, it provides a rather better one than the presence of withdrawal symptoms because, as was pointed out earlier, we have not found a strong association between the severity of withdrawal symptoms and relapse. It is that 'forgetting', the process by which the association between the cue and the response weakens over time if the response is not made, is a gradual process but is never complete.

Explaining relapse triggers

The model also provides an additional explanation, if one were needed, for why certain situations more commonly provoke relapse. Some of these are situations that have been cues for the response in question and therefore stimulate the pathways that would previously have led to the behaviour. Others, such as unpleasant experiences, appear to act on the pathways concerned to increase the propensity to enact the addictive behaviour by a direct neurochemical route.

Explaining individual differences in susceptibility to addiction

Operant learning also offers additional explanations for differences between individuals in susceptibility to addiction generally and specific addictions in particular. There are many differences across individuals in the way in which the brain pathways operate. There are differences in the number of particular kinds of dopamine receptor which will influence the susceptibility to the kinds of reinforcement provided by drugs, gambling, and so on. Some of these will affect a range of different drug-taking and other activities while others may affect only one or a small class of drugs. At least some of these differences are inherited. Some of these differences could also underlie behavioural traits that make people more or less likely to become addicted, such as a tendency to engage in antisocial behaviour.

Explaining the link between antisocial personality and addiction

In fact, this is an interesting story so it is worth a slight diversion. Antisocial traits involve repeatedly doing things that cause harm such as picking fights, stealing and being disruptive. This kind of behaviour starts to become manifest within the early years of life. A striking thing about it is that the children concerned seem not to learn very well from the punishments they are repeatedly receiving (though interestingly they do seem to learn rather better than others from rewards). The children react aggressively to punishment, so one presumes that they find it aversive but they do not appear to learn very well from it. Some experimental studies suggest that this may reflect a rather more general difficulty with learning from punishment, a process that we must presume is normally built into our make-up (Dadds and Salmon 2003). There is also interesting evidence that reduced ability to learn from punishment is linked to higher testosterone concentrations which opens up interesting hypotheses about why antisocial behaviour is more common in males than females (van Honk et al. 2004).

This provides a further explanation for the link between antisocial personality and drug addiction. The positive and immediate rewards are not being offset by the punishing consequences; under this view, it is not a wilful disregard of punishment, it is a failure of the mechanism by which we learn from punishment. Having made this connection, it is interesting to see that Finn et al. (1994) have reported that alcoholic men had poorer conditioned learning between stimulus and mild electric shock than non-alcoholic men.

Explaining environmental factors that promote addiction

Actually, once one embraces the idea that operant learning is an important driving force behind addiction, a panoply of additional explanations for big observations opens up rather nicely. These observations are very diverse, ranging from income differences in nicotine dependence to differences in the patterning of different addictive behaviours.

For example, it was already pointed out that animals such as rats will press a lever at a very high rate if it leads to delivery of cocaine. What was not stated is that the unfortunate animal is typically in a small cage with nothing else to do. It has been shown that the rate of lever pressing for cocaine is reduced when an animal is placed in a more 'interesting' environment with other sources of reward, an effect that is mirrored by experiments with cocaine users who respond less for cocaine when there are alternative reinforcers available (see Hart et al. 2000).

Many people on a low income have a very restricted range of opportunities for rewards, and a drug that provided a reliable reward would therefore be expected to be used at a higher rate. In the case of nicotine this is exactly what happens. People on low incomes in the United Kingdom, United States and other countries where there is societal pressure not to smoke are more likely to remain as smokers even though there is relatively little difference in the rate at which they experiment with smoking.

This observation in itself can also be explained easily by Choice Theory: smoking provides a source of pleasure for these people. But that does not explain a very interesting observation which is that the amount of nicotine taken in *per cigarette* is higher in low-income smokers and the number of cigarettes is higher and they smoke earlier in the morning – essentially in all respects they are ingesting nicotine at a higher rate (Jarvis and Wardle 1999). This higher rate is unrelated to the level of enjoyment from smoking – they do not report enjoying smoking more.

Explaining the patterning of addictive behaviour

The other example concerns the patterning of the behaviour. If we take cocaine, for example, its mode of action in the brain is directly on dopamine concentrations in the NAcc. It reduces the ability of the nerve cells to take back inside them the dopamine that they released as part of their normal activity, so the dopamine stays around for longer in the space between the cells and the level builds up.

This is a powerful effect that occurs within minutes of taking cocaine. When this happens in the accumbens shell, it provides a strong sense of well-being and euphoria as though something excellent had just happened. But once it has occurred there is a rapid adaptation so that more cocaine taken soon afterwards has less of an effect. In the accumbens core, this increase in dopamine strengthens the link between whatever response preceded it and the cue that preceded that response, and what is more this effect does not diminish, it actually increases: there is sensitisation. So when someone takes cocaine, they will get an initial rush of euphoria and an increase in the urge to do it again which will persist even though the pleasurable effect of subsequent doses is diminished. The result is a pattern of use in which people binge until they are exhausted or their supply runs out. However, they do not generally feel the need to do this all day, every day.

We can contrast this with smoking, for example, in which the pattern is much more one of regular use throughout the day, usually starting within an hour of waking. The explanation being offered is that nicotine has a different neuropharmacology. Nicotine does not increase dopamine levels directly but does so by stimulating bursts of firing of the cells that release dopamine in the accumbens. It does this by attaching to nicotinic acetylcholine receptors in the ventral tegmental area. When it does so, it has an immediate effect of increasing activity in those cells but the nicotinic receptor has a very special property which is that almost immediately it 'desensitises', which stops nicotine from having any further effect.

Smoking will therefore typically not produce much by way of dopamine release in the NAcc except after at least a few hours of abstinence. In any event the increase in accumbens, dopamine is nothing like as big as one observes with cocaine. Nicotine does produce a feeling that many smokers find pleasant but no one would claim that it is anything like as strong as that produced by cocaine, or even cannabis.

However, the increased dopamine in the core of the accumbens does link the act of smoking to the cues that preceded it and thus has the potential to set up operant learning. The fact that the effect is weaker than with cocaine and occurs at more irregular intervals, that is, when the desensitised receptors have recovered, means that it will be different from cocaine. The behaviour will show less bingeing and take longer to establish, but because it is on a very high variable ratio reinforcement schedule it will be surprisingly strongly established. We probably also need to consider the fact that the weak subjective effect of smoking makes it a more suitable accompaniment to everyday activities than cocaine.

Surely we now must have enough elements in the theory to explain the big observations? (In fact, we have a surfeit of explanations for many of the phenomena.) Unfortunately not.

But before we can get into why the elements of the model are not yet all in place, there is a need to tackle something that will be in the minds of some behavioural pharmacologists reading this passage. These people are scientists and many of them would prefer to eschew mentalist concepts such as choice, attitudes and other things that cannot be observed directly and are subject to differing interpretations anyway. The science of behaviour should restrict itself to things that can be observed and recorded objectively. In the case of addiction, these things are behaviours and physiological events. Perhaps, we can therefore turn to operant learning for a complete and simple explanation of the whole shooting match and discard the previous notions of rational conscious choice, whether stable or unstable. Those things are fine for everyday language but have no place in scientific discourse.

Habit is not enough

Can we explain addiction in terms of cue–response patterns underpinned by the activity of the nervous system? Unfortunately not, at least not at the moment.

Ultimately we may have a good-enough understanding of neural circuitry to achieve this but that day looks a long way off. The problem is that it will require us to apply this level of explanation to what are in the real world very complex and variable behaviour patterns. To explain this, it is useful to introduce the term 'foraging'.

Plans and 'foraging'

Under a cue–response explanation, we postulate learned associations between cues and responses: the dog trainer says 'sit', the animal 'sits' and is rewarded with a pat on the head or food. The drug addict may show some of this relatively simple cue–response behaviour but addiction goes far beyond this. A heroin addict will often be resourceful and adaptable in first of all getting the funds to get his next fix or two, and then in finding a dealer from whom to get the supplies. The action chain that leads to the eventual reward is flexible and capable of being adjusted to meet the demands of the situation. In principle, the addict may do something he has never ever done if he has a vision that it will bring his goal closer. What we have is foraging behaviour in which an addict has a need or a goal, and engages in activities that use whatever mental and physical resources he or she has at his or her disposal to achieve that goal.

For a non-human animal that activity might involve moving about, going to places that have served it well in the past, or setting up in a favourable location, such as a waterhole if that animal happens to be a lion and waiting for food to come to it. For a human it could involve something as simple as trying to find a shop that is open at 3 a.m. so as to buy a packet of cigarettes, to something as complex as conning a posh restaurant out of a bottle of champagne so that one can sell it and obtain money for a heroin fix. It frequently requires mental calculation of what will happen if certain things are tried.

These kinds of behaviours would be all but impossible to explain or understand in cue–response terms. However, they are extremely easy to understand by the simple expedient of assuming that the individual has a goal in mind and uses the means at his or her disposal to reach that goal. The individual has a plan of some sort.

What mentalist concepts give us, therefore, is an ability to explain and predict behaviour simply that can only be predicted badly or not at all by models of cue–response associations. Preferences and choices and all the other elements of the theory we started with did not establish themselves as the dominant common-sense model for no reason: they are simple and they work a lot of the time.

So operant learning provides us with a necessary set of concepts to explain elements of addiction but it cannot reasonably do the whole job of explaining and predicting addictive behaviour. In the process of demonstrating this, the term 'foraging' was introduced and the term 'plan' was also sneaked in.

The fact that people make plans is uncontroversial. It is therefore strange how little the notion of plans features in theories of motivation in general and addiction in particular (with some notable exceptions; see e.g. Miller et al. 1960 and Mook

1996). If you step back and look at our behaviour, most of it is guided at some level by plans. We look ahead to things that we want to achieve and work out how to get them. Those plans are subject to interruption, change, frustration and elaboration. Sometimes they are fully formed and detailed and sometimes they are incomplete and vague. None of this is controversial and it is impossible to interact with each other without recognising these basic facts of life.

Routines

While we are looking at the big picture we must also recognise that much of our life is governed by routines. There are various things we normally do that occupy our days. Our lives are more or less compartmentalised into personal routines such as showering, domestic routines such as preparing breakfast, taking the children to school, and so on, working and leisure. Routines are not habits because they can involve many different behaviours related to the same routine and they usually involve conscious acts of will. Routines are plans that are triggered automatically by particular conditions, including time of day, as a result of repetition.

This is all obvious but that does not stop it from having to be factored into the understanding of motivation and even addiction. Heroin addicts, like the rest of us, develop routines. Many of them have some kind of structure in their lives around getting funds, obtaining supplies and using those supplies. Smoking behaviour is different in that it can accompany many behaviours but as the social rules change and smoking restrictions increase, smokers need to set aside time to engage in the activity and that time will tend to become routine. For example, many smokers in offices will have a routine for taking smoking breaks.

Addiction, choice, compulsion and habit

It seems that addiction needs more than a simple theory of choice and more than operant learning. It requires a range of elements to be postulated, none of which is fanciful and in fact all of which are known to exist. The development of the theory has followed the rule of parsimony but has ended up with a theory with a large number of elements, so many in fact that, for many of the big observations, there are several possible explanations within the terms of the theory.

There seems to be no way of avoiding this. In the book thus far, we have considered a range of different theories that have invoked a still greater range of concepts to understand addiction. The list of key concepts provided in Table 7.2 is not comprehensive (that would constitute a dictionary of addiction) but conveys the variety and diversity of concepts involved. Yet, none of the individual constructs or ideas presented constitutes a conceptual advance on what is out there already. The only contribution that has been made is to collect together the disparate elements that are needed for the theory: we have the ingredients but we do not have the recipe.

What we need now is a set of guiding principles to pull the whole thing together.

Table 7.2 Key concepts used in theories of addiction (adapted from West 2013)

Abstinence violation effect (AVE)	A psychological process whereby a lapse leads to relapse. It involves a loss of motivation and self-efficacy.
Actions (also 'behaviours')	Discrete, coordinated chunks of behaviour
Analysis	Thought processes involving calculation, inference and comparison
Anxiety	An aversive and also motivational trait or state involving worry about adverse future events. Addictive behaviours may reduce it acutely but increase it chronically.
Associative learning	A process whereby patterns of brain activity representing perceptions, emotions or response organisation become linked so that when a particular pattern occurs, another is made more likely to occur. In addiction, associative learning plays a pivotal role with drug cues coming to generate feelings of desire or impulses.
Attentional bias	A non-conscious tendency to focus attention on particular types of object or features of objects; a form of cognitive bias
Automatic processes	Events in the brain that do not involve self-conscious reflection and analysis; and mental states arising from these, including feelings
Autonomy	Part of identity: a belief in one's independence or freedom
Behaviour	The continuous flow of activity involving voluntary muscles
Behaviour pattern	Repeated occurrences of behaviours
Beliefs	Mental representations of objects, events or situations in the form of propositions held to be true
Choice	A process whereby alternative courses of action are imagined and one of them selected through a process of reflective analysis
Cognition	Strictly, the process of creating and modifying mental representations but often specifically limited to beliefs
Cognitive bias	A non-conscious tendency to preferentially process information or form mental representations of particular types of object or features of objects in the environment
Cognitive control	Influence of reflective thought on responses
Compulsion	Experience of a strong, sometimes irresistible, impulse to perform an act

Table 7.2 (*Continued*)

Consciousness	The content of subjective experience when awake; includes feelings, perceptions, memories, beliefs and abstract ideas; distinguished from self-consciousness
Cost	Negative consequence or consequences of performing an act
Craving	Strong desire or feeling of powerful urge to do something
Decision	The process involved in determining a course of action following reflective analysis; also the outcome of that process
Decision framing	A way of representing a decision problem and the possible outcomes from each option
Depression	Feeling of gloom often accompanied by belief in own inadequacy and worthlessness; can involve physical symptoms of tiredness and motor retardation
Desire	Feeling of want or need for some imagined state of affairs
Dissonance	A feeling of discomfort attached to conflict between beliefs
Dopamine	A neurotransmitter which, when it attaches to receptors in the nucleus accumbens is believed to lead to experience of pleasure (in the shell of the accumbens) or increased incentive salience (in the core of the accumbens)
Ego-depletion	Lowered mental energy needed for the exercise of self-control
Emotion (generalised)	Experience of generalised feelings of happiness, anger, anxiety, etc.
Emotion (targeted)	Experience of feeling about something such as liking, hating and enjoying
Environmental stress	Events or conditions that can lead to anxiety or depression
Evaluations	Beliefs about the degree to which something is good or bad in some way, for example, harmful versus beneficial, morally right or wrong
Executive dysfunction	Impaired ability for reflective control over behaviour
Expectancy	Expected outcome from an action and the expected utility of that outcome
Feelings	Experiences of emotions, desires and urges
Habit	A process whereby, as a result of learning, stimuli influence responses without the requirement for reflective thought

(*continued*)

Table 7.2 (*Continued*)

Habituation	Reduced responsiveness as a result of repeated or continuing exposure to a stimulus
Hyperbolic discounting	A tendency to discount (attach reduced utility to) costs and benefits to a greater degree early in the imagined future
Goal	An imagined state of affairs that is the object of desire (affective goal) or evaluation (cognitive goal)
Identity	Mental representations (thoughts and images) of the self as one is or aspires to be and feelings associated with these
Imitation	A process whereby an individual copies all or some of the features of another person; the process may not be intentional
Impulse	A coordinated action schema which, if unopposed will result in an action
Impulsivity	A tendency to react to stimuli without, or despite, reflection
Incentive salience	An attribute of 'wanting' attached to reward-predicting stimuli
Inhibition	A process by which a response is suppressed
Intention	A self-conscious decision to undertake an action
Lapse	An instance in which a personal rule is violated but the rule is still considered to be in operation
Liking	A feeling of anticipated pleasure or enjoyment associated with an object or event
Modelling	A process whereby a behaviour occurs and all or some of its features are copied by another
Motivation	Processes within the brain that energise and direct behaviour; not limited to reasoned choice
Motivational bias	A tendency to favour a given course of action or value a given outcome as a result of factors that lie outside of conscious awareness
Motive	A feeling of desire (i.e. want or need) to attain an imagined state of affairs
Need	A kind of desire involving anticipated relief from mental or physical discomfort
Negative reinforcement	A process whereby a behaviour is induced or maintained in anticipation (not necessarily conscious) of avoidance of or escape from an aversive stimuli
Norms	Behaviour patterns or beliefs that are widely enacted or held within a population, subpopulation or group
Norms (descriptive)	Beliefs about how widespread a behaviour pattern or belief is in a population, subpopulation or group

Table 7.2 (*Continued*)

Norms (prescriptive)	Beliefs about what a population, subpopulation or group considers to be good or bad
Norms (subjective)	Beliefs about what significant others consider to be good or bad weighted by the importance one attaches to such views
Observational learning	Acquisition of information or skills through observation of the behaviour of others and the outcomes of those behaviours
Opportunity	A set of environmental factors that make a behaviour possible
Perceived control	The extent to which people believe they can enact a given behaviour (similar to self-efficacy)
Physical dependence	In relation to a drug, a condition of the CNS such that reduced concentrations or absence of the drug results in an adverse physiological reaction
Plan	A self-conscious intention to perform an act in the future
Pleasure	Addicts gain pleasure from their addictive behaviour and that motivates them to engage with the behaviour in future
Positive reinforcement	A process whereby a behaviour is induced or maintained in anticipation (not necessarily conscious) of experience of a positive stimulus
Price	The amount of money needing to be paid to acquire something or benefit from a service
Reflective thought	Self-conscious analysis of information in the form of propositions and thoughts arising from these
Relapse	Abandonment of a personal rule governing behaviour
Relief	A positive feeling that follows removal of mental or physical discomfort
Response	Reaction to a stimulus in the form of feeling, thought or behaviour
Reward	An event that increases the probability of a behaviour that it follows, often involving pleasure, satisfaction or relief
Risk taking	Behaviours as a result of which there is a significant probability of harm or failure to mitigate harm
Rule	A plan that is applicable beyond just one occurrence
Self-consciousness	Experience of the self that is necessary for reflective, executive control of thoughts and actions
Self-control	A process whereby intentions are enacted in the face of desires or impulses arising from other sources; part of self-regulation

(*continued*)

Table 7.2 (*Continued*)

Self-determination	A belief in one's power to control one's own behaviour and experience
Self-efficacy	A belief in one's capability to enact a behaviour or achieve a particular outcome
Self-regulation	A process in which plans and reflective choices govern behaviour
Sensitisation	An increase in magnitude of a response as a result of continued or repeated exposure to the stimulus
Social influence	A process whereby thoughts, feelings and behaviour are influenced by other people. This can be through a variety of mechanisms including actual or anticipated reinforcement and modelling.
Stress	A negative feeling arising from adverse environmental conditions or events, or expectation of these
Subjective expected utility	The expected perceived value of an outcome from choosing an option that takes into account the likelihood that it will occur if that option is chosen
System	A set of causally interacting elements
Temporal discounting	A tendency to attribute lower utility to outcomes of similar objective value as a function of how far in the future they are expected to occur
Urges	Feelings of impulse to engage in an action
Utility (also subjective utility)	Perceived personal value attaching to an outcome
Value	Objectively specified worth of something
Values	Beliefs about what is morally or ethically right or wrong
Want	A feeling of anticipated pleasure or satisfaction attaching to an imagined future
Well-being	A feeling of being content and happy
Withdrawal symptoms	Temporary adverse reportable changes to physical or mental functioning resulting from reduction or termination of a drug to which the body has become adapted

The definitions represent an attempt to capture the essence of the constructs as used by researchers in the field rather than choose between different explicit formulations.

References

Adan, A., Prat, G. and Sánchez-Turet, M. (2004) Effects of nicotine dependence on diurnal variations of subjective activation and mood. *Addiction* 99(12): 1599–1607.

Ajzen, I. (1991) The theory of planned behavior. *Organ Behav Hum Decis Process* 50(2): 179–211.

Baker, T.E., Stockwell, T., Barnes, G. and Holroyd, C.B. (2011) Individual differences in substance dependence: at the intersection of brain, behaviour and cognition. *Addic Biol* 16(3): 458–466.

Balfour, D.J. (2004) The neurobiology of tobacco dependence: a preclinical perspective on the role of the dopamine projections to the nucleus accumbens [corrected]. *Nicotine Tob Res* 6(6): 899–912.

Bandura, A. (1977) Self-efficacy: toward a unifying theory of behavioral change. *Psychol Rev* 84(2): 191–215.

Baron, J. (2000) *Thinking and Deciding*, Cambridge University Press, Cambridge.

Baumeister, R.F., Heatherton, T.F. and Tice, D.M. (1994) *Losing Control: How and Why People Fail at Self-regulation*. Academic Press, San Diego, CA.

Baumeister, R.F. and Vohs, K.D. (2007) Self-Regulation, ego depletion, and motivation. *Social Personal Psychol Compass* 1(1): 115–128.

Baxter, B.W. and Hinson, R.E. (2001) Is smoking automatic? Demands of smoking behavior on attentional resources. *J Abnorm Psychol* 110(1): 59–66.

Becker, G.S. and Murphy, K.M. (1988) A theory of rational addiction. *J Polit Econ* 96(4): 675–700.

Berridge, K.C. and Robinson, T.E. (2011) Drug addiction as incentive sensitization. In *Addiction and Responsibility*, (eds. J. Poland and G. Graham), pp. 21–54. MIT Press, Cambridge, Massachusetts.

Bickel, W.K., Miller, M.L., Yi, R., Kowal, B.P., Lindquist, D.M. and Pitcock, J.A. (2007) Behavioral and neuroeconomics of drug addiction: competing neural systems and temporal discounting processes. *Drug Alcohol Depend* 90(Suppl. 1), S85.

Blaszczynski, A. and Nower, L. (2002) A pathways model of problem and pathological gambling. *Addiction* 97(5): 487–99.

Blume, A.W. and Schmaling, K.B. (1996) Loss and readiness to change substance abuse. *Addict Behav* 21(4): 527–530.

Borland, R., Young, D., Coghill, K. and Zhang, J.Y. (2010) The tobacco use management system: analyzing tobacco control from a systems perspective. *Am J Public Health* 100(7): 1229–1236.

Brewer, J.A. and Potenza, M.N. (2008) The neurobiology and genetics of impulse control disorders: relationships to drug addictions. *Biochem Pharmacol* 75(1): 63–75.

Cacioppo, J.T. and Petty, R.E. (1984) The elaboration likelihood model of persuasion. In *Adv Consum Res Volume 11*, (ed. T. C. Kinnear), 673–675. Association for Consumer Research, Provo, Utah.

Cawley, J., Markowitz, S. and Tauras, J. (2004) Lighting up and slimming down: the effects of body weight and cigarette prices on adolescent smoking initiation (Research Support, Non-U.S. Gov't). *J Health Econ* 23(2): 293–311. doi: 10.1016/j.jhealeco.2003.12.003

Cooper, M.L., Frone, M.R., Russell, M. and Mudar, P. (1995) Drinking to regulate positive and negative emotions: a motivational model of alcohol use. *J Pers Soc Psychol* 69(5): 990–1005.

Dadds, M.R. and Salmon, K. (2003) Punishment insensitivity and parenting: temperament and learning as interacting risks for antisocial behavior. *Clin Child Fam Psychol Rev* **6**(2): 69–86.

Dalley, J.W., Everitt, B.J. and Robbins, T.W. (2011) Impulsivity, compulsivity, and top-down cognitive control. *Neuron* **69**(4): 680–694.

de Savigny, D. and Adam, T. (2009) *Systems Thinking for Health Systems Strengthening*. World Health Organization, Geneva.

de Wit, H. and Phan, L. (2010) Positive reinforcement theories of drug use. In *Substance Abuse and Emotion*, (ed. J.D. Kassel), pp. 43–60. American Psychological Association, Washington, DC.

Deci, E.L., Eghrari, H., Patrick, B.C. and Leone, D.R. (1994) Facilitating internalization: the self-determination theory perspective. *J Pers* **62**(1): 119–142.

Deci, E.L. and Ryan, R.M. (2012) An overview of self-determination theory. In *The Oxford Handbook of Human Motivation*, (ed. R.M. Ryan). pp. 85–107. Oxford University Press, Oxford.

Di Chiara, G. (1999) Drug addiction as dopamine-dependent associative learning disorder. *Eur J Pharmacol* **375**(1–3): 13–30.

Eddy, N.B., Halbach, H., Isbell, H. and Seevers, M.H. (1965) Drug dependence: its significance and characteristics. *Bull World Health Organ* **32**(5): 721–733.

Edwards, W. (1961) Behavioral decision theory. *Annu Rev Psychol* **12**(1). 473–498.

Einstein, S. and Epstein, A. (1980) Cigarette smoking contagion. *Int J Addict* **15**(1): 107–114.

Evans, W.D. (2006) How social marketing works in health care. *BMJ* **332**(7551): 1207–1210.

Everitt, B.J., Belin, D., Economidou, D., Pelloux, Y., Dalley, J.W. and Robbins, T.W. (2008) Neural mechanisms underlying the vulnerability to develop compulsive drug-seeking habits and addiction. *Philos Trans R Soc Lond B Biol Sci* **363**(1507): 3125–3135.

Everitt, B.J. and Robbins, T.W. (2005) Neural systems of reinforcement for drug addiction: from actions to habits to compulsion. *Nat Neurosci* **8**(11): 1481–1489.

Fernández-Serrano, M.J., Pérez-García, M., Perales, J.C. and Verdejo-García, A. (2010) Prevalence of executive dysfunction in cocaine, heroin and alcohol users enrolled in therapeutic communities. *Eur J Pharmacol* **626**(1): 104–112.

Ferrence, R. (1996) Using diffusion theory in health promotion: the case of tobacco. *Can J Public Health* **87**(Suppl. 2): S24–S27.

Ferrence, R. (2001). Diffusion theory and drug use. *Addiction* **96**(1): 165–173.

Festinger, L. (1957) *A Theory of Cognitive Dissonance*. Stanford University Press, Stanford, CA.

Fidler, J.A. and West, R. (2011) Enjoyment of smoking and urges to smoke as predictors of attempts and success of attempts to stop smoking: a longitudinal study. *Drug Alcohol Depend* **115**(1–2): 30–34.

Field, M. and Cox, W.M. (2008) Attentional bias in addictive behaviors: a review of its development, causes, and consequences. *Drug Alcohol Depend* **97**(1–2): 1–20.

Finn, P.R., Kessler, D.N. and Hussong, A.M. (1994) Risk for alcoholism and classical conditioning to signals for punishment: evidence for a weak behavioral inhibition system? *J Abnorm Psychol* **103**(2): 293–301.

Flores, P.J. (2004) *Addiction as an Attachment Disorder*. Jason Aronson Incorporated, New York.

Foltin, R.W. and Fischman, M.W. (1991) Smoked and intravenous cocaine in humans: acute tolerance, cardiovascular and subjective effects. *J Pharmacol Exp Ther* 257(1): 247–261.

French, M.T., Browntaylor, D. and Bluthenthal, R.N. (2006) Price elasticity of demand for malt liquor beer: findings from a US pilot study. *Soc Sci Med* 62(9): 2101–2111.

Gallet, C.A. and List, J.A. (2003) Cigarette demand: a meta-analysis of elasticities. *Health Econ* 12(10): 821–835.

Gariti, P., Alterman, A.I., Barber, W., Bedi, N., Luck, G. and Cnaan, A. (1999) Cotinine replacement levels for a 21 mg/day transdermal nicotine patch in an outpatient treatment setting. *Drug Alcohol Depend* 54(2): 111–116.

Gelkopf, M., Levitt, S. and Bleich, A. (2002) An integration of three approaches to addiction and methadone maintenance treatment: the self-medication hypothesis, the disease model and social criticism. *Isr J Psychiatry Relat Sci* 39(2): 140–151.

George, O., Le Moal, M. and Koob, G.F. (2012) Allostasis and addiction: role of the dopamine and corticotropin-releasing factor systems. *Physiol Behav* 106(1): 58–64.

Gerrard, M., Gibbons, F.X., Houlihan, A.E., Stock, M.L. and Pomery, E.A. (2008) A dual-process approach to health risk decision making: the prototype willingness model. *Dev Rev* 28(1): 29–61.

Goldstein, R.Z. and Volkow, N.D. (2011) Dysfunction of the prefrontal cortex in addiction: neuroimaging findings and clinical implications. *Nat Rev Neurosci* 12(11): 652–669.

Gollwitzer, P.M. (1999) Implementation intentions: strong effects of simple plans *Am Psychol* 54(7): 493–503.

Hariri, A.R. (2009) The neurobiology of individual differences in complex behavioral traits. *Annu Rev Neurosci* 32: 225–247.

Harris, P.R. and Epton, T. (2009) The impact of self-affirmation on health cognition, health behaviour and other health-related responses: a narrative review. *Social Person Psychol Compass* 3(6): 962–978.

Hart, C.L., Haney, M., Foltin, R.W. and Fischman, M.W. (2000) Alternative reinforcers differentially modify cocaine self-administration by humans. *Behav Pharmacol* 11(1): 87–91.

Hastings, G. (2007) *Social Marketing: Why Should the Devil Have all the Best Tunes?* Butterworth-Heinemann, Oxford.

Hastings, G. and McDermott, L. (2006) Putting social marketing into practice. *BMJ* 332(7551): 1210–1212.

Hayes, S.C., Strosahl, K.D. and Wilson, K.G. (1999) *Acceptance and Commitment Therapy: An Experiential Approach to Behavior Change*. Guilford Press, New York.

Hendershot, C.S., Witkiewitz, K., George, W.H. and Marlatt, G.A. (2011) Relapse prevention for addictive behaviors. *Subst Abuse Treat Prev Policy* 6(1): 17.

Hester, R. and Garavan, H. (2004) Executive dysfunction in cocaine addiction: evidence for discordant frontal, cingulate, and cerebellar activity. *J Neurosci* 24(49): 11017–11022.

Heyes, C. (2011) Automatic imitation. *Psychol Bull* 137(3): 463.

Hussong, A.M., Jones, D.J., Stein, G.L., Baucom, D.H. and Boeding, S. (2011) An internalizing pathway to alcohol use and disorder. *Psychol Addict Behav* 25(3): 390–404.

Janis, I.L. and Mann, L. (1977) *Decision Making: A Psychological Analysis of Conflict, Choice and Commitment*. The Free Press, New York.

Jarvis, M. and Wardle, J. (1999) Social patterning of individual health behaviours: the case of cigarette smoking. In *Social Determinants of Health*, (eds M. Marmot and R. Wilkinson). Oxford University Press, Oxford.

Jellinek, E.M. (1960) *The Disease Concept of Alcoholism.* Hillhouse Press, New Brunswick, NJ.

John, R.M. (2008) Price elasticity estimates for tobacco products in India. *Health Policy Plan* **23**(3): 200–209.

Jones, B.T., Corbin, W. and Fromme, K. (2001) A review of expectancy theory and alcohol consumption. *Addiction* **96**(1): 57–72.

Kanayama, G., Brower, K.J., Wood, R.I., Hudson, J.I. and Pope, H.G. Jr. (2009) Anabolic–androgenic steroid dependence: an emerging disorder. *Addiction* **104**(12): 1966–1978.

Kandel, D.B. (2002) *Stages and Pathways of Drug Involvement: Examining the Gateway Hypothesis.* Cambridge University Press, New York.

Kandel, D.B., Yamaguchi, K. and Chen, K. (1992) Stages of progression in drug involvement from adolescence to adulthood: further evidence for the gateway theory. *J Stud Alcohol* **53**(5):447–57.

Kearney, M.H. and O'Sullivan, J. (2003) Identity shifts as turning points in health behavior change. *West J Nurs Res* **25**(2): 134–152.

Keeney, R.L. and Raiffa, H. (1993) *Decisions with Multiple Objectives: Preferences and Value Trade-offs.* Cambridge University Press, Cambridge.

Khantzian, E.J. (1997) The self-medication hypothesis of substance use disorders: a reconsideration and recent applications. *Harv Rev Psychiatry* **4**(5): 231–244.

Koob, G.F. (2008) Hedonic homeostatic dysregulation as a driver of drug-seeking behavior. *Drug Discov Today Dis Models* **5**(4): 207–215.

Koob, G.F., Maldonado, R. and Stinus, L. (1992) Neural substrates of opiate withdrawal. *Trends Neurosci* **15**(5): 186–191.

Larimer, M.E., Palmer, R.S. and Marlatt, G.A. (1999) Relapse prevention. An overview of Marlatt's cognitive-behavioral model. *Alcohol Res Health* **23**(2): 151–160.

Latour, B. (2005) *Reassembling the Social—An Introduction to Actor-Network-Theory.* Oxford University Press, Oxford.

Liu, J.L., Liu, J.T., Hammitt, J.K. and Chou, S.Y. (1999) The price elasticity of opium in Taiwan, 1914-1942. *J Health Econ* **18**(6): 795–810.

Lubman, D.I., Yucel, M. and Pantelis, C. (2004) Addiction, a condition of compulsive behaviour? Neuroimaging and neuropsychological evidence of inhibitory dysregulation. *Addiction* **99**(12): 1491–1502.

Madoz-Gúrpide, A., Blasco-Fontecilla, H., Baca-García, E. and Ochoa-Mangado, E. (2011) Executive dysfunction in chronic cocaine users: an exploratory study. *Drug Alcohol Depend* **117**(1): 55–58.

Marlatt, G.A. and George, W.H. (1984) Relapse prevention: introduction and overview of the model. *Br J Addict* **79**(3): 261–273.

McAuliffe, W.E. and Gordon, R.A. (1974) A test of Lindesmith's theory of addiction: the frequency of euphoria among long-term addicts. *AJS* **79**(4): 795–840.

McCusker, C.G. (2001) Cognitive biases and addiction: an evolution in theory and method. *Addiction* **96**(1): 47–56.

Miller, E.K. and Cohen, J.D. (2001) An integrative theory of prefrontal cortex function. *Annu Rev Neurosci* **24**(1): 167–202.

Miller, G., Galanter, E. and Pribram, K. (1960) *Plans and the Structure of Behaviour.* Holt, Rinehart & Winston, New York.

Mook, D.G. (1996) *Motivation: The Organization of Action.* W.W. Norton, New York.

Muller, D.J., Likhodi, O. and Heinz, A. (2010) Neural markers of genetic vulnerability to drug addiction. *Curr Top Behav Neurosci* **3**: 277–299.

Mytton, O., Gray, A., Rayner, M. and Rutter, H. (2007) Could targeted food taxes improve health?. *J Epidemiol Community Health* **61**(8): 689–694.

Mytton, O.T., Clarke, D. and Rayner, M. (2012) Taxing unhealthy food and drinks to improve health. *BMJ* **344**: e2931.

Nevin, J.A. and Grace, R.C. (2000) Behavioral momentum and the law of effect. *Behav Brain Sci* **23**(1): 73–90.

Norcross, J.C., Krebs, P.M. and Prochaska, J.O. (2011) Stages of change. *Br J Clin Psychol* **67**(2): 143–154.

Norregaard, J., Tonnesen, P. and Petersen, L. (1993) Predictors and reasons for relapse in smoking cessation with nicotine and placebo patches. *Prev Med* **22**(2): 261–271.

Nower, L. and Blaszczynski, A. (2004) The pathways model as harm minimization for youth gamblers in educational settings. *Child Adolesc Social Work J* **21**(1): 25–45.

O'Riordan, W. (1969) Price elasticity of demand for tobacco in Ireland. *Econ Soc Rev* **1**: 109–115.

Orford, J. (2001) Addiction as excessive appetite. *Addiction* **96**(1): 15–31.

Pates, R., McBride, A. and Arnold K, eds. (2005). *Injecting Illicit Drugs*. Blackwell Publishing, Oxford.

Pattij, T., Broersen, L.M., Peter, S. and Olivier, B. (2004) Impulsive-like behavior in differential-reinforcement-of-low-rate 36 s responding in mice depends on training history. *Neurosci Lett* **354**(2): 169–171.

Perkins, K.A., Jetton, C., Stolinski, A., Fonte, C. and Conklin, C.A. (2003) The consistency of acute responses to nicotine in humans. *Nicotine Tob Res* **5**(6): 877–884.

Petty, R.E., Baker, S.M. and Gleicher, F. (1991) Attitudes and drug abuse prevention: implications of the elaboration likelihood model of persuasion. In *Persuasive communication and drug abuse prevention* (eds. L. Donohew, H.E. Sypher and W.J. Bukoski). Lawrence Erlbaum Associates, Hillsdale, NJ.

Petty, R.E. and Briñol, P. (2012) The elaboration likelihood model. In *Handbook of Theories of Social Psychology*, (eds P.A.M. Van Lange, A. Kruglanski and E.T. Higgins). pp. 224–245. England: Sage, London.

Prochaska, J.O., DiClemente, C.C. and Norcross, J.C. (1992) In search of how people change. Applications to addictive behaviors. *Am Psychol* **47**(9): 1102–1114.

Rende, R., Slomkowski, C., Lloyd-Richardson, F. and Niaura, R. (2005) Sibling effects on substance use in adolescence: social contagion and genetic relatedness. *J Fam Psychol* **19**(4): 611–618.

Rigotti, N.A., McKool, K.M. and Shiffman, S. (1994) Predictors of smoking cessation after coronary artery bypass graft surgery. Results of a randomized trial with 5-year follow-up. *Ann Intern Med* **120**(4): 287–293.

Riley, W.T., Rivera, D.E., Atienza, A.A., Nilsen, W., Allison, S.M. and Mermelstein, R. (2011) Health behavior models in the age of mobile interventions: are our theories up to the task? *Transl Behav Med* **1**(1): 53–71.

Rogers, R.W. and Prentice-Dunn, S. (1997) Protection motivation theory. In *Handbook of Health Behavior Research: Personal and Social Determinants* (eds. D.S. Gochman), pp. 113–132. Plenum Press, New York.

Ryan, R.M. and Deci, E.L. (2000) Self-determination theory and the facilitation of intrinsic motivation, social development, and well-being. *Am Psychol* **55**(1): 68–78.

Schultz, W. (2011) Potential vulnerabilities of neuronal reward, risk, and decision mechanisms to addictive drugs. *Neuron* **69**(4): 603–617.

Sheeran, P., Milne, S., Webb, T.L. and Gollwitzer, P.M. (2005) Implementation Intentions and Health Behaviour. In *Predicting Health Behaviour*, (eds. M. Conner and P. Norman). pp. 276–323. Open University Press, New York.

Sher, K.J., Walitzer, K.S., Wood, P.K. and Brent, E.E. (1991) Characteristics of children of alcoholics: putative risk factors, substance use and abuse, and psychopathology. *J Abnorm Psychol* 100(4): 427–448.

Skog, O.J. (2000). Addicts' choice. *Addiction* 95(9): 1309–1314.

Skog, O.J. (2003). Addiction: definition and mechanisms. In *Choice, Behavioural Economics and Addiction*, (eds R.E. Vuchinich and N. Heather). pp. 157–175. Pergamon, Amsterdam.

Slovic, P., Finucane, M.L., Peters, E. and MacGregor D.G. (2002) The affect heuristic. In *Intuitive Judgment: Heuristics and Biases*, (eds T. Gilovich, D. Griffin and D. Kahneman). pp. 397–420. Cambridge University Press, New York.

Slovic, P., Finucane, M.L., Peters, E. and MacGregor, D.G. (2007) The affect heuristic. *Eur J Oper Res* 177(3): 1333–1352.

Smith, K.P. and Christakis, N.A. (2008) Social networks and health. *Annu Rev Sociol* 34(1): 405–429.

Solomon, R.L. (1980). The opponent-process theory of acquired motivation: the costs of pleasure and the benefits of pain. *Am Psychol* 35(8): 691–712.

Solomon, R.L. and Corbit, J.D. (1973) An opponent-process theory of motivation. II. Cigarette addiction. *J Abnorm Psychol* 81(2): 158–171.

Solomon, R.L. and Corbit, J.D. (1974) An opponent-process theory of motivation. I. Temporal dynamics of affect. *Psychol Rev* 81(2): 119–145.

Swan, G.E., Ward, M.M. and Jack, L.M. (1996) Abstinence effects as predictors of 28-day relapse in smokers. *Addict Behav* 21(4): 481–490.

Tversky, A. and Kahneman, D. (1992) Advances in prospect theory: cumulative representation of uncertainty. *J Risk Uncertainty* 5(4): 297–323.

van Honk, J., Schutter, D.J., Hermans, E.J., Putman, P., Tuiten, A., and Koppeschaar, H. (2004) Testosterone shifts the balance between sensitivity for punishment and reward in healthy young women. *Psychoneuroendocrinology* 29(7): 937–943.

Van Ours, J.C. (1995) The price elasticity of hard drugs: the case of opium in the Dutch East Indies, 1923-1938. *J Polit Econ* 103(2): 261–279.

Vangeli, E., Stapleton, J., Smit, E.S., Borland, R. and West, R. (2011) Predictors of attempts to stop smoking and their success in adult general population samples: a systematic review. *Addiction* 106(12): 2110–2121.

Vangeli, E., Stapleton, J. and West, R. (2010). Smoking intentions and mood preceding lapse after completion of treatment to aid smoking cessation. *Patient Educ Couns* 81(2): 267–271.

Vohs, K.D. and Baumeister, R.F. (2011) *Handbook of Self-regulation: Research, Theory, and Applications*. The Guilford Press, New York.

Walters, G.D. (1996) Addiction and identity: exploring the possibility of a relationship. *Psychol Addict Behav* 10(1): 9–17.

West, R. (1995) Nicotine is addictive: the issue of free choice. In *The Effects of Nicotine on Biological Systems II*, (eds P. Clarke, M. Quik, P. Adlkofer and P. Thuraux). pp. 265–272. Birkhauser, Berlin.

West, R. (2009) The multiple facets of cigarette addiction and what they mean for encouraging and helping smokers to stop. *COPD* 6(4): 277–283.

West, R. (2013) Models of Addiction. European Monitoring Centre for Drugs and Drug Addiction, Lisbon, Portugal.

West, R. and Shiffman, S. (2004) *Smoking Cessation*. Health Press, Oxford.

West, R.J., Hajek, P. and Belcher M. (1989) Severity of withdrawal symptoms as a predictor of outcome of an attempt to quit smoking. *Psychol Med* **19**(4): 981–985.

Wonnacott, S., Sidhpura, N. and Balfour D.J. (2005) Nicotine: from molecular mechanisms to behaviour. *Curr Opin Pharmacol* **5**(1): 53–59.

Young, D., Borland, R. and Coghill, K. (2010) An actor-network theory analysis of policy innovation for smoke-free places: understanding change in complex systems. *Am J Public Health* **100**(7): 1208–1217.

Young, D., Borland, R. and Coghill, K. (2012) Changing the tobacco use management system: blending systems thinking with actor–network theory. *Rev Policy Res* **29**(2): 251–279.

Chapter 8

A SYNTHETIC THEORY OF MOTIVATION

This chapter sets out a second draft of a synthetic theory of motivation (PRIME Theory) to provide a basis for a theory of addiction. It sets this within a broader model of behaviour, the COM-B model, which recognises that capability, opportunity and motivation all interact with behaviour as a dynamic system. The motivational theory needs to be able to provide a common framework for conscious choice processes and non-conscious motivational systems. It also needs to describe common mechanisms underlying apparently diverse patterns of addictive behaviour. Finally, it needs to set out the principles underlying the developmental process by which addiction and recovery from addiction occur.

Understanding behaviour in context: the COM-B model

We have now arrived at the point in the journey where we can put what we have discovered together in an attempt to understand why some people develop powerful motivations to behave in ways that harm themselves or others even though that is not what they particularly want. Before focusing on their motivation, it is important to set this in the context of a broader model of behaviour.

The model that we adopt takes a general form that has been re-iterated over centuries in one form or another (Michie et al. 2011). It is referred to as the COM-B model because it recognises that for any BEHAVIOUR to occur, three conditions must be present: the person must have the physical and psychological CAPABILITY to perform it; they must have the physical and social OPPORTUNITY to engage in it; and they must be more MOTIVATED to engage in it at the relevant moment than some other behaviour (see Figure 8.1).

This simple analysis leads to a conceptualisation of behaviour that has been present in society for many centuries, and indeed is embedded in the legal system. In order to convict someone of a crime in the United States, one has to show means (or capability), motive and opportunity. If any of these three are lacking, then the defendant cannot have committed the crime. Of course, there is nothing special about criminal acts in this regard; capability, motivation and opportunity must be present for any behaviour to occur.

Theory of Addiction, Second Edition. Robert West and Jamie Brown.
© 2013 John Wiley & Sons, Ltd. Published 2013 by John Wiley & Sons, Ltd.

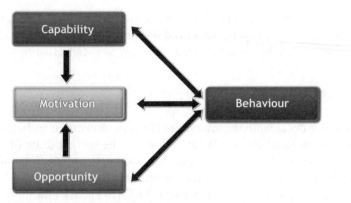

Figure 8.1 The COM-B system for analysing behaviour in context.

Capability refers to the physical or psychological capacity to engage in the behaviour in question. This capacity resides within the individual. It includes knowledge and understanding as well as physical and mental skills and facilities such as strength and stamina. It also includes the capability to resist impulses to engage in an action as well as the ability to engage in an action.

Opportunity refers to the environmental factors that permit a behaviour to occur or that promote it. This may involve the physical environment, including, for example, availability of a given drug or cues that prompt people to consider taking the drug as an option. It also includes time and financial resources. It also involves the social environment including social mores, which make it possible to entertain the idea of using a drug.

Motivation will be dealt with in more detail in the remainder of this chapter, but it refers to all those brain processes that energise and direct behaviour including 'reflective' processes of conscious thought and analysis, and 'automatic' processes that we share with other species involving feelings and impulses.

The COM-B system provides a way of generating a high-level analysis of an ongoing behaviour pattern as well as a way of identifying what would need to change in order to change that pattern. It can be applied at the level of populations, sub-populations, social groups or individuals. Therefore, in principle, it could form the basis for an individual assessment of an addict or a generalisation about a population. It is not a psychological model, a sociological model nor an environmental one. It seeks to treat the individual or population as part of a system with interacting components.

The systems approach that the COM-B model represents is reflected in arrows denoting potential influence between the components as well as patterns of influence within each component (Figure 8.1). Thus, it is clear that capability to engage in a behaviour can influence motivation to engage in it, as can opportunity. Engaging in the behaviour then can influence motivation, capability and opportunity.

With regard to addictions, powerful motivation lies at the heart of the problem but there may be different contributions from capability and opportunity for different individuals in different circumstances. Thus, one individual may experience an overwhelming desire to drink alcohol and seek out opportunities to do so while another may only experience those desires when opportunities present themselves. Similarly, some smokers experience a need to smoke as soon as they wake up while others experience equally powerful needs but only in social situations.

Focus on motivational theory

Let us now delve deeper into the mysteries of human motivation and start to develop the broad motivational theory. What follows is the second draft of the PRIME theory of motivation. The first draft was described in the first edition of Theory of Addiction. In terms of explication, the second draft is aimed at providing a better description of the correspondence between PRIME Theory and modern theories that distinguish automatic and reflective processes and its main tenets are set out as laws of motivation. In terms of substantive changes, the main one is that it recognises the role of imitation as an adaptive process (for which we must thank Simon Christmas for identifying that oversight), and develops the concept of identity.

The theory uses a psychological level of analysis but with a view to providing a 'pegboard' into which can be plugged theories at other levels (including economic theories and neurophysiological theories). The theory is painted with a broad brush and does not attempt to capture what is known about the details of drug actions, social forces and so on. However, it does seek to provide a coherent framework within which existing knowledge and future findings can be integrated.

When giving a psychological account of motivation, it is impossible to avoid making statements that just sound like common sense. The advance on common sense that is being offered here is bringing these ideas together in a coherent framework, together with non-common-sense ideas that have been developed through formal study and critical observation.

The human motivational system

Understanding addiction requires an understanding of the human motivational system. This is the system of brain processes that energise and direct our actions; it shapes the flow of behaviour on a moment-to-moment basis. There are many theories of motivation (for an excellent overview, see Mook 1996). Surprisingly none has sought to integrate all of its major modes of operation from conscious decision-making through to classical and instrumental learning processes. Therefore, it is necessary to develop a synthetic theory of motivation as the basis for a theory of addiction.

A synthetic theory of motivation

The theory specifies the key elements of the 'motivational system' (structure), how they react to input, and interact with each other to generate behaviour (function), and how their properties change over time through maturation, internal interactions and external influences (ontogenesis). It recognises that the motivational system is a product of evolution and that we share many processes with other

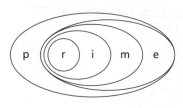

The human motivational system
p: plans (conscious mental representations of future actions plus commitment)
r: responses (starting, stopping or modifying actions)
i: impulses/inhibitory forces (can be consciously experienced as urges)
m: motives (can be consciously experienced as desires)
e: evaluations (evaluative beliefs)

Figure 8.2 A schematic of the five subsystems that make up the human motivational system.

species. It describes how the uniquely human and more generic animal parts of the system interact.

When it comes to the structure of the human motivational system, the theory identifies five major interacting subsystems of which any can function abnormally in addiction. The system as a whole is captured by the acronym PRIME, which stands for plans, responses, impulses, motives and evaluations.

Figure 8.2 shows the five subsystems of the motivational system. Plans are self-conscious intentions; responses involves starting, stopping or modifying actions; impulses and inhibitions are the final common pathway to behaviour; motives are feelings of want or need and evaluations are beliefs about what is good or bad.

Opportunities for influence between the subsystems involved in generating these mental activities are shown by their being adjacent to each other in the schematic. For example, motives can only exert influence on responding through impulses, and evaluations can only influence responses through motives and then impulses. Plans provide a structure to our actions and influence them primarily through evaluations operating at the time when they are to be executed.

The subsystems generate mental events that come into and out of existence as a result of the influences within the system, together with the ever-changing matrix of stimuli and information and overall level of arousal that 'bathe' it. Thus stimuli and information coming from our senses and from our memory have direct influence on all five subsystems. Our overall level of arousal similarly affects the operation of the whole system and all its subsystems.

The motivational system is shown in more detail in Figure 8.3 and described below. The five subsystems can also be thought of as 'levels' of varying complexity conferring varying levels of adaptation. As one moves from reflex responses, though impulses, then motives and evaluations, one allows greater flexibility of responding, consideration of a wider range of factors and anticipation of future consequences. At the highest level, plans allow action sequences to be prepared in advance of the circumstances when they are needed.

Structure and function of the human motivational system

The 'response system'

If we 'chunk' the continuous flow of activity that we call 'behaviour' into discrete 'actions' (also called 'behaviours'), we can think of 'responses' as starting, stopping

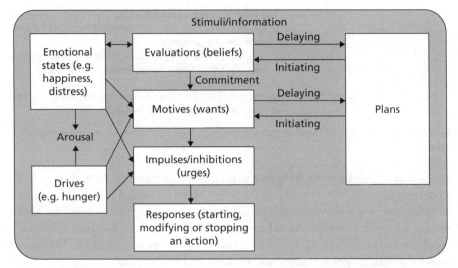

Figure 8.3 Subsystems and their main paths of influence in the PRIME Theory of motivation.

or modifying those actions. Thus, we can identify snorting a line of cocaine as an action with a beginning and end, just as we can eat a hamburger, or drink a glass of beer. The 'response system' is then the brain structures and mechanisms that underpin this. The study of how actions are organised is clearly of major importance but is outside the scope of this book. We are interested in what leads to responses.

Some parts of the response system can receive input directly from internal or external stimuli. We refer to responses thus created as 'reflexes'. Thus reflexes arise from innate or learned associations between stimuli and responses. Reflexes do not involve significant integration of inputs. They are the simplest level of motivation.

We need to introduce another term here as well: 'behaviour pattern'. Many types of behaviour are repeated for days, months or years. Any behaviour that we can identify may also be characterised in terms of this repeated patterning – hence the term 'behaviour pattern'. Thus smoking an individual cigarette or drinking a glass of beer is a behaviour but 'smoking' and 'drinking beer' are behaviour patterns. This distinction is important because it is often behaviour patterns that form the focus of attempts at behaviour change rather than individual behaviours – though of course ultimately it is the individual behaviours that are of interest. Thus someone may decide to 'drink less alcohol', that is, to change a behaviour pattern. Yet when it comes to instances of individual behaviours, when they encounter situations where they would normally drink they end up drinking the same as before. Addictive behaviours are clearly behaviour patterns, but to address them we need to understand how motivation underpinning these patterns translates into motivation relating to specific instances of behaviour.

So responses can arise directly from learned and unlearned reflexes, but most animals also have the capacity to prioritise behaviour in the light of compet-ing demands. At the very least this means having responses controlled by the strongest of competing 'impulses' and 'inhibitory' processes. So a major input into the 'response system' is output from a system that aggregates these impulses and inhibitions.

The 'impulse–inhibition system'

Thus the next level, which allows greater flexibility of responding, involves 'impulses' and 'inhibitions'. These can be thought of as motivational forces that compete or combine to generate a 'resultant force' that starts, modifies or stops an action (such as the impulse to laugh in response to a joke). They are generated by internal and external stimuli/information, drives and emotional states and by input from higher levels of the motivational system. Impulses come to conscious awareness when for some reason they are not immediately translated into action. They are then experienced as 'urges'. When they come to conscious awareness they can, in principle, be measured using self-report rating scales.

Impulses and urges

In this theory, urges are not the same as desires although in practice the two are often confused by people and indeed they are often associated with each other. Thus, an itch will create an urge to scratch it and the 'itcher' will often talk in terms of wanting to scratch the itch but the feeling is different from, say, wanting to eat a banana or watch TV. It has a quality of urgency and immediacy, of something impelling us to perform the action.

Another way of putting it is that it represents activation of the action schema (the high-level schematic representation of the action that would, if left uncontested, trigger the specific pathways that perform the muscle contractions) – that is, it involves part of the brain associated with the execution of actions.

Inhibition

Inhibition can be generated directly by stimuli or arise from repelling motives. Thus at one extreme, there are stimuli that 'stop us in our tracks' without any mental effort and at the other we sometimes require a strong act of will to exercise restraint over an impulse to do something such as strike out at someone who has annoyed us or accept a drink that is offered. In this theory, the conscious act of will and the automatic interruption of behaviour act through a final common pathway.

Drives and emotional states

'Drives' (such as hunger) and 'emotional states' (such as happiness, distress, liking, disliking) are of fundamental importance in the motivational system.

Drives come in various guises and can follow some rather complex dynamics. The obvious homeostatic ones are hunger, thirst, the need to breathe and so on. It is also probably useful to talk of 'sex drive', a drive to express one's thoughts and feelings ('expressive drive'), a drive to explore and so on. The reason for classifying these as drives is that they involve a motivational tension that is reduced by 'consummatory behaviour'.

Drives are influenced by two sources: internal stimuli that signal physiological needs and external stimuli that amplify or draw attention to or suppress or draw attention away from them. At high levels of physiological need, little or no external stimulus is required for the drive to be experienced as a feeling; at lower levels external stimuli may act as a trigger, drawing attention to the feeling and at even lower levels external stimuli are the dominant factor in creating the drive state.

Drives can create impulses to engage in actions that reduce them through direct causal links that are inbuilt (e.g. the impulse to drink when thirsty). They can also do so by creating emotional states (see below). Finally, drives can influence motives by stimulating mental operations that deduce a course of action that it is believed will achieve drive reduction.

Emotional states come in two types: 'generalised' (such as happiness and sadness) and 'targeted' (such as liking and disliking). They derive from stimuli/information that we perceive as affecting our well-being, the well-being of things we care about, our identity and our sense of what is right and wrong. They are also affected by 'hedonic' experiences (pleasure and discomfort).

It is well recognised that we are made content by, and therefore tend to like, things that we perceive as enhancing our well-being and give us pleasure and are distressed by, and tend to dislike, things that do the opposite.

Emotional states can also be created by changes in drive levels. Drive reduction can be pleasurable and so create both generalised and targeted emotional states. Generalised emotional states (e.g. contentment and distress) can directly influence impulses, for example, an instinctive impulse to laugh or cry. They also create impulses by acting as rewards and punishments through associative learning (see later discussion). Targeted emotional states are generated by generalised ones – the difference is that they are directly attached to mental representations of objects, events, actions, experiences or indeed anything that can be represented. Targeted emotional states lead to motives (see later discussion); most obviously liking leads to wanting and disliking leads to not wanting.

To some readers, the distinction between drives and emotional states and motives may seem unnecessary. The fact that it is necessary is illustrated by the statement: 'He was hungry but he did not want to eat.' Wanting to eat and being hungry are often talked about as though they were the same thing but clearly they are not, otherwise this statement would make no sense.

The language of emotional states

Grammar can often provide insights into the way we think and feel about things. An example is that it can be used to establish whether a feeling is a generalised or targeted emotional state. We talk about being 'excited about...', 'bored with...', 'disgusted by...', 'happy for...', 'angry with...', 'curious about...' and so on. The fact that these emotions can only take 'indirect objects' in our language tells us that these states are caused by something but not necessarily how we feel about that thing. These are generalised emotional states.

Targeted emotional states can take direct objects. We can talk of 'liking X, 'hating X' and so on. This conveys the idea that we have feelings towards the object in question and all that it entails.

The role of expectations

Expectation plays a critical role in emotional states. At every moment, our brain is generating mental representations of what is going to happen. At the very least this involves a representation of the immediate future but we also have the capacity to generate longer-term predictions. These mental representations can take any form including non-verbal images and beliefs that can be expressed in language.

Generating expectations: Expectations are generated by two processes: associative learning and inference. The capacity for associative learning is a very general feature of the brain in which patterns of activity that represent information, emotional states, or indeed anything at all, change the connections between elements in those patterns to create a propensity for elements to be activated when some subset of the original pattern occurs (for a neural network account of this, see Fiori 2005).

Associative learning: Manifestations of associative learning are discussed in more depth later but for the present we just note that when a set of stimuli is followed by another set, associative learning later creates a mental representation derived from the second set (the expectation) in response to exposure to elements of the first set (the cue). The stability and detail of the 'expectation' are dependent on a host of factors including the extent to which the cue stimulus was distinctively associated with it.

Inference: Inference, as a mental process, involves the application of 'if–then' rules to derive beliefs that can be expressed in linguistic terms. It need not be logical or rational. It is typically based on assumptions about causality which may or may not be accurate.

Expectations and emotional states

Expectations can directly generate emotional states. An obvious example is that expectation of negative events can induce anxiety or fear. Equally importantly they provide a reference point for what is actually experienced which affects the emotional state attaching to those experiences. The most obvious example of this is that an experience that is more positive than expected will result in a number of positive emotional states (such as relief and delight) and one that is more negative will result in a number of negative emotional states (such as disappointment and anger).

Arousal

Drives and emotional states influence and are influenced by our overall level of 'arousal'. This can be thought of as a generalised level of energy imparted to the motivational system. It affects the sensitivity of all the elements to other elements within it and external inputs such as stimuli picked up by our senses.

Arousal has important effects on the way in which elements of the system operate. For example, very high levels of arousal lead to interference by emotional states of analytical thinking being used to arrive at evaluations. It also tends to cause our attention to become more focused.

Inputs to the impulse–inhibition system

So the impulse–inhibition system receives input from emotional states, drives and external stimuli – these generate impulses and inhibitions and at any one time there are multiple such inputs competing for input to the response system. To take a simple example, when top sportspeople win an important event their feeling of relief generates an impulse to cry while their elation leads them to smile – sometimes one wins out while sometimes another does and sometimes they manage to do both at the same time.

Everything we have talked about thus far can be thought of as an S-R (stimulus-response) behaviour as opposed to goal-directed behaviour. Goal-directed behaviour arises because a higher order system also provides an input to the impulse–inhibition system. This is the 'motive system'.

The 'motive system'

The next level of the motivational system allows us to take into consideration the possible consequences of our actions. This is the level of the 'motive'. When motives come to conscious awareness because of factors that draw attention to them, they are experienced as feelings of 'want' or 'need' (such as the want or need to smoke crack, inject heroin, drink a glass of beer or smoke a cigarette). Motives comprise a mental representation of something and a degree of 'valence' – attraction or repulsion – attaching to it.

Motives can be thought of as lying at the heart of purposeful behaviour. A child quickly learns to associate the terms 'want' and 'need' with feelings of attraction towards or repulsion away from anticipated experiences that it can imagine. The feelings themselves pre-date those labels. The moment a child, or another animal, experiences pleasure or satisfaction on the one hand and mental or physical dis-comfort on the other, it begins to learn to want or need. As soon as the child learns the labels attaching to these feelings it can express them to people and so help to shape its social environment to get what it wants or needs. Thus the core of our motivational experience consists of wanting or needing things and our language reflects this.

Motives are generated by drives, emotional states and evaluations (see later discussion). Past experience plays a central role in their generation. It generates mental representations that have emotional states attached to them and when these are brought to mind they lead to motives. In an obvious example, recalling that something was pleasurable leads us to want it. The intensity of the motive is depen-dent on the intensity of the emotional state attaching to the mental representation of the target.

Competing motives

More than one motive can co-exist at one time – even for the same target. The strength of motives stems from the strength of the drives or emotional states that are generating them at the time. The more contentment something has created the more we like the thought of it and the more we want it; the more distress it has created the more we are repelled by the thought of it; the hungrier we are the more we want to eat, and so on.

When motives co-occur, those with more powerful valence prevail in generating an impulse to action, or inhibiting action. Impulses and inhibitions then compete or combine with any other impulses and inhibitions that are directly generated by current stimuli to start, stop or modify actions.

Competing motives create a particular kind of generalised emotional state: a feeling of 'conflict'. This is unpleasant and like any other adverse emotional state creates a motive to escape or avoid it.

The 'evaluation system'

The next level of motivation involves 'evaluations'. Humans have the capacity to represent the world in terms of 'beliefs'. These are conscious mental representations that can be expressed in language; that is, as propositions. They are propositions about what is true or not true or what might be true with varying degrees of likelihood.

Beliefs have attached to them a feeling of greater or lesser 'confidence'. It is necessary to differentiate 'likelihood' from 'confidence'. The former forms part of the content of beliefs as in 'It is highly likely that my horse will win the race' while the other is a feeling attaching to a belief as in 'I feel confident that my horse will win the race.' The need to differentiate these is made obvious from the statement 'I feel confident that there is a very small chance of an earthquake.'

Types of evaluation

Many of our beliefs state or imply the value that should be ascribed to things. There are many kinds of evaluation: 'global' (generally good or bad), 'aesthetic' (pleasing or displeasing), 'functional' (performing well or badly), 'ethical' (right or wrong) and 'utilitarian' (useful or detrimental). Global evaluations usually involve a more or less well-defined link with benefit and harm. Aesthetic evaluations involve judgements about taste and what is pleasing. Functional evaluations involve skill and technical performance. Ethical evaluations involve moral judgements. Utilitarian evaluations involve judgements relating to more or less specific goals.

According to this theory, evaluations do not influence behaviour directly but only through motives. Thus believing something to be good will not cause us to act unless something turns that into a motive (e.g. a desire) to do so. Put another way, beliefs drive actions by way of feelings.

How evaluations are arrived at

Evaluations have a positive or negative dimension – 'value' – which makes the object attractive or unattractive to varying degrees. Value derives from a number of sources: emotional states that we associate with the object in question; acceptance of statements of other people; by observation and by inference.

Thus, for example, we evaluate positively things that bring contentment and that we like, and we ascribe negative value to things that bring us distress and that we dislike. We also adopt evaluations communicated to us by others when we are not motivated to distrust what we are being told. We make evaluations when we experience things that match certain evaluative criteria. Finally, we arrive at evaluations through a process of generalisation and deduction.

For example, if we believe that having a drink was useful in helping with anxiety on one occasion, we assume it will be useful on other occasions; and if we believe that alcoholic drinks are useful we assume that a specific drink will be useful. We assume that if something is good in one respect it will be good in other respects. We also readily generalise from specific instances to categories. This is of course one of the ways in which stereotypes are formed.

How evaluations influence motives

Evaluations influence motives directly (by generating representations of things that we find attractive or repulsive) and indirectly by generating emotional states (making us feel good or bad about these things) which then create motives.

The direct route: This is moderated by a feeling of 'commitment'. In some cases, commitment is influenced by our 'identity'. For example, if we form the view that drinking alcohol is morally wrong, we may or may not become motivated not to drink or to take actions to prevent consumption in others depending on how far morality forms part of our sense of 'identity'. In other cases, commitment is influenced by acceptance of a 'task'. For example, having established that prescribing a particular drug to a patient is a good thing to do, physicians will generally want to do this in accordance with their role.

The indirect route: This involves the creation of emotional states. One common example of this involves the motive to punish or reward. Things that threaten our well-being or that of things we care about, or violate our sense of what is right, make us feel angry and anger leads to a desire to punish the agent of this state of affairs. Things that enhance our well-being or that of things we care about or have moral worth enhance our contentment and we are motivated to reward the agent of this state of affairs. The states of affairs in question can be directly perceived or can be represented as evaluations. For example, if we believe we are being treated unfairly, we get angry and are motivated to dislike and punish the perpetrator.

Competing evaluations

Evaluations of the same object can co-exist. When they do, they reinforce each other if they are all positive or all negative, and they conflict with each other if some are positive and others are negative. Where there is conflict (often called dissonance), we are motivated to reduce this by suppressing beliefs, changing them or adding new beliefs. We do whichever is easier. If a belief can be changed without creating other conflicts, that is the route generally adopted. If not, then suppression is favoured.

In many cases, it is not possible to resolve conflicting evaluations. When evaluations have conflicting implications for actions, and when these conflicts are not resolved by suppression, addition or modification, there are a wide variety of different ways in which they can come to affect our motives.

Analytical reasoning and choice

Analytical reasoning and cost–benefit analysis represent just one class of activities. Even within this class, there is a wide variety of different paths to assigning a value to a particular course of action. This is the province of Choice Theory and 'decision analysis'. Numerous accounts have been proposed as to how conflicting evaluations contribute to actions (for an excellent review, see Baron 2000). Two of these classes of theory are expectancy-value theories and multi-attribute utility theories, but there are many more.

Expectancy-value theories: There are what are known as 'expectancy-value' theories such as 'Subjective Expected Utility Theory' in which our evaluations of possible outcomes of a course of action are represented numerically (as utilities) and weighted by our judgement of the likelihood of these outcomes if a given course of action is followed. The theory proposes that we behave as though we sum the weighted utilities for each course of action and follow the course of action with the highest weighted utility. For example, when facing a conflict between evaluations relating to trying to stop smoking, we are presumed to weigh the very negative but uncertain prospects of getting lung cancer, heart disease, and so on against the positive but guaranteed enjoyment of smoking.

Multi-attribute utility theories: There are 'multi-attribute utility theories' in which the competing courses of action are compared on a number of qualities that are judged as more or less important. For example, when choosing between the nicotine patch and nicotine gum as an aid to smoking cessation, it is proposed that smokers give a weighting to things such as ease of use, embarrassment when using, cost, effectiveness and so on. They then ascribe a value on each of these dimensions to each of the options and choose the option with the highest total weighted value.

Variability in methods used to address competing evaluations: There are many more theories about the analytical methods we might use to deal with conflicting evaluations but even cursory observation of the behaviour of people in the real world shows that decision-making rarely follows such rules exclusively. It is much more haphazard and variable. Somewhere along the line, people engage in some kind of calculus of preferences but it involves any number of different rules and is influenced by memory limitations, imperfect logical reasoning and emotional forces. The role of emotion in analytical judgement and choice is addressed in the Conflict Theory by Janis and Mann (1977).

Probably the most important thing to note is that we can use an analytical method to calculate the value attaching to a course of action but this can then fail to translate into a motive because it conflicts with emotional states generated by one or more of the evaluations involved. For example, a smoker may weigh up the costs and benefits of attempting to give up and work out that the benefits outweigh the costs, but the idea of giving up the pleasure of smoking creates a negative emotional state that overrides everything else.

The 'planning system'

The highest level of adaptation in the motivational system involves plans. Plans arise when thought or forethought is required for an action to occur. 'Immediate plans' are formed when the action occurs straight away but is sufficiently complex that it requires at least some self-conscious reflective thought to construct it or get it going. Probably most of our actions are self-consciously constructed and then automated at the level of the component actions that combine to make these. 'Delayed plans' are formed when the circumstances that make the action appropriate are not present (it is 'not the right time or place'), but they can also be because other actions are taking priority, the starting conditions have not been specified or it is not clear what the appropriate course of action is.

Plans are mental representations of actions or action sequences, together with at least some degree of commitment to them and some form of mental representation of the starting conditions – however vaguely specified. Delayed plans are often formulated in anticipation of events or circumstances that will arise and sometimes they are formulated in response to the current situation. An insightful account of plans is given by Miller et al. (1960). The rest of this chapter will focus primarily on delayed plans and use the term 'plans' for shorthand.

Diaries and routines

Many of us have diaries in which we mark appointments. These are obviously plans about what we are going to do at particular times. Within the structure provided by our diaries, there is clearly plenty of scope for other kinds of plans, both short and long term. When we get up in the morning we make more or less detailed plans for the day. This often includes activities that fulfil work or domestic commitments, or leisure activities.

These plans provide 'structure' to our lives. They are worked out according to evaluations and motives and they are subject to change as new stimuli and information come to light or in response to events.

Even when we do not have a written diary, it is useful to think of many of our plans in terms of a mental diary and a 'to-do' list. The mental diary is a list of actions with their starting conditions while a 'to-do' list does not have particular starting conditions but might have a level of priority.

Mental diaries can be thought of as stored representations that have to be regenerated at appropriate times in order to influence behaviour. This involves the same recall processes as those that occur with other stored information including associative learning mechanisms and cues.

Routines are a particular kind of entry in our mental diaries in which the starting conditions are regularly occurring events, for example, linked to times of day and days of the week. Because of their degree of repetition, routines involve a habitual element that helps to maintain them in the face of competing priorities (see later discussion on associative learning).

Plans to make lifestyle changes

Of particular interest are plans to make lasting changes to our behaviour, such as stopping smoking, cutting down on drinking or changing our diet. Plans of this kind are quite special in a number of ways.

First, the starting conditions are not usually dictated externally. We can make an attempt to stop smoking at any time, and we can usually put it off to another day. Secondly, they are not discrete action sequences with specific immediate objectives to be met and tasks to be undertaken. Thirdly, they can remain in effect even when specific actions are not in accordance with them. Thus a person can still be 'making an attempt to stop smoking' if they smoke a cigarette. Fourthly, they relate to long-term behaviour patterns and so the commitment to them needs to be maintained indefinitely.

Plans about lifestyle have characteristics that make them particularly vulnerable to a disjunction between the plan and the actual behaviour, and this is of course what is observed. Only a minority of stated intentions to make changes within a given time frame actually involve initiation of that change, and even once initiated they are more often than not rescinded or put into abeyance.

Plans and behaviour

It is particularly obvious with plans to make lifestyle changes, but it is true of any plan that, in order to influence behaviour, it needs to be recalled and to generate motives. Those motives will be combining or competing with other motives that may be present at the time. For a plan to influence behaviour it must be remembered at the opportune time and the commitment to it must generate motives that outweigh any competing motives and impulses.

The chain of influence in the motivational system gives an inherent though not paramount priority to simple impulses over wants and desires, and wants and desires over evaluations, and current situational factors over stored plans.

The 'head model'

Figure 8.4 provides another depiction of the structure of the human motivational system which makes explicit that all external input needs to be sensed and interpreted at some level in order to feed into the system. Internal states such as drives and emotions are important in that process.

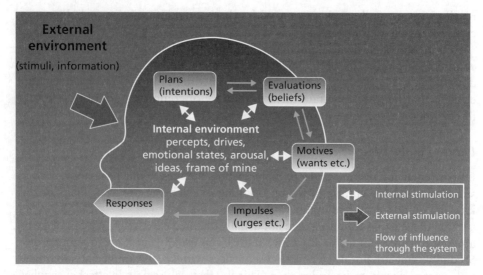

Figure 8.4 The 'head' model of the human motivational system

The head model is schematic but goes further than the diagram in Figure 8.3 to reflect what may be anatomical structures involved in motivation. Thus, the planning systems finds itself in the frontal cortex, the evaluation system is also firmly situated in the cortex while the motive system spans the cortex and mid-brain and the impulse–inhibition system is a mid-brain structure. The head model breaks down somewhat by depicting all responses coming out of the mouth – except that a lot of our behaviour does appear to involve talking!

Note that under this model, plans can influence responses without going through evaluations and motives by virtue of their interaction with other processes such as drives, emotional states and so on. For example, the fact that someone plans to make an attempt to reduce their alcohol consumption may lead to anxiety which then influences any of the other levels of the system directly.

Momentum and inertia

There are two more concepts to add – 'momentum' and 'inertia' – in order to understand certain features of behaviour, and particularly differences in what is required to start an action or stop it starting and to stop an action or prevent it from stopping. The motivational system can be thought of as a system of forces, like physical forces. Observation of behaviour seems to suggest that once an action sequence has begun it is often brought to a conclusion in the face of events that would have prevented it starting if they had occurred in time (for an experimental analysis, see Nevin 1992). It seems as though, once started, actions are less responsive to outside influence.

It is also apparent that there are occasions when it seems particularly difficult to initiate actions, even when the motivation to do so is present. A particularly clear case is patients with Parkinson's disease. While it is widely believed that Parkinson's disease is a disorder of the motor system in the brain, it goes far wider than that and sufferers experience greater physical and mental fatigue (Lou et al. 2001). It has also been noted that some patients with multiple sclerosis suffer from high levels of behavioural inertia (Grigsby et al. 1993).

Adaptation: ways in which experience affects motivational disposition

Apart from causal links between emotional states, evaluations and motives, there are four general ways in which our motivational system is affected by past experience. What follows is an overview of these processes (for more details, see Mook 1996).

Habituation/sensitisation

Possibly the simplest way in which our motivational system is influenced by experience is habituation/sensitisation to a given stimulus. Mere repetition of a stimulus can alter its hedonic value. In some cases, it can reduce it or even reverse it and in others it can exaggerate it. There are complex dynamics to this phenomenon so that a stimulus to which we have become habituated can, after a delay, recover its hedonic value. In some cases, repetition will make a stimulus more pleasurable but further repetition will lead it then to become unpleasant.

Numbing and amplification: There are numerous examples of simple habituation. For example, a beautiful scene will lose its ability to evoke emotion after a while. There are equally numerous examples of sensitisation. Thus a noise that is mildly annoying at first can, with repetition, become more and more annoying.

Reversal: Reversals are also common, as in the case of 'acquired tastes'. The taste of fruit such as avocado can be unpleasant at first but then become very pleasant. By the same token, in most cases, if we experience a pleasing sensation or collection of sensations often enough in sufficiently quick succession, we become 'bored' with them and they can become aversive.

Adaptation and boredom: Adaptation and ultimately boredom are ubiquitous consequences of repeated experiences with important implications for the way that we behave. What once delighted us at first often loses its ability to generate a positive emotional response and then becomes unpleasant. What was once regarded positively, such as a pay increase, soon becomes the expected level against which future events are judged.

Balance and enhancement: The mechanisms underlying these changes are complex and not well understood. However, there do seem to be two pervasive adaptive principles at work: maintenance of balance and striving for improvement. With regard to balance, in order to function adequately, we need to be motivated by rewards but we cannot afford to become attached to those to the exclusion of other needs and motives. We need to be able to switch our behaviours to attend to long- and short-term needs. We need balance and variety. With regard to the need for improvement, there is a clear adaptive advantage to becoming dissatisfied with the *status quo* and being motivated to improve on it.

Explicit memory

The second way in which our motivational system changes with experience involves explicit memory. That is, we recall things that happened in the past, plans we formed, how we felt and so on. These recollections create 'mental representations' that form current elements within the motivational system and influence our actions accordingly. Mental representations are more or less attenuated and indistinct versions of experiences including visual images, sounds, feelings, smells, linguistic representations and so on.

Anything that can be experienced can be recalled, and that includes mental constructions such as plans. For example, a smoker who is trying to stop and who is offered a cigarette may or may not recall at that moment what it was that led them to make the attempt and this may affect the response.

It is well recognised that memory does not involve retrieving a stored engram. Rather it involves reconstruction of a mental representation from cues. The more specific and detailed the cue, the greater the likelihood of successful recall. That is why police mount reconstructions to trigger the memory of potential witnesses.

Associative learning

The third way in which experience affects our motivational system is by 'associative learning'. Associative learning is a pervasive feature of brain functioning and has many manifestations. What follows is a highly schematic account.

The best documented of the associative learning mechanisms are 'Pavlovian conditioning' (also called 'classical conditioning') and 'instrumental learning' (also known as 'operant conditioning').

Pavlovian learning

Pavlovian conditioning involves a stimulus (the conditioned stimulus) that precedes and predicts another one (the unconditioned stimulus) triggering a mental representation of that second stimulus which can then form an element in the motivational system. This can mean that the conditioned stimulus causes an anticipatory response (e.g. fear to a warning signal) or a response similar to that which would occur to the unconditioned stimulus (e.g. pleasure to a melody that is associated with a pleasant experience).

Instrumental learning

Instrumental learning influences the effect of cues on actions depending on what happened when those actions were performed in the past. It can lead to generation of impulses or inhibitory forces, or reduction of inhibitions.

Generating impulses: Looking first of all at impulses, instrumental learning involves a stimulus (the cue) triggering an impulse to perform a particular action if, in the presence of that cue, the action previously satisfied a motive (e.g. reduced a drive). A stimulus that satisfies a motive is called a 'reinforcer'. The classic example is the hungry rat learning to press a lever in the presence of a particular coloured light if it repeatedly gives access to food. The dynamics of this process are complex but the strength of the impulse is (up to a point) positively related to the number of times the sequence has been repeated in the past and the strength of the motive that was satisfied.

Generating inhibition: Turning to inhibitory forces, instrumental learning involves a stimulus (the cue) triggering inhibition of an action if, in the presence of that cue, the action previously generated a negative emotional state. Frequently, though not always, the negative emotional state (e.g. distress, disliking) will have been created by a negative hedonic state (e.g. discomfort). Inhibitions are also created when actions fail to create desired outcomes.

Reducing inhibitions: The mechanism of instrumental learning can reduce inhibitions when an expected punishment does not occur. This is in addition to other factors that reduce inhibitions such as some mental disorders and drugs and factors that reduce self-awareness.

This theory predicts that, if the probability of punishment for a regularly occurring behaviour is too low and so the perpetrator 'gets away with it' on a sufficient number of occasions, failure to be punished will be rewarding and will lead to reduced inhibitions to the extent that a habit develops that will then be unresponsive to punishment when it does occur.

Conscious awareness: It is important to note that instrumental learning does not require conscious awareness of pleasure or discomfort and neither does it require us to be consciously aware of the fact that the cue, activity and reward or punishment are connected. That is to say, it does not require evaluations or propositional knowledge.

Habit

The term 'habit' has been used to describe actions that, because of associative learning, have become to a large degree under the control of non-conscious forces. It is probably more accurate to think of habit, not as an entity, but in terms of a quality that attaches to actions by virtue of their associative learning history. Thus, for any action it is possible to assess to what degree it is 'habitual'.

Routines can be thought of as behaviours that have a significant habitual aspect, usually linking them to times and days. They are not 'automatic' in the sense that they occur without a self-conscious intention to enact them – but situation reminds the individual to form the intention and habitual mechanisms support enactment of the sequence of actions involved.

Imitation learning

The fourth way in which experience affects our motivational system is by 'imitation learning'. Thorndike defined imitation as 'learning to do an act from seeing it done' (Thorndike 1898). Psychologists have long known it is far easier to learn through observation than by description. However, the ease with which people imitate presents a 'correspondence problem' (Heyes 2001). We witness the outcome of a series of muscle activations but how do we easily match visual information with motor output? Specialist theories propose a unique learning system dedicated to imitation whereas generalist theories propose that the general mechanisms of associative learning and action control suffice (Brass and Heyes 2005). The discovery of mirror neurons favours the generalist solutions with input from a unique neural architecture (Catmur et al. 2009).

Our capacity for imitation is an extremely useful adaptation for learning new skills and actions efficiently. However, like much associative learning, imitation learning can automatically influence behaviour, which in certain contexts can contribute to addictions. For example, smokers automatically imitate the smoking of strangers. During an apparently incidental break from a psychological experiment, the amount smoked by a confederate explained 35% of the variance in the number of cigarettes smoked by participants (Harakeh et al. 2007). Furthermore, passive imitation is a better predictor of young adult smoking than whether they are actively offered a cigarette (Harakeh and Vollebergh 2012).

The 'representational system', consciousness and dual process models

Having provided an overview of the structure and function of the human motivational system at a very broad brush level of analysis, and the main ways in which it adapts over time and through experience, we can examine some specific issues related to it. One of these is what is the role of consciousness?

Reference has been made to stimuli, information and mental representations. We now need to consider this in a little more detail. For heuristic purpose, we can think of the 'representational system', like the motivational system, as a set of elements that interact with each other and with the external environment.

The human brain can represent entities (things, materials, scenarios, events and features of these) iconically or propositionally. Iconic representations encode the features of the entity derived from the senses. Thus visual images in our heads, whether recalled, imagined or deriving from our immediate senses, are iconic. When we remember or imagine feelings such as pleasure or pain, these are also iconic representations. Propositional representations are symbolic representations that can be expressed through language.

Mental representations are the link between stimuli and motivation

The first thing to say is that, like the motivational system, it is mental representations active at a given time that influence actions. Internal and externally generated stimuli create representations and it is these which 'bathe' the motivational system in a fluid matrix of information at multiple levels from simple sensory experiences to complex propositions. Information that is latent in the representational system by virtue of having been experienced in the past and altering the connections between neural elements only influences the motivational system by virtue of creating mental representations that are active at the time.

Mental representations involve much more than the stimuli that immediately give rise to them. They involve 'interpretation' and this interpretation is fundamental to the effect that these have on the motivational system. An obvious example is that a feeling of pain can be distressing, tolerable or pleasurable depending on the interpretation placed on it which in turn is related to what it signals.

The importance of 'change'

The motivational system in humans and other animals is responsive to change, not steady states. For external steady states to influence our actions, they must create change in some internal state (such as physical discomfort, boredom, hunger, etc.). The change must be detectable by some element of the system which means that slow transitions usually have less of an effect than the same change achieved more rapidly. Part of the role of the representational system is to create a representation of change from the inputs it receives.

Motivational states can be represented

By definition anything that can be experienced can be represented. It can also be regenerated (recalled). This includes feelings of want and urge as well as the fact that we have formed beliefs about things.

This capacity to represent motivational states allows us to take account of these when formulating new wants and evaluations. It also allows us to express our wants and evaluations. However, it is essential to recognise that the experience of a want or other motivational element is not the same as the motivational element itself. The experience of the motivational element does not influence behaviour unless it is used to create another motivational element, for example, by inference. Thus, we can recognise that there is something we want and formulate a plan to achieve it but then it is the plan that motivates behaviour.

Consciousness

A distinction has been made between conscious and non-conscious processing. Only a very small proportion of information and forces that act on our behaviour are represented consciously at any one time. The conscious mind has a very limited capacity.

The elements that have been described are brought to conscious awareness either through an act of will (which itself comes about through the same motivational forces that operate within the system) or because of the nature of the elements themselves. What happens here is that non-conscious processing of the information creates a representation that has particular properties, often called salience, that cause conscious attention to be focused on it.

Conscious awareness is required for particular mental functions, especially the development of beliefs through inference and communication through language. Inference is undertaken by means of an inner monologue in which a kind of short-hand language is used to generate and represent states of the world and calculate possible new states from these.

PRIME Theory and dual process models

PRIME Theory recognises the value of distinguishing between 'automatic' and 'reflective' processes. However, it differs from classical dual process models (e.g. Strack and Deutsch 2004) in (i) positing that there is a multi-level hierarchy of influence and that reflective processes have to act upon processes that can proceed automatically rather than having a direct pathway to behaviour and (ii) recognising a fundamental distinction between automatic processes that involve affective goals (wants and needs) and those that involve stimulus–impulse associations. Figure 8.5 shows which of the motivational constructs invoked by PRIME theory are described as 'reflective' and which as 'automatic'.

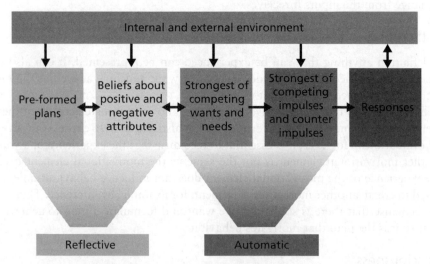

Figure 8.5 A representation of PRIME theory with the different constructs labelled as either reflective or automatic.

Self and self-control

Self and identity

We are able to form mental representations of ourselves. These constitute our 'identity' or 'self'. Like other mental representations, they come into existence when attention is drawn to them, vary over time, vary in how coherent and well defined they are, and involve evaluations, emotional states and motives. When we think of ourselves, we have beliefs about what we are, whether we are good or bad, moral or immoral, useful or useless. We also have a sense of whether we like ourselves or not, whether we are happy with what we are or not, and what we would like to be and not to be.

Self-consciousness

Most of the time we are not self-conscious. We may be *conscious* of impulses, motives, evaluations and plans but we do not at the time have a mental representation of ourselves. There are occasions, however, when attention is drawn to mental representations involving ourselves as objects and that provides the possibility of self-control.

The 'self' is not an enduring homunculus that sits inside our heads telling us what to do, sometimes with limited success. It appears to be enduring just because, by definition, it is always there when we think about it. Rather, it is a set of mental representations of ourselves as objects that, like any mental event, is generated, held in mind for a while and then replaced when other representations come to our attention.

Self-control

Self-control is the influence of mental representations involving ourselves and evaluations and motives that we ascribe to ourselves in the motivational system. For example, if I decide that I will be a non-smoker and I want to be a non-smoker, when a cigarette is offered to me, as long as that mental representation is triggered it will influence my decision as to whether or not to accept. The decision does not just rely on any impulses I may have to smoke, any desire I may have for a cigarette or any evaluations I may form as to the costs and benefits of smoking that cigarette.

There are many occasions in which self-control plays an important role, both in leading us to do things we do not want to do and in inhibiting impulses to do things that will be harmful. It is important to note that self-control does not just involve the domination of evaluations over wants or impulses, or long-term goals over short-term needs. It involves any evaluation, plan or motive that derives from a representation of how or what we want to be. An excellent account of the operation of self-control is given in Baumeister et al. (1994).

These representations and the associated emotional states and evaluations are developed through our childhood by means of the processes already described.

Under this theory, we would not consider it to be an example of self-control if a person unselfconsciously refrains from lashing out at someone who has annoyed him or her. It would only be an example of self-control if the restraint involved some mental representation of the self and a commitment to moral or other attributes of the self that overrode the impulse.

Identity and self-worth

Of fundamental importance is our overall self-evaluation, our sense of self-worth (see McIntosh and McKegany 2001; Crocker and Nuer 2004; Crocker and Park 2004; DuBois and Flay 2004; Pyszczynski and Cox 2004; Pyszczynski et al. 2004; Sheldon 2004). This has a pervasive and powerful effect on and is powerfully affected by generalised emotional states such as depression and targeted emotional states such as liking or disliking what we are. The full panoply of causal connections within the motivational system influence and are influenced by identity as with any other object that we can think of.

People who are depressed tend to think of themselves as worthless. When it comes to motivation, such a belief can have a profound influence on wants and evaluations. If you think you are worthless, you will value your own welfare less and be less inclined to exercise restraint when it comes to activities that harm you. If you think you are worthless, you will find activities, including drug taking, that numb that feeling, distract you from it or even bolster your self-esteem more rewarding than someone who has a high sense of self-worth.

It is striking how many people who become injecting heroin users and show evidence of addiction have been abused as children and have a very low self-esteem. Of course, as with any other single observation, there are other explanations, but low self-worth is certainly a good candidate for an explanation of this link. In such cases, the pathology may not be in the development of a compulsive pattern of use but in the sense of self in the context of which harmful drug injecting is a rational choice.

Self and categorical labels

From the point of view of self-control, there is an aspect of our identity that can be particularly important: 'categorical labels'. These are self-beliefs that have clear and definite boundaries.

Vegetarianism

For example, a person may label himself as a vegetarian. On the other hand, he likes the taste of some meats and occasionally wants to experience that taste. If he were not a 'vegetarian' he would occasionally give in to that desire and assuming that the taste was as pleasant as he imagined it would be, there would be no particular reasons to stop there and very soon he would be eating quite a lot of meat.

The fact that he is a vegetarian puts an absolute block on eating even the tiniest amount of meat. If he were to eat one beef or tuna sandwich he would not be a vegetarian; he would be someone who does not usually eat meat but sometimes does. That is not what he wants to be. Being a vegetarian is important to the value that he places on himself. This is notwithstanding that he realises that in wearing leather shoes and benefiting from a society that exploits the rearing and slaughtering of animals he is drawing an arbitrary line in the sand.

The point is that this is his line in the sand and he is committed to it. His identity has an effect on his behaviour that is over and above the ebb and flow of wants and evaluations regarding specific acts. It sets absolute limits on what he can do. Categorical self-labelling is a means of preventing what may be called 'behaviour creep': the tendency for single activities to become a regular pattern that the individual wants to avoid.

The label of 'ex-smoker'

Let us now consider an example closer to the topic of addiction. It is apparent that most people think of themselves as either smokers or non-smokers. Not all people who smoke think of themselves as smokers and some people who no longer smoke still think of themselves as smokers. But there is reason to believe that thinking of oneself as a smoker or non-smoker influences one's behaviour.

In one study, for example, it was found that approximately half of smokers who were trying to stop smoking and who had lasted a week thought of themselves as 'ex-smokers' (West, in preparation). This may seem optimistic given that three-quarters of people who last a week will not make it to the 1-year point. However, almost half of those who labelled themselves as ex-smokers lasted at least 6 months, whereas of those who did not make that mental transition not a single person did.

As with so many observations of human behaviour it is easy to think of reasons why that should be the case. For example, perhaps those who had not made the mental transition were going from experience – they were people who had tried before many times and failed. In fact other evidence indicated they had no more reason to believe they would fail than those who declared themselves as non-smokers.

Alternatively, perhaps they had in fact smoked the occasional cigarette even though they said they had not – we would not know for sure. However, there was no particular reason in this study why they would not tell the truth, or why they would not tell the truth about their smoking one week into the quit attempt and then own up later; there was no moral or financial inducement to being non-smokers in this study. We can entertain the possibility that the explanation lies in the fact that 'ex-smokers' were subject to an additional motivational force not to smoke which was the fact that they now identified themselves as such. This gave them a substantial amount of additional commitment.

Identity and 'persona'

Identity can influence behaviour beyond self-imposed taboos and beyond the wants and evaluations concerning good or bad things that could happen to us. Identity causes us to act in particular ways that we think will affect how others regard us.

We dress in a particular way, walk in a particular way, adopt a particular hairstyle and so on. We develop a 'persona' that we project to the world and to ourselves. Why and how we develop such a persona and how it changes over the life course is a field of study in itself, but there is no doubt that it affects us profoundly. It is well recognised that the persona of a rebel, an outlaw, even a figure of fear and loathing in the eyes of 'respectable, boring, hypocritical middle-class, middle-aged, middle-America' is desirable for many young people and some older people. This representation of oneself often includes reckless abandon for one's own welfare and that of others, and this in turn can make the risk attached to certain behaviours such as injecting drugs a desirable thing rather than an undesirable one.

Selves as future possibilities

Like any other object, we can form mental representations of ourselves as future possibilities; what we might become. And like other imagined objects, those representations can be attractive or repulsive to us; they can be the targets of motives.

Thus many of the elements of our identity are linked to desire: this is who I want to be; this is who I ought to be. As with any representation, it can have any level of specificity and completeness and any kind of desire or evaluation attached to it. But identity is special because it is a representation of ourselves, and in some sense we are at the centre of our own world. Therefore, identity is usually imbued with a higher degree of commitment and desire than other representations or imaginings.

Mental effort and motivational resources

The exercise of self-control requires 'effort' (see Gaultney et al. 1999). This concept is similar to that of physical effort in that it results in 'fatigue/tiredness'. It requires 'motivational resources' that become depleted with continued expenditure.

One may speculate about the physiological basis of this effort and its perception but it could involve internal sensory systems capable of monitoring the energy utilisation and reserves of cells in neural pathways involved in thought. The susceptibility of cells in neural pathways required for conscious (not necessarily self-conscious) thought to depleted resources may underpin the need for humans and many other animals to sleep.

Many factors may deplete motivational resources apart from the exercise of mental effort. Of these, the one that is probably of greatest significance is depressed mood.

Mental and physical fatigue can perhaps be thought of as drive states that work to retard thought or action and allow recovery.

What motivates us

In all the above discussion, there has been only scant attention paid to the specifics of what motivates us – what impels us, what drives us, what it is that we want and what we think of as good and bad. This has been the subject of considerable debate for centuries in the writing of philosophers and more recently psychologists, sociologists and economists. What follows is the briefest of outlines of how these ideas fit into the current theory.

The cart metaphor

The present theory proposes examining this in terms of what *pushes* behaviour, what *pulls* it and what *retards* it. Once in motion the behaviour or the system underlying it has a certain *momentum*. Perhaps a useful metaphor is a cart that is pulled by a horse, pushed by some very strong farm labourers, retarded by mud and its own weight but once moving has an inertia that can sometimes make it difficult to stop.

Pushing

Reflexes and automatic impulses and emotional responses to the immediate environment push behaviour. Frustration and threats to our self-esteem or things we care about induce feelings of anger that lead to aggressive impulses. There is no consideration of the consequences.

Pulling

Motives and evaluations pull behaviour. Whether conscious or not, mental representations of future events feed into impulses to engage in actions that experience or inference leads us to assume will bring these about or prevent them. The two dominant experiences here are contentment and distress. What causes contentment and distress varies from person to person.

Contentment

Contentment derives from pleasant sensations which may be tactile, visual and so on. It also derives from the creation, preservation or enhancement of things we care about. What we care about varies from person to person but usually includes ourselves, people whom we are close to, often other animals and often inanimate objects such as possessions or works of art. Contentment also derives from self-respect or the respect of others. It often derives from feeling superior in some way to others. It derives from exerting influence. In some people it can derive from achieving dominance. It can also derive from submission to a higher authority. It derives from relief of mental or physical discomfort. It also derives from events that satisfy our personal sense of moral justice. It derives from attaining goals that we have set ourselves or that have been set for us. It derives from good things happening to people with whom we identify. Of particular importance is the fact that it derives from receiving affection from those to whom we feel affection.

Distress

Distress derives from unpleasant sensations and harm to people and things we care about or with which we identify. It derives from shame, embarrassment and feelings of low self-worth and loneliness. It derives from failing to achieve goals. It can derive from being treated unfairly as we see it, and it also derives from events that violate our personal sense of what is right.

Prediction and explanation

With all these sources of contentment and distress to consider, the calculus of forces operating on motives can be very complex and very often we do not have the necessary information to make a confident prediction. When one adds to this the habits and impulses that push our behaviour, the difficulty in predicting behaviour becomes even more clear.

By the same token, with all these factors potentially influencing behaviour, it is generally easy to explain behaviour once it has occurred. Therefore, we are often in a situation where we cannot formulate accurate predictions of behaviour but we can offer a multitude of explanations when it does occur.

The complexity of the motivational system and the individual differences in what motivates us mean that we often have to take shortcuts when making predictions. Probably the most important shortcut is summed up by one of the enduring truths in psychology: 'The past predicts the future'. If someone behaved in a particular way before when encountering a particular situation, there is a good chance he or she will do the same thing again in the same situation. This is true even when the person himself or herself fervently and honestly declares that he or she has changed.

The unstable mind

The description of the motivational system provided so far has included only a very sketchy idea of its dynamics. It has focused on the importance of considering the moment-to-moment influences within the system and a brief outline of the plasticity of the system in terms of habituation/sensitisation, explicit memory, associative learning and imitation learning.

Consideration of the motivational system would be incomplete, however, without mention of a pervasive feature of the functioning of physiological systems and indeed the human mind which has profound implications on how we think, feel and behave. This is the concept of the 'unstable mind'.

Fly-by-wire systems

The proposition is that the human mind has evolved to be inherently unstable. It is steered and manoeuvred by constant balancing input. This is analogous to the design of modern 'fly-by-wire' fighter aircraft. These are designed to be inherently unstable and are controlled by continual adjustments to their control surfaces. This can only be achieved by computers and electronic activation of the motors that control these surfaces.

The advantage of this approach is that the planes are extremely manoeuvrable. Their instability means that the slightest movement of the control surface sends them off in a new direction. The disadvantage is that without continual balancing input they spiral out of control.

It seems that the human mind has evolved along these lines such that it is extremely adaptable, creative and exquisitely sensitive to environmental inputs and contingencies. However, it needs continual balancing input to prevent it from spiralling out of control.

Randomness and 'homeodynamics'

The unstable mind concept proposes that the instability in mental functioning stems ultimately from an inherent 'pseudo-randomness' that is observed in all biological systems (Yates 2002). In this case randomness means that the momentary state of the system is subject to a multitude of small influences that make it all but impossible to predict, just like the position that a leaf will arrive at when it falls from a tree or the number that will come up when a die is rolled.

Thus nerve cells do not sit silently waiting for input. They typically fire more or less unpredictably at a given low rate, and the rate and pattern of firing are influenced by nerves to which they are connected. Aggregating up to the level of nerve bundles, the inherent randomness in the process means that our central nervous system cannot be construed as electrical circuitry with pathways switched on and off but rather as what has been called a 'homeodynamic' system in constant flux and capable of springing surprises when by chance the confluence of influences puts the system into an unusual state. Aggregating up still further, the inherent randomness is in some sense smoothed out but the sensitivity of the system to inputs and occasional unpredictability remains.

The importance of 'balancing input'

There are normally enough checks and balances in the system to ensure that it does not descend permanently into chaos, but there are circumstances when a single extreme event can put the system into a very different state, others where a single small event can send the system down a different path at which point the checks and balances maintain the system in the new state, and still others where a succession of small events can progressively lead the system to become more firmly established in a new state.

Figure 8.6 shows these possibilities schematically. A critical feature of this concept is that it postulates that change can occur, not only because of reactivity to stimuli but also because of the *absence* of balancing input (see Figure 8.6e).

(a) Stability

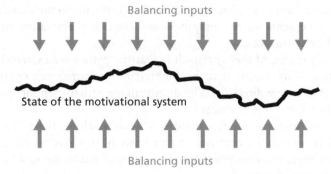

Balancing inputs

State of the motivational system

Balancing inputs

(b) Sudden change

Balancing inputs

Balancing inputs

State of the motivational system

Balancing inputs

Balancing inputs Major
event

(c) Triggered change

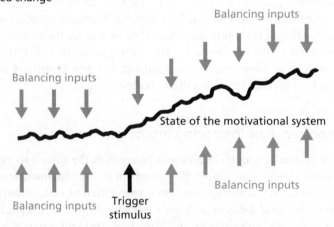

Balancing inputs

Balancing inputs

State of the motivational system

Balancing inputs

Balancing inputs Trigger
stimulus

Figure 8.6 Examples of different trajectories in the unstable mind.

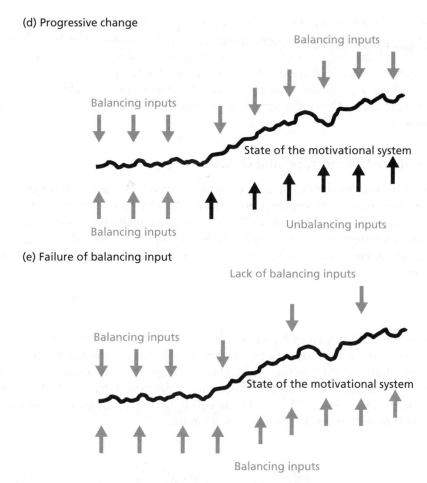

(d) Progressive change

(e) Failure of balancing input

Figure 8.6 (*Continued*)

Examples of patterns of instability

The manifestations of this are all-pervasive, from the difficulty we have in achieving coherent thought without providing structure by talking or writing our ideas down; to the development of neurotic patterns of thought; a tendency in some people to become anxious about small things when there is not enough to occupy their minds; the way in which, when members of a couple are too alike, they can develop what seem from the outside to be peculiar habits and views; the effects of sensory deprivation; the phenomenon known as 'groupthink' in which an isolated group can become out of touch with reality; 'superstitious behaviours' in which we believe there are connections between what we do and events that are not real, and so on.

At one level, the concept of the unstable mind is so non-specific that it is neither testable nor useful for prediction. However, as a principle it can be applied to more specific models of mental functioning that can generate predictions and be tested. It can also guide the design of interventions designed to change unwanted behaviour patterns or prevent them from developing.

The broad guiding principle in terms of understanding how an unwanted behaviour pattern has developed is to look either for the *presence* of influences that take it in a particular direction or equally importantly the *absence* of balancing input from other influences. It is this latter contribution that can easily be overlooked.

The epigenetic landscape and chaos theory

A model for understanding the development of behaviour patterns through plasticity of the motivational system is provided by Waddington's concept of the 'epigenetic landscape' (Waddington 1977). This was originally proposed to help in understanding the way in which embryos develop in the context of varying environmental circumstances but has since been applied more widely to topics from decision analysis to economics.

Chreods

The concept is illustrated in Figure 8.7. It represents the state of an organism at a given time as the position of a ball and potential future states determined by a landscape down which it is travelling. This landscape involves a series of valleys (which Waddington calls 'chreods') which vary in depth and shape and which may divide at critical periods. Which path the ball follows depends on environmental forces that move it from side to side in that landscape.

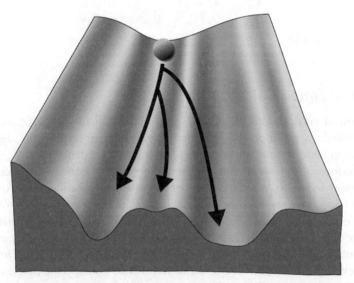

Figure 8.7 Example of the epigenetic landscape proposed by Waddington (1977) to represent how genes and environment interact in ontogenesis.

The concept of the epigenetic landscape provides a way of thinking about how environmental factors influence behaviour through the motivational system and how the motivational system itself changes in response to experiences. We can think of the condition of the motivational system at a given time with respect to a given set of behaviours in terms of the landscape.

Types of landscape

The landscape may be quite flat in which case small environmental forces can send behaviour in markedly different directions. At the other extreme it may constitute a deep V-shaped valley in which case powerful motivational forces will move the behaviour some way off its original path but as soon as the forces are removed it will revert to its original course. The landscape may involve a valley with a flat bottom in which case small environmental forces will easily move behaviour about within a certain range but it would require very powerful forces to move it outside that 'normative' range. The landscape may involve a bifurcation so that a very small environmental force at a critical period can send the behaviour down very different paths.

With this model in mind, we can think of stimuli and information acting on the landscape of our motivational system in varying ways to shape the energy and direction of our actions. In doing so, it sends us down paths in that landscape that dictate what effects future stimuli will have. A single experience can dramatically alter the landscape that we subsequently encounter if either it is very powerful or, if it is quite small, it occurs when the landscape is flat but on the point of bifurcating.

Flat-bottomed valleys and rating scales

There are many occasions when our behaviour can be characterised in terms of a ball rolling down a flat-bottomed chreod. This is a valley in which the smallest of environmental influences can swing the ball from one side to another. There is an example of this that is of relevance to anyone using rating scales to measure attitudes, feelings or any subjective state.

Spuriously precise response scales can appear to be highly sensitive to experimental manipulations while doing nothing more than providing a vehicle for intrusion of experimental artefacts. Consider this example. Suppose you are asked how much you want to drink a glass of beer on a 20-point scale. You know that you have, let us say, quite a strong desire and are inclined to use the middle of the scale – but which point to choose? There is little to guide you, so after a small delay you arbitrarily pick 12. But you would have been quite happy to pick anything between 9 and 15. We might call 9 to 15 your 'range of uncertainty'.

Of course it does not have definite boundaries but the range can be specified approximately. Now let us say that you are shown a film of someone drinking and, for the sake of this example, we state that this had no actual effect on your desire for a beer. However, you have a sense that the film might be expected to increase your desire for a beer and when you are asked to rate your desire

---

again you choose a different figure *within your range of uncertainty,* perhaps you choose 14 or 15.

The experimenter may think he has influenced your desire for a beer but all he has done is to influence what for you is an arbitrary choice between different points within your range of uncertainty. This is dealt with in more detail in West (1983). It is slightly worrying to consider how many of the findings that we have observed in experimental studies on self-reported motivation reflect this kind of effect.

Chaos theory

This model is very powerful. It can be applied at many levels of analysis from the initiation of individual actions through to chronic behaviour patterns. However, it needs to be borne in mind that it is no more than a metaphor. In theory it may be possible one day to apply mathematical models to these processes as has been done in other areas of science such as physics, but for the present we have to content ourselves with the conceptual account. Where mathematical equations have been applied to this kind of model it is referred to as 'non-linear systems dynamics' of which a well-known branch is chaos theory (see www.imho.com/grae/chaos/chaos.html for an excellent introduction).

Chaos theory is a mathematical approach to modelling particular kinds of events in the world. It developed from the accidental discovery that a minuscule difference in the initial state of a computer program designed to model atmospheric conditions led to massive differences in the output of the program after it had been running for a while. This led to the famous notion of the flapping of butterfly wings in Asia potentially being responsible for storms in America.

'Chaotic systems' (such as weather) exhibit characteristic patterns: they involve periods of short- to medium-term stability punctuated by apparently unpredictable switches in state or periods of violent instability resulting from apparently small events; the paths that two systems follow can diverge markedly as a result of very small differences in their starting points; on occasions the system can become fixed in a particular state without the possibility of escape under any realistic conditions, while on other occasions it can apparently show this pattern only to suddenly switch state.

Human behaviour appears chaotic in much the same way as do weather patterns (see e.g. Robertson and Combs 1995). We can find ourselves heading inexorably down a particular path without any obvious difference except perhaps for something minor that happened in the past. Yet having gone down that path, sometimes we switch dramatically from one state to another (e.g. 'finding religion'). We are also prone to sudden outbursts that seem to come from nowhere. Sometimes we fluctuate in an unpredictable manner from one state to another, in terms of preferences, opinions or how we see ourselves and behave.

Thus at a general level, chaos theory looks quite useful as a metaphor for the operation of motivational systems, and the epigenetic landscape looks like a useful pictorial representation of the process.

Motivational forces as we experience them

It is worth considering what kind of force it is that we *experience* either directly or through observation of our behaviour. That is to say what are the forces that we can describe? At a common-sense level of analysis there seem to be three that are 'mindful': *wants*, *urges* and *evaluations*. These are accompanied by two that are 'mindless': *reflexes* and *habits*.

The mindful forces are conscious feelings and beliefs that drive our choices. They only exist when they are created by the right circumstances. When they are not operating, they do not exist. What exists is the potential for them to be created. This is already a departure from most current motivational accounts. Current theories typically treat these forces as though they had a continuous existence. Thus when we ask the question 'How much do you want to control your drinking?', the presumption is that there is some kind of motivational quantity residing in the respondent's head which that person can examine and report on. What happens in reality (and this is obvious if you think about it) is that the person was probably not thinking about the issue at all until asked the question. Then having been asked the question he has to call upon whatever cues he can to offer an answer. One cue might be recollection of an answer he gave the last time the question was asked. Another might be a recollection of feelings that were generated when he last gave the matter some thought, such as after a particularly heavy binge. Another might be a rapid analysis of the costs and benefits of controlling his drinking, projecting himself into a future with and without controlled drinking and inspecting the feelings that each prospect arouses. Such stability as is observed in responses to this kind of question can arise from any number of processes, including a desire to appear consistent.

A summary: key propositions from PRIME theory

1. At every moment we act in pursuit of what we most desire ('want' or 'need') at that moment.
2. Wants and needs involve imagined futures and associated feelings of antici-pated pleasure/satisfaction (wants) or relief from mental or physical discom-fort (needs). They form part of our conscious experience, but we are not necessarily conscious of them.
3. Beliefs (propositions that we hold to be true) only influence actions if they generate desires that are strong enough to overwhelm those arising from other sources (e.g. drives and emotions) or impulses and inhibitions arising automatically out of learned or unlearned associations; imagery plays a key role in this.
4. Plans (self-conscious intentions to undertake actions in the future) provide overarching structure to our actions but in order to direct our behaviour, they need to be recalled and generate desires at relevant moments that are suffi-ciently powerful to overcome desires and impulses arising from other sources.

5. The motivational system can be characterised in terms of dispositions for its components to respond in particular ways to internal and external inputs. Processes that lead to changes in dispositions include associative learning, habituation, sensitisation, direct imitation, analysis and inference. A wide variety of patterns of change can occur with sudden large changes resulting from apparently small triggers.

6. Identity (our mental representations of ourselves and the feelings attached to these) is an important source of desires and provides a degree of stability to our behaviour by virtue of the labels we apply (e.g. ex-addict) and the rules that govern our behaviour (e.g. no longer using drugs).

7. Identity change is a starting point for deliberate behaviour change (in terms of a new label and a new set of rules governing our behaviour) and can be regarded as an 'act' that occurs when the desire to make the change is momentarily greater than the desire not to.

8. Deliberate behaviour change is sustained when the desires arising from the new identity are stronger at each relevant moment than the desires arising from other sources to revert to the previous behaviour pattern, or are able to overwhelm habitual or instinctive impulses.

9. When identity change results from self-conscious beliefs about what is good and bad, maintaining behaviour change requires 'self-control': the effortful generation of desire to adhere to a rule that is sufficiently powerful to overcome desires arising from other sources.

10. Personal rules that have clear boundaries and a strong connection with components of identity that involve strong emotional attachments will generate more powerful desires when required and better suppress countervailing desires and so have a stronger lasting impact on behaviour.

These 10 key principles can be reframed for the purposes of designing interventions into five laws of motivation:

First law of motivation

At every moment we act in pursuit of our strongest motives (wants or needs) at that moment. Wants are anticipated pleasure or satisfaction and needs are anticipated relief from, or avoidance of, mental or physical discomfort.

Second law of motivation

Evaluations (beliefs about what is good and bad) and plans (self-conscious intentions to do or not do things) can only control our actions if they create motives at the appropriate moments that are stronger than competing motives coming from other sources.

Third law of motivation

Self-control (acting in accordance with plans despite opposing motives) requires mental energy and depletes reserves of that energy.

Fourth law of motivation

Our identities (thoughts, images and feelings and feelings about ourselves) can be a powerful source of motives and involve labels (the categories we think we belong to), attributes (the features we ascribe to ourselves) and personal rules (imperatives about what we do and do not do).

Fifth law of motivation

Motives influence actions by creating impulses and inhibitions, which are also generated by habitual (learned) and instinctive (unlearned) associations; behaviour is controlled by the strongest momentary impulses and inhibitions.

References

Baron, J. (2000) *Thinking and Deciding*. Cambridge University Press, Cambridge.

Baumeister, R.F., Heatherton, T.F., and Dice, T.M. (1994). *Losing Control: How and Why People Fail at Self-regulation*. Academic Press, San Diego.

Brass, M. and Heyes, C. (2005) Imitation: is cognitive neuroscience solving the correspondence problem?. *Trends Cogn Sci* **9**(10): 489–495.

Catmur, C., Walsh, V. and Heyes, C. (2009) Associative sequence learning: the role of experience in the development of imitation and the mirror system. *Philos Trans R Soc Lond B Biol Sci* **364**(1528): 2369–2380.

Crocker, J. and Nuer, N. (2004). Do people need self-esteem? Comment on Pyszczynski et al. (2004). *Psychol Bull* **130**(3): 469–472; discussion 483–488.

Crocker, J. and Park, L.E. (2004). The costly pursuit of self-esteem. *Psychol Bull* **130**(3): 392–414.

DuBois, D.L. and Flay, B.R. (2004). The healthy pursuit of self-esteem: comment on and alternative to the Crocker and Park (2004) formulation. *Psychol Bull* **130**(3): 415–420; discussion 430–434.

Fiori, S. (2005). Nonlinear complex-valued extensions of hebbian learning: an essay. *Neural Comput* **17**(4): 779–838.

Gaultney, J.F., Kipp, K., Weinstein, D J. and McNeill, J. (1999). Inhibition and mental effort in attention deficit hyperactivity disorder. *J Dev Phys Disabil* **11**(2): 105–114.

Grigsby, J., Kravcisin, N., Ayarbe, S.D. and Busenbark, D. (1993). Prediction of deficits in behavioral self-regulation among persons with multiple sclerosis. *Arch Phys Med Rehabil* **74**(12): 1350–1353.

Harakeh, Z., Engels, R.C., Van Baaren, R.B. and Scholte, R.H. (2007) Imitation of cigarette smoking: an experimental study on smoking in a naturalistic setting. *Drug Alcohol Depend* **86**(2–3): 199–206.

Harakeh, Z. and Vollebergh, W.A. (2012) Young adult smoking in peer groups: an experimental observational study. *Nicotine Tob Res* **15**(3):656–661.

Heyes, C. (2001) Causes and consequences of imitation. *Trends Cogn Sci* **5**(6): 253–261.

Janis, I.L. and Mann, L. (1977) *Decision Making: A Psychological Analysis of Conflict, Choice and Commitment*. The Free Press, New York.

Lou, J.S., Kearns, G., Oken, B., Sexton, G. and Nutt, J. (2001) Exacerbated physical fatigue and mental fatigue in Parkinson's disease. *Mov Disord* **16**(2): 190–196.

McIntosh, J. and McKegany, N. (2001) Identity and recovery from dependent drug use: the addict's perspective. *Drugs (Abingdon Engl)* 8(1): 47–59.

Michie, S., van Stralen, M.M. and West, R. (2011) The behaviour change wheel: a new method for characterising and designing behaviour change interventions. *Implement Sci* 6: 42.

Miller, G., Galanter, E. and Pribram, K.A. (1960). *Plans and the Structure of Behaviour.* Holt, Rinehart & Winston, New York.

Mook, D.G. (1996) *Motivation: the Organization of Action.* W.W. Norton, New York.

Nevin, J.A. (1992) An integrative model for the study of behavioral momentum. *J Exp Anal Behav* 57(3): 301–316.

Pyszczynski, T. and Cox, C. (2004) Can we really do without self-esteem? Comment on Crocker and Park (2004). *Psychol Bull* 130(3): 425–429; discussion, 430–434.

Pyszczynski, T., Greenberg, J., Solomon, S., Arndt, J. and Schimel J. (2004). Why do people need self-esteem? A theoretical and empirical review. *Psychol Bull* 130(3): 435–468.

Robertson, R. and Combs, A. (1995) *Chaos Theory in Psychology and the Life Sciences.* Lawrence Erlbaum Associates, Mahwah, NJ.

Sheldon, K.M. (2004) The benefits of a "sidelong" approach to self-esteem need satisfaction: comment on Crocker and Park (2004). *Psychol Bull* 130(3): 421–424; discussion, 430–434.

Strack, F. and Deutsch, R. (2004) Reflective and impulsive determinants of social behavior. *Pers Soc Psychol Rev* 8(3). 220–247.

Thorndike, E.L. (1898) Animal Intelligence: An Experimental Study of the Associative Processes in Animals. *Psychological Monographs: General and Applied* 2(4). i–109.

Waddington, C. (1977) *Tools for Thought: How to Understand and Apply the Latest Scientific Techniques of Problem Solving.* Basic Books, New York.

West, R. (1983) Self-report measures in psychology experiments: ratings versus natural language measures. Ph.D. thesis, Psychology Department, London University.

West, R. (in preparation) Self-labelling as a non-smoker as a predictor of success in maintaining abstinence.

Yates, F.E. (2002). From homeostasis to homeodynamics: energy, action, stability and senescence. URL: http://www.biodynamichealthaging.org/Abstracts/YatesNIAsynopsis.pdf [06 February 2005]

Chapter 9
A THEORY OF ADDICTION

This final chapter returns to the concept of addiction and examines how the PRIME Theory of motivation can help in understanding the various manifestations of addiction and how this can be used to develop more effective intervention strategies.

With a broad-brush description of the motivational system and the context in which it exists in mind, we can now examine what kinds of abnormality become manifest in addiction. The first thing we need to do is to revisit the definition of addiction.

Addiction is

Addiction is a social construct, not an object that can be uniquely defined. According to the proposed theory, addiction can be usefully viewed as a chronic condition involving a repeated powerful motivation to engage in a rewarding behaviour, acquired as a result of engaging in that behaviour, that has significant potential for unintended harm. It often forms part of a well-defined syndrome such as the 'alcohol dependence syndrome' (Edwards and Gross 1976) involving cravings and withdrawal symptoms. Physical dependence can contribute to addiction as an important source of motivation to engage in the activity but it is not an essential or necessary condition for addiction.

Addiction can arise from many different underlying abnormalities and so perhaps is better regarded as a symptom more than a unitary disorder. It varies in strength and severity and is also manifest in different patterns of behaviour from irregular bingeing to a sustained chronic level of activity.

As a social construct, addiction has fuzzy boundaries. There are cases where there is a clear consensus that addiction is present and others where it is not. There are also cases where there is legitimate disagreement concerning whether this is a case of addiction or something that has 'addiction-like' qualities. In this respect, it is no different from other taxonomies in biology and social science. The important thing to note is that the label is not paramount. What is important is the set of phenomena that are observed and how best to address them.

Theory of Addiction, Second Edition. Robert West and Jamie Brown.
© 2013 John Wiley & Sons, Ltd. Published 2013 by John Wiley & Sons, Ltd.

The pathologies underlying addiction

The pathologies underlying addiction involve three main types of abnormality interacting with each other:

1. Abnormalities in the 'motivational system' of the individual that exist independently of the addictive behaviour such as a propensity to heightened sensitivity to reward, low ability to learn from punishment, anxiety, depression or impulsiveness;
2. Abnormalities in the motivational system that stem from the addictive behaviour itself such as acquisition of a strongly entrenched habit or an acquired drive; and
3. Abnormalities in the individual's social or physical environment such as the presence of strong social or other pressures to engage in the activity.

These pathologies become manifest in a range of ways in which we think about ourselves, and the way we behave towards ourselves and the objects of our addiction. They can affect the way we plan our lives as well as the way we respond to our immediate environment.

Thus addiction affects the choices we make but cannot be understood solely in terms of those choices; it affects our needs and desires but cannot be understood solely in terms of those; it affects our emotional attachment to the object of the addiction but involves more than this; it involves our sense of identity but cannot be understood solely in terms of this; it can involve non-conscious impulses as well as conscious urges but cannot be understood solely as a disorder of impulse control; finally it often involves a habitual element but is more than just a habit. In short, understanding addiction in its varying manifestations requires an understanding of the whole motivational system.

An example: PRIME theory and cigarettes

Since the first edition, PRIME theory has been used to understand cigarette addiction and the process of smoking cessation (West 2009). We hope the general explanatory value of the theory will be illuminated by considering a concrete application. Cigarette addiction, like most addictions, requires an understanding that there are several mechanisms underlying it.

Impulses and inhibitions
The delivery of nicotine from each puff of a cigarette leads to dopamine release in the core of the nucleus accumbens that appears to generate stimulus–impulse associations (Balfour 2004; Benowitz 2010). Consequently, cues that are regularly associated with the action leading to this release generate the impulse to repeat the associated action without the need to experience positive feelings. This impulse does not require any anticipated pleasure, satisfaction or relief. Thus smokers can feel urges to smoke in the presence of smoking cues

that seem to arise without any obvious reason or anticipation of pleasure from smoking.

Additionally, during nicotine withdrawal, smokers have impaired functioning of the low-level brain mechanisms that underlie inhibition (Dawkins et al. 2007). This means that smokers trying to stop not only experience the impulse to smoke in the presence of smoking cues but also have a reduced capacity to inhibit this action.

Motives

Nicotine also leads to dopamine release in the shell of the nucleus accumbens that results in pleasant sensations (Balfour 2004), and therefore positively reinforces smoking behaviour. This enjoyment is enhanced by the presence of all the stimuli associated with cigarettes such as the aroma, the touch of the cigarette and the packaging. Many of these stimuli originally elicit little affect, however, over time people are conditioned to like them as a result of many pairings with the 'unconditioned' nicotine reward (Balfour 2009). Finally, nicotine amplifies the positive affect associated with any reinforcer, either conditioned or unconditioned (Caggiula et al. 2009), and therefore magnifies whatever pleasure is generated from smoking.

Repeated nicotine ingestion from cigarettes also leads to chronic functional changes in several parts of the brain that lead smokers to feel a need to smoke – to relieve a kind of 'nicotine hunger'. Thus while nicotine acutely increases the release of dopamine in the nucleus accumbens, after chronic use there appears to be abnormally low levels of dopamine released when central nervous system nicotine concentrations are depleted (Foulds 2006). It creates an acquired drive to smoke.

Chronic neural adaptation also leads smokers to experience unpleasant withdrawal symptoms when they abstain (irritability, depressed mood, anxiety, restlessness, difficulty concentrating and increased appetite; Hughes 2007). As a consequence, the actions associated with not smoking are negatively reinforced, while the relief from the removal of these aversive symptoms positively reinforces the behaviour involved in smoking following abstinence.

Evaluations

Smokers readily form beliefs about the benefits of smoking. In particular, they believe that it helps to control stress, is enjoyable, helps weight control and aids concentration (McEwen et al. 2008). It is likely that these beliefs result from the repeated experience that smoking is effective at relieving withdrawal symptoms resulting from abstinence. As a consequence, smokers tend to over-generalise and many come to believe (mistakenly) that smoking is effective at relieving these symptoms even when the source is not nicotine withdrawal.

These beliefs will lead the smoker to want or need to smoke at times when circumstances make them relevant (e.g., at times of stress). Thus, a smoker who feels miserable and wants to be 'cheered up', or who is stressed and needs to feel better, will on those occasions experience a want or need to smoke (Yong and Borland 2008). These beliefs will deter smokers from attempting to quit if they are anticipating a particular stressful or miserable time ahead. Additionally, the beliefs can persist for many months and sometimes years after having stopped. If, at the same time, the same individual has low reserves of mental energy, the self-imposed rule of not smoking may not be sufficient to prevent the behaviour. Often individuals do not intend to resume smoking permanently but only long enough to address the particular need at that time. However, once the cigarette is smoked, it rekindles the other sources of motivation, including the stimulus–impulse associations and the 'nicotine hunger'; and usually eventually leads to a full resumption of smoking.

Plans and self-control
Stopping smoking requires the exercise of self-control. The many sources of motivation to smoke listed above can be mitigated by medication and various behavioural change techniques (West et al. 2010; Michie et al. 2011). However, there are many occasions on which an urge, want or need to smoke still generated by the sources listed above must be countered by a want or need to not smoke. Plans, the self-imposed rule that smoking is not permitted, and a change in identity are all important sources of a desire to not smoke and maintain the motivational balance in favour of the changed behaviour.

Smoking cessation
Overcoming addiction to cigarettes involves (a) making a serious quit attempt and then (b) maintaining abstinence in the face of motivation to smoke coming from multiple sources. Therefore, the process is likely to begin by forming a personal rule not to smoke followed by self-conscious implementation of that rule in the face of impulses, wants and needs to smoke. Smokers will form that rule when at the precise moment they have the idea of making the rule and feel more attracted to it than the idea of continuing to smoke.

In approximately half the cases where this occurs, the smoker implements the quit attempt as soon as the decision is made (West and Sohal 2006). In other cases, the smoker defers implementation, usually for just a few days, for example, to give time to prepare mentally or practically for what is ahead.

This intention to stop is quite variable and dependent on a variety of stimuli and factors (Ussher et al. submitted). This means that smokers can be prompted to make quit attempts who were not thinking of doing so beforehand. They will also accept the offer of help and many will go on to succeed.

PRIME theory predicts that the nature of the not-smoking rule may have a major bearing on the outcome of the quit attempt. If the rule is that the smoker will 'try not to smoke', it would be expected that it would not generate sufficiently strong motivation on all relevant occasions to prevent smoking. On the other hand, if the rule is that smoking is not permitted at all, the boundaries are more clearly defined and the inhibition of smoking will be more powerful and consistent. However, for the rule to be able to generate sufficiently strong wants or needs to inhibit smoking, it needs to be linked to what might be termed 'deep identity': self-ascribed labels and attributes to which the individual is emotionally attached.

Therefore, the process of smoking cessation can be encapsulated in a simple four-state model in terms of the rule that is in operation (Figure 9.1):

1. Smoking (no rule),
2. Not smoking (I do not smoke),
3. Attempting to stop (I am trying not to smoke) and
4. Planning to stop (I have made a definite plan to stop in the near future)

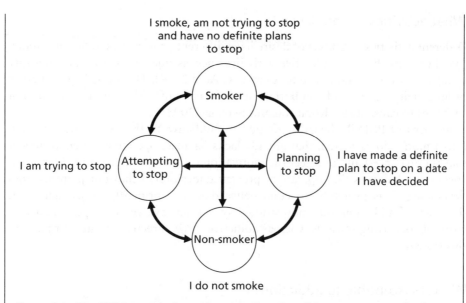

I smoke, am not trying to stop and have no definite plans to stop

Smoker

I am trying to stop

Attempting to stop

Planning to stop

I have made a definite plan to stop on a date I have decided

Non-smoker

I do not smoke

Figure 9.1 The SNAP model of smoking cessation. Transitions occur as result of a combination of tension and triggers. Tension is a feeling of a desire to change (want or need) arising from a combination of dissatisfaction with current situation or hope that change can be achieved. Triggers are events that momentarily either raise the tension (including increasing urgency), reduce barriers, simply put the idea of change in the person's mind or show a pathway by which the change can occur.

By contrast with stages of change of models, transitions can occur suddenly between any state and any other state, depending on the momentary balance of wants and needs. Particular factors make certain transitions more likely. For example, wanting to smoke (enjoyment of smoking) deters quit attempts while needing to smoke (anticipated relief from nicotine hunger) and cue-driven impulses to smoke (experienced as 'urges') leads to relapse after the quit attempt has been started (Fidler and West 2011). If the would-be ex-smoker maintains complete abstinence, then the cue-driven impulses to smoke, nicotine hunger and withdrawal symptoms decline which substantially reduces the risk of relapse with each week of abstinence that passes (West and Stapleton 2008).

A return to some 'big observations' about addiction

We now return to some 'big observations' in the field of addiction and in each case, examine how these relate to the theory of motivation that has been developed. The questions posed are now slightly different from those that were posed in the first chapter so as to frame them more closely in the conceptual system that has been developed. With such major observations, the choice of citations is problematic; those that are used are illustrative only.

What activities are addictive?

Different activities or objects of desire have different propensities to become addictive, but even the most addictive activities such as injecting heroin are minority occupations among those who try them (e.g. Atha 2004). The rewarding properties of an activity appear to be important in the genesis of addiction but they are not sufficient to cause it (see Robinson and Berridge 2003).

In terms of PRIME theory, activities are addictive to the extent that they tap into a motivational system that already lacks balance, operate in an environment that is unbalanced and/or affect the motivational system to undermine the normal checks and balances that operate to prevent undesirable behaviour patterns from developing. It is probably no coincidence that it is primarily drugs that lie at the heart of addiction: our motivational system has evolved to apply balance to naturally occurring rewards whereas addictive drugs directly tap into just parts of this system.

Who is susceptible to addiction?

There are individual differences in propensity to become addicted to activities and, moreover, there is at least a moderate heritability to this (in the order of 50%) (e.g. Han et al. 1999). In terms of behavioural traits, the differences are at least partly manifest in terms of propensity to antisocial behaviour, impulsivity and depression (e.g. Ball and Schottenfeld 1997; Blaszczynski et al. 1997; Burt et al. 2000). There are also differences in terms of physiological and metabolic responses to ingestion of potential drugs of addiction (e.g. Batra et al. 2003).

In terms of the synthetic theory, individuals are susceptible to particular addictive activities in so far as their motivational system is already unbalanced or transformed into an unbalanced state by the activity. Thus individuals are susceptible to an activity becoming addictive if for them it has the capacity to be continually or increasingly rewarding. This can be at the level of conscious feelings or habit. Susceptibility is also increased by low self-control, or a susceptibility to the effect of the activity in lowering self-control. Individuals will also be susceptible if they have little reason as they see it to exert self-control, or they are less responsive to the punishing effects of the activity. Some of these susceptibilities will increase propensity to become addicted to a wide range of rewarding activities while others will be more specific.

What circumstances promote addiction?

Different environmental conditions are more or less conducive to the development and maintenance of addictive behaviours. Critical variables include the extent of opportunities to engage in the activity, cost of the activity, other sanctions and rewards relating to the activity, environmental stressors, opportunities to achieve personal goals in other ways, and social and microcultural norms about the activity (see Vuchinich and Heather 2003).

For existing addicts, these variables may undermine genuine attempts to abstain even when they do not influence conscious decisions to try to abstain. For example, in the United Kingdom, economic deprivation is more strongly related to the success in attempts to stop smoking than the rate at which those attempts are made (Lader and Goddard 2004).

According to PRIME theory, environmental conditions that fail to provide balancing input will promote addiction. This will occur if an activity is seen as normal within the social group with which the person identifies. That immediate social group will tend to be more influential than the wider society.

A lack of opportunities for other sources of contentment will unbalance the motivational system towards whatever rewards are available, including reliable sources of reward such as addictive drugs.

Environmental conditions that create distress will promote addictive behaviours that provide escape or reduce the mental resources available for the exercise of self-control.

Conditions that reduce sense of self-worth will promote addiction by reducing the critical balancing influence of desire for self-protection. It will also obviously promote ways of engaging in the addictive behaviour that are more damaging (such as needle sharing).

When and how does addiction develop?

Experimentation with behaviours that have addictive potential typically begins in the teenage years or early adulthood though it can start earlier or later (see Chambers et al. 2003). Initiation of a behaviour that has addictive potential and transition from non-addictive to addictive behaviour is more likely in individuals who experience adverse life events such as break-up of a relationship or involuntary job loss (e.g. Gorelick 1992).

The trajectories into addiction are varied, even within the same behaviour type such as smoking and drinking alcohol. Movement from initial experimentation to addiction can be very rapid, a slow progression or even initial experimentation followed by a period of dormancy and then movement to addiction (e.g. Robinson et al. 2004; Vitaro et al. 2004). The trajectory has been found to be related to factors that would be expected to promote addiction such as pre-existing psychopathology (e.g. Shaffer and Eber 2002).

In terms of the current theory, the development of addiction appears to follow a 'chaotic' pattern in which in some cases an event, which may at the time appear significant or insignificant, can send an individual down a particular path. In others, it sets up a susceptibility to which other triggers are needed for the addictive pattern of behaviour to develop. The particular trajectory will depend on a host of factors and chance events.

What other symptoms accompany addiction?

The experience of a repeated powerful motivation to engage in a rewarding but harmful activity is accompanied by different symptoms in different individuals and across different activities. There are characteristic withdrawal syndromes associated with addictive drugs, though the prevalence, severity and duration of these vary, as do their relationship with failure to exercise restraint (Hughes et al. 1994). The addiction is also often accompanied by mood disturbance, increased stereotypy of the behaviour and emotional and motivational conflict. In the case of alcohol dependence, the syndrome has been well characterised (Edwards and Gross 1976). Parallel descriptions of a cocaine dependence syndrome and an opiate dependence syndrome have been proposed (Sutherland et al. 1988; Washton 1989). However, these are strongly parallel and are influenced by the alcohol dependence syndrome, although the authors did not use the same methods. A nicotine dependence syndrome based on the model by Edwards and Gross (1976) and using a factor analytic approach to questionnaires has also recently been proposed (Shiffman et al. 2004).

In terms of PRIME theory, the syndromes of dependence that accompany addiction give clues as to the mechanisms underlying it – the sources of unbalanced input. These may be mood disturbances that are temporarily relieved by the addictive behaviour, powerful urges even when there is no very strong desire, or anticipation of pleasure. The increasing stereotypy, for example, points to a powerful associative learning mechanism in operation.

However, these syndromes are descriptive rather than theoretically driven and are also themselves social constructs that simplify the pattern of experiences encountered by individual addicts. They, therefore, do not obviate the need for a principled system for directing the detailed investigation of underlying pathologies such as is proposed in this volume.

How do addicts describe their experience of addiction?

Reports of the experience of addiction vary widely across individuals, types of addictive behaviour and occasions. In some cases, addicted individuals deny that the activity is problematic and make no effort to exercise restraint. In other cases, they report making an effort to exercise self-control but with limited or no success (see Quintero and Nichter 1996).

Under some accounts of addiction, someone could not be addicted unless he or she has attempted to exercise control over the behaviour. In others, he or she would need to experience cravings. In choice-based theories, the experience would have to be one of changing preferences. In habit-based theories, addictive behaviour can be established even though the addict experiences no conflict and never attempts to exercise self-control. PRIME theory attempts to capture the diversity of the experience in all its shades.

How do different addictive behaviours relate to each other?

It is common, though not universal, for initiation of one pattern of addictive behaviour to be associated with later development of another one that involves greater costs and more extreme rewarding effects – the so-called 'gateway phenomenon' (e.g. Kandel et al. 1992; Fergusson and Horwood 2000). It is also

common, but again not universal, for less invasive, harmful methods of drug administration to precede more invasive and harmful forms that produce stronger effects,
for example, movement from smoking to injecting heroin (e.g. Davies et al. 1985).
Adults who engage in one addictive activity are much more likely to engage in
others (e.g. Miller and Gold 1990). This is not universally the case, however.

In the current theory, addictive behaviours co-occur to the extent that they share a
common aetiology in terms of their effects, the susceptibilities of individuals to them
and environmental conditions. They can also obviously be mutually reinforcing in
terms of their effects on the balance of the motivational system or the addict's
environment.

When do addicts attempt to overcome their addiction?

Attempts to overcome addictive behaviours vary widely from behaviour to
behaviour and person to person. In the case of smoking, for example, there is
evidence that attempts are made to give up within a few years of starting (McNeill
et al. 1986). In other cases, it may be many years before attempts are made to
control or stop the activity.

These attempts are often prompted by experience of harmful effects or fear
of future harmful effects of the activity (see Hanninen and Koski-Jannes 1999).
However, there are many other factors that can trigger the change, including new
circumstances that make the behaviour less attractive or necessary or are incompatible with the behaviour. Social pressure and changes in self-concept can also trigger
attempts at restraint. It is rare for attempts to overcome addiction to be effective
first time (e.g. Lader and Goddard 2004).

PRIME theory emphasises the 'chaotic' nature of change. A motivational system that has become less sensitive to the rewarding effects of the activity, either
physiologically or psychologically, can lead to a reduction in the 'depth' of the
addictive chreod. The environment may normalise, for example, with the advent
of a new personal relationship. There may be a major change in identity which is
incompatible with the addictive behaviour or even highly rewarding of overcoming
that behaviour. A very small trigger can initiate an attempt at change in individuals,
who at the moment it occurs are receptive.

What form does the transition from addicted
to non-addicted state take?

The transition varies widely (see Dennis et al. 2005). In some cases, it involves a
relatively orderly sequence from making a decision to change within a particular
timescale followed by preparatory actions and then a definite transition point (e.g.
'the quit date' for smokers).

On other occasions, it involves no very clear decision point and a more or less
haphazard process involving an attempt to reduce or control the activity, then
perhaps an attempt at abstinence. On other occasions, an event triggers a firm

decision to change that is implemented immediately without there having been any planning (Larabie 2005).

Once an attempt to control or stop an activity is more or less definitively under way, its progress is also subject to wide variation. In a small minority of cases, the activity ceases and does not occur again, at least for several months or years. In some cases, there are lapses but eventually the activity ceases. Most often, there are lapses that are followed after varying amounts of time by resumption of the addictive behaviour (see Marlatt 1996). The likelihood of relapse is greatest early in the attempt at restraint and decreases over time (e.g. Hughes et al. 2004). However, it probably never reaches zero.

Once addiction has developed, attempts to control the behaviour without abstaining from it completely are successful on occasions but it is quite rare. In most cases, the only form of control that is stable is abstinence (e.g. Hajek et al. 1995; Vaillant 2003).

Like the attempt at changing addictive behaviours, the process of change appears to follow a 'chaotic' pattern. If we think in terms of an addicted state and a non-addicted state, propensities and triggers interact so that in some cases there is a sharp transition with no movement backwards or forwards while in other cases a chaotic series of transitions occurs depending on the precise balance of forces operating at the moment leading either back into the original addicted state or progressing further and further down a new chreod. In most cases, we can think of this chreod as relatively shallow and running right next to the addictive one so that even minor triggers can tip the individual over the ridge into the addicted chreod at any time.

What predicts success of attempts to recover from addictive behaviours?

Ability to exercise sustained restraint over an addictive activity is not the same thing as recovery from the addiction. Individuals may continue to feel motivations to engage in an activity and need to expend effort to exercise restraint for a long period or indefinitely. Other individuals may genuinely recover, at least partially, in the sense that the abnormal motivation to engage in the activity no longer occurs or is greatly weakened.

Reduced likelihood of continued abstinence or control over the addictive behaviour is not necessarily related to reported enjoyment of the activity but is typically related to the intensity and frequency of the activity, levels of distress and psychological problems in the individual (e.g. Miller et al. 1999; Pettinati et al. 1999; West et al. 2001).

Relapse occurs more often in situations of high temptation (when the opportunity presents itself together with reminders of the positive rewards offered by the activity) or perceived need (situations in which it is believed that the activity serves some purpose such as relief of stress), or during periods of boredom. However, it can also occur without any obvious external trigger (e.g. Shiffman et al. 1996).

In PRIME theory, the depth of the addicted chreod represents the plethora of motivational elements that have come to support the behaviour. Where there remain significant conflicting elements or the elements maintaining the addictive pattern are less strong or there are fewer of them, the exercise of self-control will be more likely to be successful.

The degree to which the addictive behaviour is entrenched will be signalled by the regularity with which it occurs in particular situations, the breadth of situations in which it occurs and the efforts made to set up situations in which it can occur. This will be one of the strongest and most reliable predictors of the likely success of attempts to exercise restraint.

Triggers for relapse can be construed in terms of factors that tip the recovering addict out of his or her shallow recovery chreod back into his or her addicted one. An important implication of the current theory is that triggers for urges or desires will not be a simple consequence of associative learning but will be responsive to higher level expectations and interpretations. For example, a stimulus that has been associated with smoking will be effective primarily in situations where the smoker knows that he or she could smoke if he or she wanted to.

The current theory also provides a basis for understanding why addicts talk in terms of 'missing' their addictive activity. This must be seen in terms of an integrated motivational system in which affectionate memory for something that has provided pleasure is triggered by reminders and this can set up a cascade of rekindling elements of the motivational system through associative learning and the opportunity to engage in the activity.

What treatments for addiction are effective?

Some pharmacological interventions improve the likelihood of addicts being able to maintain control over the behaviour (see Lingford-Hughes et al. 2012).

- Methadone and buprenorphine help heroin users to reduce or abstain from heroin use for as long as these drugs are provided. There is no good evidence that they promote long-term abstinence after they have ceased to be administered.
- Acamprosate and naltrexone help people addicted to alcohol to maintain abstinence for at least a period of months.
- Nicotine in the form of transdermal patches, chewing gum, nasal spray or other devices helps a proportion of smokers to maintain abstinence. Combining nicotine patches with a faster acting form improves success rates. Relapse rates after termination of treatment seem to be slightly higher in the treated smokers than in untreated smokers but a residual treatment benefit is still observed many years later. Bupropion has an effect broadly similar to nicotine replacement therapies. Varenicline and cytisine, partial agonists binding with high affinity to a particular subtype of the nicotinic acetylcholine receptor, are effective in aiding cessation.

Psychological interventions to help addicted individuals abstain or control use can help in a small proportion of cases. The effect does not seem to outlast the duration of treatment but because the relapse rates are often similar after the end of treatment, a residual treatment effect is often observed months or years later.

Medications

In the language of PRIME theory, medications reduce the acquired drive that has developed as a result of the addiction. In some cases, this may allow the motivational system to normalise simply by virtue of not repeatedly being challenged by the addictive behaviour. In other cases, the motivational system does not recover sufficiently and if the medications are removed, the residual drive, together with all those other elements of the motivational system that have been supporting the addiction, will be enough to reinstate it.

Psychological interventions

These attempt to prevent the addictive behaviour from occurring by another means. They typically attempt to bolster restraint (e.g. through the use of group pressure) or even change the addict's identity to achieve a more lasting and pervasive shift in his or her network of evaluations. They also attempt to provide techniques to cope with or avoid situations that trigger motives and impulses to engage in the activity. As with medications, the hope is that abstinence for a sufficiently long period will lead to sufficient normalisation of the motivational system that the individual will be able to maintain a degree of stability outside the addicted chreod.

In terms of the current theory, the reality is that, for most addicts, the medical and psychological interventions do no more than move the addict's motivational system up the side of his or her addicted chreod and when the treatment is discontinued, the system rapidly descends to the bottom again.

Treatment is more effective when the chreod is shallow or when the individual is already close to the top and a relatively modest influence can tip him or her over the edge. Chreods may become more shallow over time if an addictive drug starts to lose pharmacological effect, perhaps because of the damage to the neural pathways involved, or it may be shallow because there are some balancing forces still in operation or because the motivational properties of the addictive behaviour are not very strong.

What population measures are effective in reducing the prevalence of addictions?

The prevalence of addictions is reduced by population measures that reduce the opportunity to engage in them or increase their cost in financial, social or other terms (e.g. Edwards et al. 1994; Grossman et al. 2002; Jamrozik 2004). However, the size of the effects varies widely and their temporal dynamics are complex.

PRIME theory proposes that population measures will reduce the prevalence of addiction at all stages in the process: by reducing experimentation, reducing the development of an addictive pattern of behaviour, encouraging attempts at abstinence, improving the chances of success at abstinence and reducing relapse rates. This is because they act on a broad front to apply balance to the addict's motivational system and environment. The size of the effects on different points in the addict's career will depend on the intervention and the addictive behaviour.

A detailed understanding of the addictive behaviour is needed to make accurate predictions. For example, price rises will typically reduce uptake of smoking and the transition from irregular to regular smoking. It will have a much more modest effect on cessation because smokers smoke fewer cigarettes but can increase the dose they receive from each cigarette to compensate.

The abnormalities underlying addiction

It is apparent from the above that there is wide variation in the manifestations of addiction across individuals and addictive behaviours. The complex emotional, motivational and cognitive experiences that accompany it require us to postulate a range of pathways into addiction and a range of abnormalities in the motivational system underpinning it.

As a unifying principle, it is postulated that the development of addiction involves the operation of environmental forces on an inherently unstable motivational system. In this system, forces that create imbalance, or the absence of, or a progressively reduced sensitivity to, forces that would restore balance, send that system down an even more entrenched pathway in the epigenetic landscape. We can now summarise some of the main principles.

What makes something addictive?

Addictive activities are those that have the potential to change the motivational system so that they become highly rewarding or habitual over time in susceptible individuals, or that reduce the individual's ability to exercise restraint. Any or all elements in the motivational system may be involved including associations between stimuli and impulses, stimuli and motives, evaluations and plans.

Even if the addictive activity (such as a drug) acts primarily on one element of the system (e.g. on impulses), connections within the system will lead to changes in other elements (such as evaluations) that will support the behaviour.

For example, cigarettes are addictive because they deliver nicotine rapidly to the brain in a form that is mostly socially acceptable, convenient, supportive of a particular identity, and accompanied by distinctive, quite pleasant stimuli (such as the smell and sensation in the throat) that can be associated with a subtle rewarding stimulus and whose negative consequences are deferred and difficult to be fearful about until it is too late. Without nicotine, cigarettes would not be smoked but addiction to cigarettes involves a network of beliefs, motives and emotions that help to maintain the behaviour.

What makes an individual susceptible?

Individual susceptibility to addiction involves a large number of potential factors. These include a drive to explore new experiences and so be exposed to a potentially harmful addictive behaviour; a lower propensity or ability to exercise restraint; a greater propensity to form associative links with rewards than with punishments; an identity in which engaging in the addictive activity is valued positively; an identity in which being addicted is viewed positively; a propensity to emotional states that make the addictive behaviour rewarding and a physiological susceptibility to the effects of the addictive activity.

For example, pre-existing psychological problems are very common in both alcohol and heroin addiction to the extent that there can be little doubt that a large proportion of addicts, as opposed to non-addicted users, are meeting an important need with their substance use. There are also differences in the balance between the rewarding and aversive effects of alcohol, at least partly determined by the efficiency with which the body deals with the major toxic effect of alcohol, acetaldehyde.

What makes an environment pathological?

The evidence strongly points to social norms, opportunity, boredom, stressors and more specific needs relating to the addictive behaviour in question being important in the development and maintenance of addiction.

For example, if most of the people in one's social world are smokers or drinkers, these behaviours will find it easier to carve a path to habitual use. If the environment changes, individuals whose motivational system has not been radically altered will be able to recover their balance but some will not.

An example of alcohol dependence

Individuals who are emotionally vulnerable and who experience relief from distress as a result of alcohol consumption, given a social environment in which it is normal are more likely to drink heavily, especially at times of personal crisis.

In many cases, there are enough balancing forces in the social and physical environment to keep the behaviour from becoming problematic. However, combining this with a relatively weak propensity to learn from punishment, and normal social and ethical controls on behaviour may be too weak to prevent escalation. Then rebound anxiety, pharmacological tolerance and onset of withdrawal symptoms during abstinence, together with instrumental and Pavlovian learning, can further entrench the behaviour, increasing its frequency, intensity and stereotypy.

Impulses, emotional states, drives, motives and evaluations are all affected and they interact with each other to maintain the behaviour. It would be wrong to ascribe the addiction to any one element in the motivational system, and intervening with just one element would be unlikely to be successful because of the network of influences within the system.

Thus counselling, which focuses on shaping the addict's evaluations, may strengthen the attempts at self-control but will not affect the links between cues, motives and impulses that have been established through associative learning.

A drug such as acamprosate may dampen an 'acquired drive' to drink but the effect will be incomplete and there will be no direct effect on other parts of the motivational system. Cue-exposure techniques, in which cues associated with drinking are presented without drinking taking place, may weaken the classically conditioned links that have been established but will not affect other parts of the system.

An example of nicotine dependence

A teenager may start smoking out of curiosity, in response to social pressures, because it serves a desire for a particular identity, or in the belief that it will be enjoyable or serve some need such as helping to control appetite or reduce stress. The teenager is likely to be aware that smoking is damaging to the health but may not consider this relevant at the time.

The first reaction will be a mixture of unpleasant sensations from inhaling smoke and from the systemic effects of nicotine. In some cases, there will also be a subtle rewarding effect of nicotine which may or may not be noticed. The balance between aversive and rewarding effects of nicotine, together with the extrinsic factors that affect the teenager's evaluations and motives, may lead to the activity being repeated soon afterwards.

Even one dose of nicotine may also act on the brain to cause lasting changes that increase the rewarding effect of the drug if it is ingested again. It can also begin to establish an associative link between the activity of smoking, the sensory aspects of smoking a cigarette and the rewarding effect of nicotine.

Thus, the pharmacological actions of nicotine on impulses and motives may combine with evaluations that are conducive to smoking to lead to the behaviour being repeated in circumstances that promote or permit it. If escalation of smoking caused immediate severe social, financial or health problems, it is unlikely that the forces promoting it would be powerful enough for an addictive pattern of behaviour to occur.

However, the primary influences that are stopping smoking are evaluations concerning financial costs and possible future health effects. These do not generate powerful enough motives to inhibit the behaviour though they may be enough to cause conflict in the mind of the smoker about what he or she is doing.

What do these two examples illustrate?

These are just two examples of how a pattern of addictive behaviour can develop. They are intended to illustrate the multiplicity of predisposing factors, successive influences and triggers that are involved in the genesis of addiction. They further illustrate that once addiction has developed, the whole motivational system is involved in its maintenance. Finally, they illustrate that addiction can arise because of the strength of forces that promote a particular behaviour (as in the alcohol dependence case) as well as the weakness of balancing forces that would lead to restraint (as in the smoking case).

Effects of interventions

Treating the symptom or the pathology

We may think of interventions in terms of whether they are simply treating the symptoms of addiction or the underlying pathology. If they are treating the symptoms, we may think of this as pushing the ball in the epigenetic landscape up the side of the valley. As soon as the pressure is released, the ball will roll back down to the bottom because the landscape has not changed. If they are treating the underlying pathology, they are directing the ball down a different path.

For example, treatments for alcohol dependence often do little more than bolster motivation to remain abstinent. For example, where group pressure bolsters motivation, the addictive pattern of consumption will re-emerge if that pressure is no longer present. Pharmacological treatments that act on the drive to drink alcohol may offer the prospect of a more lasting effect, but only if they can alter the motivational system.

Nicotine patch therapy for smoking cessation is a good example of the potential of an intervention to effect a lasting 'cure', or at least remission, in a small minority (probably about 5%) of cases.

Why interventions that assume rationality can work

Because many parts of the motivational system are involved in addictive behaviours, interventions targeted at any part of the system may have some effect. In certain circumstances, this can include interventions targeted at 'rational addicts' such as tax rises, punishments, educational campaigns and brief advice from physicians.

In general, these would be expected to be more effective in individuals whose addiction has a stronger basis in evaluations than habit or impulse control but any individual can be affected. It would be expected that the effect would be immediate rather than delayed and more likely to last if it involves a 'chaotic' shift of identity, for example, as someone who has 'had enough'.

Recommendations and predictions regarding addiction interventions

It would be difficult to claim that any theory of the kind considered in this volume can make unequivocal predictions and recommendations that could not have been made by others. However, the theory being proposed here suggests some guiding principles in the design of interventions:

1. *Interventions must reduce impulses or create inhibitions operating at the moments when the opportunities for engaging in the addictive behaviour occur.* Those designing interventions should be able to trace a causal path from the

initial focus of the intervention, such as creating a visual image by means of a mass media campaign, or creating a feeling that the activity is too expensive, to the impulses to engage in the activity in the succession of opportunities that arise for this behaviour.

2. *Preventive interventions should increase vigilance for small signs that the motivational system is getting out of balance and add, remove, strengthen or weaken elements to restore motivational balance.* It is important to be aware that the motivational system can switch suddenly in response to seemingly minor triggers and that absence of elements that would create motivational balance are as important as those that may be very strong. Restoring balance does not just involve adding elements to inhibit behaviour (punishments) but also it can involve adding elements that distract from it, complement it or substitute for it.

3. *Interventions to combat addiction should have a clear specification concerning how far they are seeking to reduce the strength or extent of excessive motivational forces or to increase the strength of forces that counter these or both.* In many cases, the only practicable option is to apply balancing forces (such as social pressure) to prevent the activity in the hope that over time the motivational system will normalise. In other cases, it will be possible to reduce the strength of motivational forces (e.g. through medications).

4. *All interventions should have a clear specification concerning how far they are seeking to move the recipients into a new chreod and what methods are being used to achieve this, bearing in mind the likely current state of their motivational system.* Unless a new path is found, the balancing inputs will need to be applied to suppress the behaviour. This is as much true of preventive interventions in schools as it is of treatment programmes. One of the most important motivational elements that can act as a potential target for this is a sense of identity and the use of 'conversion' experiences.

5. *Moving individuals into new chreods will require changes to the motivational system that propagate throughout that system.* Even quite profound changes in evaluations of the addictive behaviour will not lead to sustained change unless they propagate to other core beliefs including sense of identity as well as habitual thought patterns, feelings and impulses. Similarly, weakening of associative links between cues and addictive behaviours (through cue-exposure treatment) will not have lasting effects unless they are accompanied by changes in desires, core evaluations and habits associated with concomitant behaviours (including all the social activities related to the addiction).

What follows considers in more detail just three areas of interest: educational interventions, treatments and the process of intervention building.

Educational interventions

Educational interventions involve attempts to increase addicts' understanding of the consequences of their behaviour and of changing it, and of the possibilities for change. This includes mass media campaigns and advice from health-care professionals.

Basic principles

Educational interventions will be effective to the extent that they (a) induce a feeling of *desire* to avoid or restrain the activity; (b) translate that desire into an *impulse* to initiate a change plan before it dissipates; (c) create a lasting *commitment* to the plan based on a shift of *identity*; and (d) trigger *supporting activities* that preserve or restore balance to the motivational system.

Do not tailor to 'stage' of change

PRIME theory argues that interventions should do the opposite of what is proposed by the Transtheoretical Model (Prochaska and Velicer 1997). The model, which has become popular in the field of health promotion, states that interventions should first find out whether people are at a stage where they are thinking about changing, planning to change or in the process of changing and tailoring the content to that stage.

The current theory takes the view that there are no stages as such. Motivation to change is much more unstable and responsive to the immediate environment. Therefore, interventions should not stimulate the recipient to think about what 'stage' they are in, but rather put the maximum *tolerable* pressure on the individual to make the change.

What is tolerable depends on ethical considerations, practical resources and social constraints. A family doctor raising the topic of excessive drinking, for example, needs to exercise his or her clinical and communication skills in doing so in a way that does not harm the relationship with the patient, but within that constraint should focus clearly on attempting to generate a desire for change in the patient and initiate a change plan to which the patient is committed.

Tailoring, where it is possible, should focus on the aspects of the pattern of addictive behaviour concerned, the individual's circumstances as they relate to triggers and cues, wants and needs, and the addict's relationship with the addictive behaviour. Tailoring along some of these lines has been found to have a beneficial effect (Strecher et al. 2005).

Do not waste time on 'pros' and 'cons' analysis

Many of the current models of health promotion also propose that interventions should encourage recipients to think about the 'pros' and 'cons' of their behaviour and of making a change. The current theory takes the view that this will be at best a very weak intervention with regard to achieving behaviour change.

Simply focusing on getting addicts to think about the 'pros' and 'cons' of making a change will typically not generate the kinds of feelings needed to achieve it. The intervention needs to take account of what feelings can realistically be generated.

For example, it will be all but impossible to create genuine and lasting fear of lung cancer in teenage smokers. Increasing the immediate social and financial cost and providing alternative means of affirming their identity are more likely to be effective.

Encourage immediate action in those who feel they are ready

Population-level interventions should take advantage of the instability of motivations by encouraging those who are ready at the time of receipt of the intervention to make the change without delay. These people should not be advised to set a date for change at some time in the future: they should make the change immediately and follow this up with supportive measures.

Repeat the interventions frequently over a short space of time

Single interventions will only create a change in individuals who are in shallow chreods or near the top of chreods because of other pressures. If interventions are repeated but spaced too far apart, the recipients will have time to return to the bottom of the chreod in the interval. They should be sufficiently close together to be able to have a cumulative effect – bearing in mind that it is feelings and impulses that are the ultimate target and these dissipate over time even though beliefs causing them may still be held.

Educational interventions will typically only trigger attempts at change

It is unrealistic to imagine that educational interventions will address those aspects of addictive behaviours that operate at the lower levels in the motivational system (those relating to habits and deeply felt needs and emotions). Educational interventions are targeted at changing evaluations.

If approached intelligently using the principles already described, these interventions can lead to an action that is under the addict's control – the *attempt* to make a change. What happens after that will depend on factors relating to the addiction. That is why part of the educational intervention should involve directing recipients to evidence-based treatment programmes.

Treatment interventions

Basic principles

The guiding principles of treatment are: (a) to alter the balance of motivational forces by weakening those that are too strong, strengthening those that are weak and adding new forces; (b) applying this to the whole motivational system, not just some elements of it; and (c) applying intervention elements dynamically to take account of the current state of the system. If this can be done in a way that achieves a lasting effect, then it is ideal but very often it will be a matter of managing the condition rather than achieving a 'cure'. The application of some of these principles is now briefly outlined.

1. *Assess the behaviours across the broadest possible front*: establish the extent and pattern of the addictive behaviours including the range of targets and linkages between these. For example, how far is the pattern of behaviour one of bingeing or regular use, how much is it linked to particular situations, how far does the 'addict' focus on heroin but will use other drugs when this is not available or to meet secondary needs, etc.

2. *Examine the full range of abnormalities in the motivational system*: identify the abnormalities in the motivational system that are causing the problem, including dysfunctional beliefs, feelings, impulses, sense of identity, propensity to self-control and habits. For example, how does the addict respond to challenges about the damaging effects of the behaviour, how far do they enjoy it, how far does it meet emotional or social needs that they have, how far does the activity form a part of their sense of identity, how far are urges or desires to engage in the activity linked to particular situations and states, how close is the addict to a cusp or possible branching point, etc.

3. *Determine the prospects for altering relevant elements in the system*: determine what are the prospects for changes to those elements of the motivational system that have been identified as abnormal, how these changes might be effected and how long this might take.

    This will determine the content of any psychological treatment and what type of pharmacological treatment might be appropriate. It will also determine how much resource should be devoted to achieving change. In some cases, the best that can be achieved with the available resources is stabilisation while in other cases there may be a realistic prospect of achieving lasting change.

    For example, as noted earlier, a short course of bupropion or nicotine replacement therapy will help about 5–10% of nicotine-dependent smokers to remain abstinent for more than a year. This does not affect the associative learning that has taken place or the emotional vulnerabilities that have contributed to the addiction, or the desires that stem from beliefs about what the addictive behaviour will do.

    Similarly, we may attempt to restructure an addict's evaluations through 'motivational interviewing' but if we do not address strong emotional forces, acquired drives and habits, this will be minimally effective in achieving lasting change.

4. *Acknowledge the inherent limitations of the interventions available to us*: there are severe constraints on resources, on what is ethical, and on what those receiving treatment are willing to commit to. At the same time, we are often dealing with deeply entrenched behaviour patterns and abnormalities at all levels in the motivational system.

    Although there are some excellent treatment guides for addiction, these are based mostly on what ought to help rather than what has been shown to work (e.g. Waller and Rumball 2004). However, the idea that a particular treatment approach can be isolated and demonstrated to be more effective than other plausible approaches is probably unrealistic.

One specific example of a treatment approach that would be expected to have minimal effects is 'self-reinforcement'. It is common for treatment manuals to encourage addicts to reward themselves with praise and encouragement for achievements in maintaining abstinence. A more complete understanding of the motivational system linking conscious beliefs with associative learning suggests that this is unlikely to be effective because knowing that the reward is self-initiated would take away the hedonic tone that it can convey and hence its power to influence the wants and impulses.

The idea of matching treatment approaches to different *types* of addict also seems plausible but if PRIME theory is correct, it is unlikely to bear fruit. According to the present theory, typologies are not the way forward: if the resources allow, the treatment plan needs to be tailored to the individual.

A great deal has been written about 'relapse prevention' but to date, there is no clear evidence for the effectiveness of any such intervention approach (e.g. Hajek et al. 2005). The current theory predicts that it is unlikely that we will ever see a clear benefit for approaches to relapse that focus on just one technique. Interventions need to encompass as many of the following elements as possible: (a) setting in motion a radical change in identity, (b) where possible, remodelling the social and physical environment that the addict inhabits, and (c) providing long-term medication that dampens the addictive drives or enhances the addict's capacity for impulse control.

5. *Pay particular attention to the temporal patterning of treatment*: related to the above, the temporal patterning of pharmacological and psychological treatment will need to be tailored to the specifics of the underlying pathologies. In some rare cases, a single treatment episode that helps to 'launch' the recovery process into orbit will be sufficient. At the other extreme, chronic treatment will be needed to suppress the behaviour and minimise the imbalance in the motivational system but there will be no 'cure', just long-term management. An intermediate case will be the addict whose addiction can be helped into 'remission' but in which the conditions that led to the original imbalance remain so that the addiction will gradually re-emerge and re-treatment will be needed.

6. *Use population-level interventions as treatment*: the theory also implies that the distinction between population-level interventions to control a behaviour that for some people is addictive and treatment to assist addicts to control their behaviour needs to be reconsidered. For example, price rises, denormalisation and banning smoking in enclosed public spaces would be expected to be helpful to smokers trying to stop as it would encourage them to try.

Similarly, interdiction of illicit drug supplies that leads to a significant increase in cost and reduction in availability should be helpful to those who are seeking to restrict their use.

Building interventions

PRIME theory has consequences for the strategy behind building interventions. One implication is that interventions are likely to benefit from being sufficiently nuanced in order to address the variety of motivational constructs important in determining addiction and behaviour. However, it is extremely difficult to keep all decisions based entirely on theory or evidence when constructing large, complex interventions, and still more difficult to evaluate whether each component part has contributed to any effectiveness. An alternative approach is embodied by the multiphase optimisation strategy which prioritises making 'best bet' decisions on the basis of potentially many rounds of pragmatic experimentation using short-term outcomes (Collins et al. 2011). Efficient experimental designs are proposed as fit for purpose, such as fractionated factorial and SMART designs (Collins et al. 2009; Lei et al. 2012), that may not meet the standard for drawing scientific conclusions – the result of tolerating more false positives – but are sufficient for refining the many aspects to a complex intervention before determining the overall effectiveness of the resultant intervention in a confirmatory randomized controlled trial.

Testing the theory

The point was made at the start of this book that we need a new approach to theory development. The current approach of developing theories that are essentially for the purpose of drawing attention to ideas but which are demonstrably false as stated, while pretending that they are in some sense testable through correlational-type evidence, is not conducive to incremental science.

It was argued that we should not allow theories to stand if clear counter-examples to their explicit assumptions can be found. It was argued that the plethora of theories in behavioural and social sciences arises from an approach which gives a nod in the direction of the scientific method but actually violates its fundamental tenets. It is not acceptable that there should be so many theories purporting to deal with the same phenomena, many of them using concepts that overlap to a considerable degree with other theories and none of them encompassing the full range of concepts that even a common-sense analysis shows must be required.

The question, therefore, is whether PRIME theory falls into the same trap. We would argue that it does not. The theory went through many formulations and was changed radically on a number of occasions precisely because we or our colleagues could think of counter-examples to what was being proposed. If there remain genuine counter-examples to the theory, then those parts of the theory must be wrong and need to be altered. A radically different formulation of the way in which elements of the motivational system interact may emerge that is more parsimonious, makes better predictions and explains things that this theory does not explain while at the same time continuing to explain all the things that this theory explains. If this occurs, then this theory should be rejected in favour of the new theory.

The present theory is, therefore, arguably not just the first truly synthetic theory of motivation but also hopefully the first theory to derive from and be subject to a method of theory development that is appropriate to the behavioural and social sciences: a method in which a single counter-example of what it describes makes it false even though its predictions cannot be made with absolute certainty. If that is the case, then the acronym PRIME would be fortuitously apposite.

First results

Since the first edition of Theory of Addiction, a number of studies have been inspired by PRIME Theory. The development of a single-item scale of motivation to quit smoking was informed by PRIME theory to distinguish between differing levels of wanting and planning. In a large study of the English population, the scale provided strong and accurate prediction of quit attempts 6 months after baseline assessment (Kotz et al. 2013). In a similar study, a simple rating of strength of urges was a better predictor of succeeding at stopping smoking than well-established scales based on patterns of consumption (Fidler et al. 2011). This result supports the notion from PRIME theory that acting in pursuit of what we most want and need is a central feature of addictive behaviour and that patterns of consumption are rather indirect symptoms.

The fact that enjoyment and dependence have been identified as making important and distinct contributions to the process of smoking cessation supports the multi-faceted nature of motivation proposed in this book. There is evidence that wanting to smoke arises from anticipated enjoyment and thereby deters even the attempt to stop while the day-to-day craving that arises from abstinence is dominant in determining the success once attempts have been initiated (Fidler and West 2011).

Another study exploring the relative value of wanting, duty and intention in predicting attempts to quit smoking produced results that require further thought (Smit et al. 2011). The superiority of wanting over duty in predicting quit attempts supports the distal influence of higher-level constructs as postulated by PRIME theory. The theory is agnostic as to how the relatively minor influence exerted by duty would affect behaviour and the study suggested there is a negative association. Finally, the study also found that intention had an influence on attempts that was independent of desire. By contrast, PRIME theory suggests that the effect of intention should be mediated by generating desires. However, it remains possible that intention influences behaviour by generating a desire to quit smoking but that this process occurs in the moment in which it unfolds and is therefore undetected by a simple 2-stage longitudinal design.

Finally, considering the role of identity as a high-level source for generating desires to maintain behaviour change, one study found that there was a steep decline in the prevalence of a self-reported attraction to smoking and a smoker identity with the length of time a smoker had been abstinent (Vangeli et al. 2010). The suggestion is that smokers are more likely to relapse without the ongoing source of resolve provided by a non-smoker identity and consequently the existence of a smoker identity becomes more rare the longer people have successfully abstained. However, the absolute figures were still surprisingly high, and the non-smoker identity may not be sufficiently coherent to allow simple assessment by asking 'how do you think of yourself?' and dichotomising responses (Vangeli and West 2012).

It is still early days but work on PRIME theory is growing – the number of citations has increased year on year since its publication (in 2006:11, 2007:28, 2008:34, 2009:40, 2010:46, 2011:55) – and the theory will continue to require reformulation and development and ultimately it will be rejected in favour of a better theory. For the present, it still provides a coherent narrative that can be used to understand the diverse features of addiction and to develop intervention strategies that may improve on what is currently available.

Conclusions

This book has presented the second draft of a synthetic theory of addiction that recognises that addiction can involve any or all aspects of a motivational system that involves five levels of operation in which all motivational forces must ultimately operate through impulses and inhibitory forces. It has introduced the idea of the 'unstable mind' in which constant balancing input is required to keep our thoughts, feelings and actions from heading off in unwanted directions and which helps to explain apparently sudden switches in what appear to be deeply entrenched behaviour patterns.

It has offered a framework for understanding the heterogeneity of addiction, phenomena that lie at the fuzzy boundaries of this concept and how addiction relates to other forms of behaviour in which reasoned analysis of what is good and bad is undermined and overpowered by motives arising from identity, basic drives, emotions and habit.

It has argued that we need to make a clear distinction between addiction as a syndrome at the centre of which is a repeated powerful motivation to engage in a rewarding behaviour, acquired as a result of engaging in that behaviour, that has significant potential for unintended harm and dependence syndromes, such as the alcohol dependence syndrome, which differ considerably with the target of the addiction (e.g. the alcohol dependence syndrome is substantially different from the nicotine dependence syndrome).

It has acknowledged that in many cases an addicted lifestyle involves choices made by individuals for whom the activity is particularly attractive given their circumstances and/or emotional vulnerabilities. However, in other cases, the addiction arises out of a susceptibility to the effect of a drug on their motivational system, setting up powerful acquired drives.

The motivational theory outlined in this volume is intended as a general theory that can be developed to apply to all aspects of behaviour. For example, it is hoped that it can provide a useful framework for understanding activities as diverse as reckless driving and consumer choice.

References

Atha, M. (2004). Taxing the UK drugs market. Wigan, Independent Drug Monitoring Unit.

Balfour, D.J. (2004) The neurobiology of tobacco dependence: a preclinical perspective on the role of the dopamine projections to the nucleus accumbens [corrected]. *Nicotine Tob Res* **6**(6): 899–912.

Balfour, D.J. (2009) The neuronal pathways mediating the behavioral and addictive properties of nicotine. In *Nicotine Psychopharmacology* (eds. J. Henningfield, E. London and S. Pogun). pp. 209–333. Springer, Berlin.

Balfour, D.J. (2004). The neurobiology of tobacco dependence: a preclinical perspective on the role of the dopamine projections to the nucleus accumbens. *Nicotine Tob Res* **6**(6): 899–912.

Ball, S.A. and Schottenfeld, R.S. (1997). A five-factor model of personality and addiction, psychiatric, and AIDS risk severity in pregnant and postpartum cocaine misusers. *Subst Use Misuse* **32**(1): 25–41.

Batra, V., Patkar, A.A., Berrettini, W.H., Weinstein, S.P. and Leone, F.T. (2003). The genetic determinants of smoking. *Chest* **123**(5): 1730–1739.

Benowitz, N.L. (2010) Nicotine addiction. *N Engl J Med* **362**(24): 2295–303.

Blaszczynski, A., Steel, Z. and McConaghy, N. (1997). Impulsivity in pathological gambling: the antisocial impulsivist. *Perspect Addict Nurs* **92**(1): 75–87.

Burt, R.D., Dinh, K.T., Peterson, A.V., Jr and Sarason, I.G. (2000). Predicting adolescent smoking: a prospective study of personality variables. *Prev Med* **30**(2): 115–125.

Caggiula, A.R., Donny, E.C., Palmatier, M.I., Liu, X., Chaudhri, N. and Sved, A.F. (2009) The role of nicotine in smoking: a dual-reinforcement model. *Nebr Symp Motiv* **55**: 91–109.

Chambers, R.A., Taylor, J.R. and Potenza, M.N. (2003). Developmental neurocircuitry of motivation in adolescence: a critical period of addiction vulnerability. *Am J Psychiatry* **160**(6): 1041–1052.

Collins, L.M., Baker, T.B., Mermelstein, R.J., et al. (2011) The multiphase optimization strategy for engineering effective tobacco use interventions. *Ann Behav Med* **41**(2): 208–226.

Collins, L.M., Dziak, J.J. and Li, R. (2009) Design of experiments with multiple independent variables: a resource management perspective on complete and reduced factorial designs. *Psychol Methods* **14**(3): 202–224.

Davies, B., Thorley, A. and O'Connor, D. (1985). Progression of addiction careers in young adult solvent misusers. *Br Med J (Clin Res Ed)* **290**(6462): 109–110.

Dawkins, L., Powell, J., West, R., Powell, J. and Pickering, A. (2007) A double-blind placebo-controlled experimental study of nicotine: II—Effects on response inhibition and executive functioning. *Psychopharmacology* **190**(4): 457–467.

Dennis, M.L., Scott, C.K., Funk, R. and Foss, M.A. (2005). The duration and correlates of addiction and treatment careers. *J Subst Abuse Treat* **28**(2 Suppl): S51–S62.

Edwards, G., Anderson, P., Babor, T., et al. (1994). *Alcohol Policy and the Public Good.* Oxford University Press, Oxford.

Edwards, G. and Gross, M.M. (1976). Alcohol dependence: provisional description of a clinical syndrome. *Br Med J* **1**(6017): 1058–1061.

Fergusson, D.M. and Horwood, L.J. (2000). Does cannabis use encourage other forms of illicit drug use? *Addiction* **95**(4): 505–520.

Fidler, J.A., Shahab, L. and West, R. (2011) Strength of urges to smoke as a measure of severity of cigarette dependence: comparison with the Fagerström Test for Nicotine Dependence and its components. *Addiction* **106**(3): 631–638.

Fidler, J.A. and West, R. (2011) Enjoyment of smoking and urges to smoke as predictors of attempts and success of attempts to stop smoking: a longitudinal study. *Drug Alcohol Depend* 115(1–2): 30–34.

Foulds, J. (2006) The neurobiological basis for partial agonist treatment of nicotine dependence: varenicline. *Int J Clin Pract* 60(5): 571–576.

Gorelick, D.A. (1992). Progression of dependence in male cocaine addicts. *Am J Drug Alcohol Abuse* 18(1): 13–19.

Grossman, M., Chaloupka, F.J. and Shim, K. (2002). Illegal drug use and public policy. One can support the war on drugs' goal of reducing consumption without supporting the war itself. *Health Aff (Millwood)* 21(2): 134–145.

Hajek, P., Stead, L., West, R. and Jarvis, M. (2005). Relapse prevention interventions for smoking cessation. *Cochrane Database Syst Rev* (1): CD003999.

Hajek, P., West, R. and Wilson, J. (1995). Regular smokers, lifetime very light smokers, and reduced smokers: comparison of psychosocial and smoking characteristics in women. *Health Psychol* 14(3): 195–201.

Han, C., McGue, M.K. and Iacono, W.G. (1999). Lifetime tobacco, alcohol and other substance use in adolescent Minnesota twins: univariate and multivariate behavioral genetic analyses. *Addiction* 94(7): 981–93.

Hanninen, V. and Koski-Jannes, A. (1999) Narratives of recovery from addictive behaviours. *Addiction* 94(12): 1837–48.

Hughes, J.R. (2007) Effects of abstinence from tobacco: valid symptoms and time course. *Nicotine Tob Res* 9(3): 315–327.

Hughes, J.R., Higgins, S.T. and Bickel, W.K. (1994) Nicotine withdrawal versus other drug withdrawal syndromes: similarities and dissimilarities. *Addiction* 89(11): 1461–70.

Hughes, J.R., Keely, J. and Naud, S. (2004) Shape of the relapse curve and long-term abstinence among untreated smokers. *Addiction* 99(1): 29–38.

Jamrozik, K. (2004) Population strategies to prevent smoking: *BMJ* 328(7442): 759–762.

Kandel, D.B., Yamaguchi, K. and Chen, K. (1992) Stages of progression in drug involvement from adolescence to adulthood: further evidence for the gateway theory. *J Stud Alcohol* 53(5): 447–457.

Kotz, D., Brown, J. and West, R. (2013) Predictive validity of the Motivation To Stop Scale (MTSS): A single-item measure of motivation to stop smoking. *Drug Alcohol Depend* 128(1–2): 15–19.

Lader, D. and Goddard, E. (2004). *Smoking Related Attitudes and Behaviour, 2003*. Office of National Statistics, London.

Larabie, L. (2005) To what extent do smokers plan quit attempts? *Tob Control* 14(6): 425–428.

Lei, H., Nahum-Shani, I., Lynch, K., Oslin, D. and Murphy, S.A. (2012) A "SMART" design for building individualized treatment sequences. *Annu Rev Clin Psychol.* 8: 21–48.

Lingford-Hughes, A., Welch, S., Peters, L., Nutt, D., et al. (2012) BAP updated guidelines: evidence-based guidelines for the pharmacological management of substance abuse, harmful use, addiction and comorbidity: recommendations from BAP. *J Psychopharmacol* 26(7): 899–952.

Marlatt, G.A. (1996) Taxonomy of high-risk situations for alcohol relapse: evolution and development of a cognitive-behavioral model. *Addiction* 91(Suppl): S37–S49.

McEwen, A., West, R. and McRobbie, H. (2008) Motives for smoking and their correlates in clients attending Stop Smoking treatment services. *Nicotine Tob Res* 10(5), 843–850.

McNeill, A.D., West, R.J., Jarvis, M., Jackson, P. and Bryant, A. (1986) Cigarette withdrawal symptoms in adolescent smokers. *Psychopharmacology (Berl)* 90(4): 533–536.

Michie, S., Hyder, N., Walia, A. and West, R. (2011) Development of a taxonomy of behaviour change techniques used in individual behavioural support for smoking cessation. *Addict Behav* 36(4): 315–319.

Miller, N.S. and Gold, M.S. (1990) The contemporary alcoholic. *N J Med* 87(1): 35–39.

Miller, N.S., Ninonuevo, F., Hoffmann, N.G. and Astrachan, B.M. (1999) Prediction of treatment outcomes: lifetime depression versus the continuum of care. *Am J Addict* 8(3): 243–253.

Pettinati, H.M., Pierce, J.D., Jr, Belden, P.P. and Meyers, K. (1999) The relationship of Axis II personality disorders to other known predictors of addiction treatment outcome. *Am J Addict* 8(2): 136–147.

Prochaska, J.O. and Velicer, W.F. (1997) The transtheoretical model of health behavior change. *Am J Health Promot* 12(1): 38–48.

Quintero, G. and Nichter, M. (1996) The semantics of addiction: moving beyond expert models to lay understandings. *J Psychoactive Drugs* 28(3): 219–228.

Robinson, M.L., Berlin, I. and Moolchan, E.T. (2004) Tobacco smoking trajectory and associated ethnic differences among adolescent smokers seeking cessation treatment. *J Adolesc Health* 35(3): 217–224.

Robinson, T.E. and Berridge, K.C. (2003) Addiction. *Ann Rev Psychol* 54(1): 25–53.

Shaffer, H.J. and Eber, G.B. (2002) Temporal progression of cocaine dependence symptoms in the US National Comorbidity Survey *Addiction* 97(5): 543–554.

Shiffman, S., Paty, J.A., Gnys, M., Kassel, J.A. and Hickcox, M. (1996). First lapses to smoking: within-subjects analysis of real-time reports. *J Consult Clin Psychol* 64(2): 366–379.

Shiffman, S., Waters, A. and Hickcox, M. (2004). The nicotine dependence syndrome scale: a multidimensional measure of nicotine dependence. *Nicotine Tob Res* 6(2): 327–348.

Smit, E.S., Fidler, J.A. and West, R. (2011) The role of desire, duty and intention in predicting attempts to quit smoking. *Addiction* 106(4): 844–851.

Strecher, V.J., Shiffman, S. and West, R. (2005) Randomized controlled trial of a web-based computer-tailored smoking cessation program as a supplement to nicotine patch therapy. *Addiction* 100(5): 682–688.

Sutherland, G., Edwards, G., Taylor, C., Phillips, G.T., Gossop, M.R. and Brady, R. (1988) The opiate dependence syndrome: replication study using the SODQ in a New York clinic. *Br J Addict* 83(7): 755–760.

Ussher, M., Brown, J., Rajamanoharan, A. and West, R. (Submitted) How do factors prompting attempts to quit smoking relate to method of quitting and quit success?.

Vaillant, G.E. (2003). A 60-year follow-up of alcoholic men. *Addiction* 98(8): 1043–1051.

Vangeli, E., Stapleton, J. and West, R. (2010) Residual attraction to smoking and smoker identity following smoking cessation. *Nicotine Tob Res* 12(8): 865–869.

Vangeli, E. and West, R. (2012) Transition towards a 'non-smoker' identity following smoking cessation: An interpretative phenomenological analysis. *Br J Health Psychol* 17(1): 171–184.

Vitaro, F., Wanner, B., Ladouceur, R., Brendgen, M. and Tremblay, R.E. (2004) Trajectories of gambling during adolescence. *J Gambl Stud* 20(1): 47–69.

Vuchinich, R.V. and Heather, N. (2003) *Choice, Behavioral Economics and Addiction.* Pergamon, Cambridge.

Waller, T. and Rumball, D. (2004) *Treating Drinkers and Drug Users in the Community.* Blackwells, Oxford.

Washton, A.M. (1989) *Cocaine Addiction: Treatment, Recovery and Relapse Prevention.* Norton, New York.

West, R. (2009) The multiple facets of cigarette addiction and what they mean for encouraging and helping smokers to stop. *COPD.* 6(4): 277–283.

West, R., McEwen, A., Bolling, K. and Owen, L. (2001). Smoking cessation and smoking patterns in the general population: a 1-year follow-up. *Addiction* 96(6): 891–902.

West, R. and Sohal, T. (2006) "Catastrophic" pathways to smoking cessation: findings from national survey. *BMJ* 332(7539): 458–460.

West, R. and Stapleton, J. (2008) Clinical and public health significance of treatments to aid smoking cessation. *European Respiratory Review* 17(110): 199–204.

West, R., Walia, A., Hyder, N., Shahab, L. and Michie, S. (2010) Behavior change techniques used by the English Stop Smoking Services and their associations with short-term quit outcomes. *Nicotine Tob Res* 12(7): 742–747.

Yong, H.H. and Borland, R. (2008) Functional beliefs about smoking and quitting activity among adult smokers in four countries: findings from the International Tobacco Control Four-Country Survey. *Health Psychol* 27(3 Suppl): S21–S223.

INDEX

Note: Page numbers in *italics* refer to Figures; those in **bold** to Tables.

Theory of Addiction, Second Edition. Robert West and Jamie Brown.
© 2013 John Wiley & Sons, Ltd. Published 2013 by John Wiley & Sons, Ltd.